Embracing Multilingualism
Across Educational Contexts

Embracing Multilingualism
Across Educational Contexts

Edited by Corinne A. Seals and
Vincent Ieni Olsen-Reeder

Victoria University Press

TE WHARE WĀNANGA O TE ŪPOKO O TE IKA A MĀUI

VICTORIA
UNIVERSITY OF WELLINGTON

VICTORIA UNIVERSITY PRESS
Victoria University of Wellington
PO Box 600 Wellington
vup.victoria.ac.nz

Printed by YourBooks, Wellington

Contents

Foreword

When I first began research on minority languages (other than te reo) in New Zealand in the 1990s, very little was known about the numbers of speakers of languages such as Samoan, Greek, Dutch, Italian, Cantonese, Gujarati, and Korean, among many others. Even less was known about the contexts in which the languages of these communities were used, and the attitudes of community members to maintaining their languages. Happily this situation has been rectified and we now know a good deal more about these issues, but the issue of the use of minority languages other than te reo in the classroom remains a contentious one, often troubled by misinformation, prejudice, and a dearth of rigorous research. In this context, this book makes a very valuable contribution. Corinne Seals and Vini Olsen-Reeder are experienced researchers in minority group language issues, and especially in the complexities of the use of minority languages in educational contexts. This collection brings a wide diversity of perspectives to this issue from a number of different communities worldwide.

Many years ago, Jim Dickie, a colleague and expert in TESOL, argued passionately that Samoan children who came to school speaking Samoan as their mother tongue should be not just permitted but encouraged to discuss material with each other in Samoan. He demonstrated that their grasp of the mathematics concepts they were struggling with was enormously improved when this was allowed. In the context in which he was working, the teacher was flexible enough, with Jim's support, to encourage the use of Samoan in her classroom for discussion among her pupils. The scholarly chapters in this book bring a strong research focus to this issue of minority language use in the classroom across a wide range of current linguistic environments. Concepts such as "transacquisitional tasking" and "metashuttling" suggest ways of bringing new and productive practices into classrooms and indicate passionate intellectual engagement with the challenges involved in supporting second language acquisition in education. Together the contributors make a very strong case for the advantages of encouraging linguistic diversity and multilingualism in educational contexts.

Finally, I need to confess that I have some reservations about the term "translanguaging", which has been so enthusiastically espoused by many researchers in this area.[1] I guess the root of my discomfort is simply that I do not see that this term offers more than could be encompassed by the well-established term "code-switching", especially as developed and researched by John J. Gumperz. I take the point that translanguaging provides a wider and self-consciously political lens or perspective, just as Critical Discourse Studies did for discourse analysis. And I recognize that the approach advocated stresses dynamism and fluidity. But I personally think Gumperz's analyses frequently had the same goal; and he consistently stressed the skill with which people drew on all their linguistic and non-linguistic resources in meaning-making in interaction. Nonetheless, it is undoubtedly the case that the term "translanguaging", which is very well represented in the chapters of this book, has rejuvenated research and practice in this area, generating high levels of energy, and a raft of new concepts aimed at providing further valuable insight into the complexities of dynamic multilingual linguistic practices in educational contexts.

Janet Holmes
20 March 2019

1   Response from editors in Chapter 1.

Introducing the volume: The value of translanguaging

Vincent Ieni Olsen-Reeder and Corinne A. Seals

Nau mai ēnei kupu kōrero ki te ao nei,
he rukunga whakaaro, he rukunga manawa,
he whakairinga kōrero nō ngā reo huhua o te ao.
He reo tāmia i ngaro i ngā ngutu nōnanahi,
kua hahua ake kia mauri ora anō
hei tōiringa korokoro e waha atu nei:
Whano mai taku reo, hīkina ake ki te atakura.
Karangahia! Whaikōrerotia! Wānangahia!

Come, bathe these words in living light,
assumption carefully crafted as belief,
now intoned with the voices from many lands.
Oppressed languages once lost on yesterday's lips,
elevated from limbo with life force anew,
vibrations in my throat impel words to life:
Come my language, come face the morning.
Breath from Earth Mother! From Sky Father!

1. Introduction

Embracing Multilingualism Across Educational Contexts is an international response to the growing body of literature investigating the effects of different types of supportive languages education, from minority language immersion models to flexible multilingual education models (e.g. Cenoz & Gorter, 2015; García, 2009, 2011; García & Sánchez, 2018; Weber, 2014). These investigations have also led to the rise in popularity of investigations into translanguaging – what it means, how it can be used, who benefits and how.

Translanguaging models often work in conjunction with other models of language education, leading to a complex teaching and learning atmosphere that deserves further study. This edited collection seeks to bring together some of the vast expertise that exists internationally in the realm of multilingual education. Thus, this volume focuses on researcher-led and practitioner-led studies of translanguaging in teaching.

Additionally, we are interested in this volume in the role of translanguaging approaches as applied to traditionally immersive contexts. In all cases, this volume will pay particular attention to how one best services heritage languages, including both Indigenous and immigrant languages. To best serve the above goals, we have actively included researchers, activists, policy makers, and practitioners in this volume.

2. Translanguaging: A paradigm shift

The word translanguaging, and its application in this volume, requires some contextualization from the outset. The prefix "trans-" refers to the fluid and complex languaging of multilingual speakers, and recognizes that in reality their language choices *go beyond* the use of state-endorsed named language categories (García & Wei, 2014, p. 42). "Languaging" refers to the dynamic processes of using language to make meaning – that people do not just *use* language, they *do* language. That is to say, there is more complexity to communication than simply speaking one categorized language before speaking another.

As with any term, translanguaging as an approach to multilingualism is debated in several ways, mostly as practice, as theory, and as pedagogy. In practice, the term assists in explaining how multilinguals go about their language choices in real contexts. As García (2009, p. 45) points out, it is the "multiple discursive practices in which [multi]linguals engage in order to make sense of their [multi]lingual worlds."[1] In regards to theory, translanguaging rejects the idea that there are separate linguistic systems from which multilingual speakers strategically select and deploy features under different circumstances to accomplish different communicative and expressive ends (García & Wei, 2014; Vogel & García, 2017). Instead, there is much more room for fluidity. As Otheguy, García, and Reid (2015, p. 283) point out, "translanguaging is the deployment of a speaker's full linguistic repertoire without regard for watchful adherence to the socially and politically defined boundaries of named (and usually national and state) languages."

This definition can also be applied to education contexts. In terms of curriculum development and pedagogical practice, translanguaging refers to

> the ways in which [multi]lingual students and teachers engage in complex and fluid discursive practices that include, at times, the home language practices of students in order to 'make sense' of teaching and learning, to communicate and appropriate subject knowledge, and to develop academic language practices (García 2014, p. 112).

In summary then, translanguaging lenses, whether investigating language use in practice, theory, or pedagogy, allow one to understand how multilinguals go about *doing* their linguistic selves, without limiting understanding to recognizing a specified set of language

---

1   We have actively chosen to refer to "multilinguals" in place of "bilinguals," as we are purposefully focusing on the multiple and not the numerable.

behaviors. To put this in context, a Māori- and English-speaking multilingual can language so much more than just, say, code-switch. Their language needs are also much more complex than just double those of a monolingual. There needs to be a way to make space for the transcultural lived experiences and multimodal means of expression and communication that multilinguals navigate on a daily basis. There is much more to uncover about our multilingual selves in taking this natural linguistic fluidity for granted. It is in this space that we find translanguaging to be a particularly useful way of understanding multilinguals' interactions with the world.

Furthermore, methods and data collection practices do not necessarily change when applying a translanguaging lens, as opposed to a more traditional code-switching analysis. Rather, it is the larger perspective and approach we take to analyzing the data that changes – a paradigm shift, if you will. For this reason, this book also touches on traditional and diverse elements of multilingual research, such as: codeswitching, code meshing, polylingualism, polylanguaging, plurilingualism, hybridity, hybrid language practices, and flexible/ dynamic bilingual education. Translanguaging does not necessarily replace, criticize, or reject any of these ideas, and nor does this book. Instead, translanguaging encourages fluidity in analyzing these phenomena. This book aims to do the same, by supporting authors to make meaning out of translanguaging in their many and varied approaches.

3. Translanguaging in the literature

Translanguaging is a rapidly growing field of research. We acknowledge the numerous contributions that have been and are currently being made to this area. Many of these studies are discussed throughout the chapters in this volume. In this introductory chapter, we mention a few of the studies that have supported our own line of inquiry into translanguaging.

Firstly, we acknowledge García and Kleyn's (2016) *Translanguaging with Multilingual Students: Learning from Classroom Moments*, which presents six documented ethnographic case studies demonstrating the different ways of implementing translanguaging in transformative teaching tools, such as by providing translations as a scaffold, grouping students based on home languages, incorporating translanguaging as a literary device, and fluid multilingual "free writing" activities. Transformative literacy learning and teaching practices also support Latinx students' experiences in Spanish/English bilingual education programs. Furthermore, Gort and Sembiante (2015) illustrate that despite one program's official "one teacher / one language" policy, partner teachers crossed diglossic boundaries strategically and flexibly, and performed translanguaging practices of bilingual casting, translation, and language brokering, drawing on children's linguistic and cultural funds of knowledge. This afforded students agency in experimenting with new language forms and in becoming creative and critical language users (Wei & Wu, 2009) while recognising, validating, and expressing teachers' and children's shared multilingual identities.

Additionally, García-Mateus and Palmer (2017) have shown how translanguaging pedagogies promote the development of positive multilingual identities and critical metalinguistic awareness for both "English" dominant and "Spanish" dominant students. Further examining classroom practices, Palmer, García-Mateus, Martínez, and Henderson (2014) evidenced teachers adopting a flexible bilingual pedagogy (Creese & Blackledge, 2010), allowing for translanguaging in the classroom to help students better make sense of content. These students also used translanguaging practices in the classroom to learn language and as a legitimized means of reaffirming desired identities. These examples are some of many that show how, in spite of prevalent structural constraints in multilingual education, translanguaging pedagogies enable teachers to be agentive social actors within classrooms and schools, by allowing them to value and mirror students' voices and linguistic choices.

Translanguaging research has also been done in Aotearoa New Zealand. Firstly, Lowman, Fitzgerald, Rapira, and Clark (2007), show that when the first language of students is used to analyze texts being read in Māori educational contexts, language and literacy skills increased across languages. Furthermore, Podmore, Hedges, Keegan, and Harvey (2016), in their study on early childhood language teaching and learning strategies, show that all children, regardless of sociolinguistic background, benefited from use of translanguaging, except for cases where parents were unsure of, or did not believe in, the benefits of multilingualism. Finally, research as part of the Wellington Translanguaging Project has shown how translanguaging in Samoan and Māori early childhood education centres (aʻoga amata and puna reo, respectively) supports minority students' use of home languages, while also encouraging new speakers of the language(s) to give multilingual communication a try in a supportive atmosphere (c.f. Seals, 2018, forthcoming, 2019; Seals, Olsen-Reeder, Crawford, Pine, Wallace, Kingstone, & Ash, 2018; Seals, Pine, Ash, Olsen-Reeder, & Wallace, this volume). All of these studies highlight the need to examine the wider sociolinguistic context within which multilinguals reside, and the understandings we can glean from doing so.

4. Translanguaging: Switching codes

The term translanguaging has been challenged as a perhaps unnecessary addition to the literature. There is a growing number of scholars moving towards this lens, and it important the editors make a stance in this debate. The editors do understand that, at least on a superficial level, code-switching and translanguaging seem to be one practice; that the two terms seem synonymous. For us, the point of departure is that there is little room in the code-switching approach to analyze language behaviours, over and above the overall switch. One of the editor's own doctoral thesis (Olsen-Reeder, 2017) on Māori language choices presents an incredibly complex set of language behaviours which affect language fluidity between Māori, English, and other languages. Any number of factors can simultaneously affect language choice. Here, code-switching would certainly only allow for a binary I/O analysis of those choices to develop, and there is so much more to see in a multilingual speech act.

Furthermore, the editors also believe their multilingual experiences are, at times, invalidated by code-switching theory in ways that feel quite unjust to the multilingual reality. Translanguaging gives much more to the social justice lens of sociolinguistics, and, as this book shows, code-switching can still be a part of that lens. As far as we can tell, translanguaging lenses validate multilingual realities in the interests of deeper sociolinguistic understanding, in a way that code-switching alone has not yet managed to achieve.

5. Chapter overview

The current book is an attempt to further such translanguaging scholarship and to develop its approaches as theory, as practice, and as pedagogy. This volume presents contributions from around the world, and this recognizes the different socio–historical–political contexts our collective global multilingualism(s) are situated in. Additionally, this volume accepts there will be varying take-ups of translanguaging, in both adoption and adaptation. For example, we expect that a more critical lens is to be found in US contexts, a more sociolinguistic lens in Asian contexts, and a focus in New Zealand on ground-up understandings that are guided by each community. Translanguaging is not new in any of these contexts, not in research nor in practice. However, this is an opportunity to push our understanding of linguistic terminology and to challenge research agendas (especially in areas of social justice). Yet, at its core, this book seeks always to empower the speakers and teachers in each context, as translanguaging should do.

We look first to translanguaging in education with Indigenous languages. First, Feauaʻi Amosa Burgess and Sadie Fiti assess the introduction of translanguaging resources into a Samoan early childhood centre, which in this instance is located in Aotearoa New Zealand. Their research suggests that translingual resources allow children of diverse language backgrounds to participate confidently in the same reading exercise. Next, Corinne Seals, Russell Pine, Madeline Ash, Cereace Wallace, and Vincent Ieni Olsen-Reeder assess the role of translanguaging as a way to build bridges linguistically and culturally in a Māori-medium early childhood centre in Aotearoa New Zealand. Third, Sophie Tauwehe Tamati provides an account of transacquisition pedagogy inside Māori-medium schools in Aotearoa New Zealand and validates this approach in transitioning Māori language literacy into English literacy. Then, Madoka Hammine observes the Miyara community and its Yaeyaman speakers for inherently cultural translanguaging practices and shows that dominant monolingual values present on Ishigaki Island are quite uncomfortable for the multilingual reality of the community. Rounding out this section, Chun-Mei Chen seeks to understand how social network, dual identity, and agency play a part in the implementation of Indigenous language education for Paiwan-Mandarin children in diglossic Taiwan. Observations here include that dual lexicon resources are a necessity in this community for family language maintenance.

Then we move to translanguaging in additional language education settings. First, Judith Purkarthofer's case study examines heritage language education across languages in Austria, and concludes that traditional understandings of heritage language education are not necessarily equipped for the realities of multilingual families. In Sweden, Jenny Rosén, Boglárka Straszer, and Åsa Wedin present the attitudes of teachers who practice within the juxtaposition of a country perceived as homogenous, that also has legislation providing for home language instruction. This chapter also investigates how translanguaging approaches may provide positive inroads through the challenges such a juxtaposition might present. Next, in Germany, Simone Plöger and Galina Putjata assert that educational systems are inherently situated in monolingual norms, and they highlight the importance of multilingual teachers who are tasked with intersecting policy and supporting immigrant languages in practice, although this is not recognized as pedagogical expertise. In Sweden, Vesna Busic and Kirk Sullivan provide an important account of the transition of trainee teachers from traditional understandings of multilingualism to translanguaging as practice and pedagogy. Findings suggest a positive future for the uptake of translanguaging by these teachers, who are not limited by traditional beliefs about what is "correct" in the classroom.

Moving to the United States, Suriati Abas provides a photographic commentary to illustrate how practices both inside and outside the classroom assist in minority language learning in one midwestern college town and aims to encourage practitioners to perpetuate minority language development even in spaces with limited resource to do so. Moving to South Africa and Switzerland, Verbra Pfeiffer provides a transnational perspective on academic writing among tertiary students and suggests that heritage and home languages can be used to enrich academic writing in another language. Finally, Enrique Arias Castaño and Isabel Cristina Sánchez report on the inclusion of translanguaging in an English and Spanish classroom. Here, pre-service teachers in Latin-American education contexts note opportunities and limitations of the approach for these diglossic environments. We then conclude this volume with a look back at key themes that emerged across the chapters and diverse research contexts to see what we can learn about translanguaging in multilingual education as we move forward.

Acknowledgements

Finally, the editors wish to acknowledge the support of Victoria University of Wellington – especially our resident schools, Linguistics and Applied Language Studies, and Te Kawa a Māui. Additionally, we would like to particularly thank the Victoria University Deputy Vice Chancellor Māori and Research Offices for their generosity in funding the Wellington Translanguaging Project and its resource branch Translanguaging Aotearoa through the Mātauranga Māori Research Programme. It is from the Wellington Translanguaging Project that the impetus for this book is spurred. Furthermore, we acknowledge Victoria University Press for their keen eyes and hands in bringing this book to life. Thank you also to Sydney Kingstone for your magical copyediting skills. Special thanks as well to Professor Janet Holmes, from whom both of the editors have learned so much over the years, for writing the foreword.

We acknowledge the local Māori and Samoan communities with whom Translanguaging Aotearoa works. Without your welcoming arms, this project, and by extension this book, would not have eventuated. Tēnei e tuohu nei, fa'afetai lava.

We extend a warm message of thanks to all the contributors who worked quickly and globally to submit abstracts, chapters, and peer-reviews. We have thoroughly enjoyed working with each of you, albeit mostly electronically! We hope we have represented your words in a fitting manner and that you are as proud of this publication as we are.

Lastly, to our friends and family for always supporting late nights and accommodating the strange schedules of the academic, thank you!

Dr. Corinne A. Seals
Dr. Vincent Ieni Olsen-Reeder
Editors

References

Cenoz, K. & Gorter, D. (2015). Translanguaging and linguistic landscapes. *Linguistic Landscape, 1*(1–2), 54–74.

Creese, A. & Blackledge, A. (2010). Translanguaging in the bilingual classroom: A pedagogy for learning and teaching? *Modern Language Journal, 94*(1), 103–115.

García, O. (2009). *Bilingual education in the 21st century: A global perspective.* Malden, MA: Wiley-Blackwell.

García, O. (2011). Educating New York's Bilingual Children: Constructing a future from the past. *International Journal of Bilingual Education and Bilingualism, 14*(2), 133–153.

García, O. (2014). Countering the dual: Transglossia, dynamic bilingualism and translanguaging in education. In R. Rubdy & L. Alsagoff (Eds.), *The global-local interface, language choice and hybridity* (pp. 100–118). Bristol: Multilingual Matters.

García, O. & Kleyn, T. (2016). *Translanguaging with multilingual students: Learning from classroom moments.* New York: Routledge.

García, O. & Wei, L. (2014). *Translanguaging: Language, bilingualism and education.* New York: Palgrave Macmillan.

García, O. & Sánchez, M. T. (2018). Transformando la educación de bilingües emergentes en el estado de Nueva York. *Language, Education, and Multilingualism, 1*, 138–156.

García-Mateus, S. & Palmer, D. (2017). Translanguaging pedagogies for positive identities in two-way dual language bilingual education. *Journal of Language, Identity & Education, 16*(4), 245–255.

Gort, M. & Sembiante, S. F. (2015). Navigating hybridized language learning spaces through translanguaging pedagogy: Dual language preschool teachers' languaging practices in support of emergent bilingual children's performance of academic discourse. *International Multilingual Research Journal, 9*, 7–25.

Lowman, C., Fitzgerald, T., Rapira, P., & Clark, R. (2007). First language literacy skill transfer in a second language learning environment: Strategies for biliteracy. *Set, 2*, 24–28.

Otheguy, R., García, O., & Reid, W. (2015). Clarifying translanguaging and deconstructing named languages: A perspective from linguistics.

Applied Linguistics Review, 6(3), 281–307.

Palmer, D. K., Mateus, S. G., Martínez, R. A. & Henderson, K. (2014). Reframing the debate on language separation: Towards a vision for translanguaging pedagogies in the dual language classroom. *The Modern Language Journal, 98(3)*, 757–772.

Podmore, V. N., Hedges, H., Keegan, P. J. & Harvey, N. (Eds.) (2016). *Teachers Voyaging in Plurilingual Seas: Young children learning through more than one language.* Wellington: NZCER Press.

Seals, C.A. (2018, 13 July). *Translanguaging in New Zealand Māori and Samoan Early Childhood Education Centres.* Seminar and Master Class, Monash University, Australia.

Seals, C.A. (forthcoming, 2019). Classroom Translanguaging through the Linguistic Landscape. In S. Dubreil, D. Malinowski, and H. Maxim (Eds.) *Language Teaching in the Linguistic Landscape.* New York: Springer.

Seals, C.A., Olsen-Reeder, V., Crawford, T.O., Pine, R., Wallace, C., Kingstone, S., & Ash, M. (2018, 28 June). *He Puna Reo: Embracing New Zealand's Linguistic Diversity.* Paper presented at the 22nd Sociolinguistics Symposium, University of Auckland, New Zealand.

Seals, C.A., Pine, R., Ash, M., Olsen-Reeder, V. & Wallace, C. (2019, this volume). The use of translanguaging to bridge sociocultural knowledge in a puna reo. In C.A. Seals & V. Olsen-Reeder (Eds.) *Embracing Multilingualism across Educational Contexts.* Wellington: Victoria University Press.

Vogel, S. & García, O. (2017). Translanguaging. In G. Noblit (Ed.), *Oxford Research Encyclopedia of Education.* Oxford: Oxford University Press.

Weber, J.-J. (2014). *Flexible Multilingual Education: Putting Children's Needs First.* Bristol: Multilingual Matters.

Wei, L. & Wu, C. J. (2009). Polite Chinese children revisited: Creativity and the use of codeswitching in the Chinese complementary school classroom. *International Journal of Bilingual Education and Bilingualism, 12*(2), 193–211.

CHAPTER 2

Using both Samoan and English to shape understandings, reasoning, and appreciation during a book experience in an A'oga Amata: An example of translanguaging[1]

Feaua'i Amosa Burgess and Sadie Fiti

1. Introduction

Children are coming to our A'oga Amata (Samoan early childhood education center) with varied heritage language backgrounds. Through book experiences, children develop their oral language when they are able to engage fully with the story using preferred language practices. This requires book experiences of a different kind to those typically used in the center.

The present study looks at how understandings, reasoning, and appreciation are developed when the text of the story is presented through both Samoan and English and discussed flexibly in

1   We wish to acknowledge the work done by the authors of the story and of other resources. We have appreciated the leadership of Dr. Corinne Seals in setting up and managing the wider project, as well as communicating the findings to us. We thank the Management Committee of the A'oga Amata and our patron Rev Tauti'aga Mamea, for their interest and support. We also thank the parents for allowing us to include their children who took part in the study.

both languages. Specifically, we provide examples of emerging multilingualism on the part of the children as well as examples of teacher strategies suited to texts of this nature.

1.1 New views of multilingualism

Recent views of early multilingualism stress the need for children to have opportunities to shape experiences, understandings, and knowledge through the use of two or more languages (Baker, 2011, p. 289).

Currently, book experiences are available at the A'oga Amata in English, Samoan, te reo Māori, and various other heritage languages. Teachers usually read the story in the language of the text but discuss the story and illustrations in Samoan. The children inevitably contribute to the discussion in English, thus setting up dual language conversations. The children demonstrate more or less understanding of Samoan in the talk, or in the other languages of the source text, while using their preferred language (English) for their own contributions.

1.2 Translanguaging approach

A translanguaging approach to a book experience is based on three core ideas if claims made by García and Sylvan (2011) can be applied to our center:

1. Translanguaging may mirror better the way Samoan and English are used by families of Samoan heritage in New Zealand settings. In many of these families, both languages may be developing as a highly individual composite competence.
2. The use of Samoan and English in the storytelling may be a way to meet the cognitive, emotional, and social needs of children who vary considerably in their Samoan and English language proficiencies. Texts of this kind should enable

children to contribute to the book experience to their fullest potential.

3. Teachers have a primary obligation to respond to children's developmental needs and promote their well-being. At the same time, teachers are obliged to respect family values, beliefs, expectations, and rights (Ministry of Education, 2017).

The ability of children to use both Samoan, English (and other heritage languages) for the purpose of communication is the outcome sought from a book experience that facilitates translanguaging. Specifically, we are interested in gathering examples of talk generated by the book that addresses three questions:

1. What evidence is there that early multilingualism is emerging from interactions with the picture book written in alternating languages?
2. What multilingual language practices are being encouraged by the teacher and observed among the children?
3. What pedagogical actions recognize the children's own language practices and cultural experiences?

2. Method and background
2.1 Language and cultural diversity
The A'oga Amata currently enrolls children from many heritage language and cultural backgrounds. The parents of the children, however, have a common expectation that the children will have opportunities to acquire Samoan and experience Samoan cultural values and practices while at the A'oga Amata.

Under the initiative of Dr. Corinne Seals[2] from Victoria University

---

2 Dr. Seals is the TESOL Programme Director, Linguistics and Applied Languages Studies, VUW.

of Wellington, we have been trialing a model of language development that builds more fully on the individual language practices that children come to the center with. Examples of a resource consistent with this model are language experience stories created by the staff, children, and student teachers, and told through using both Samoan and English in different parts of the text. The question of interest is how this kind of text influences the way that the children understand, reason about, and appreciate the story while also facilitating early multilingualism.

2.2 Participants
The teachers, Savaliga Liko and Feaua'i Burgess, are native speakers of Samoan and proficient users of English. They were reading the book *O le Olaga A'oga*[3] *(School Life)* to a group of four-year-old children who were sitting with them on the mat. The children come from diverse heritage language and cultural backgrounds. English was the preferred language of six of the children at the center at the time. One of the children comes from a family with Samoan-speaking grandparents, and, when given the opportunity, usually preferred to speak in Samoan when interacting with teachers. The full text of the story appears in Appendix A. The background details of the children are summarized in Appendix B.

2.3 The resource
Three episodes involving norms of respectful and caring behavior were observed and recorded in storybook form. The text of each story alternated between English and Samoan within and between idea units. For example, the first story began this way:

---

3   Written by Fabieara Filo, Leitumalo Parsons, Honiara Salanoa, and Corinne Seals. Illustrated by Alex Hoffmans.

It was Lotu time, ua ova le fiafia o Isa because today, o ia o le a faia le tatalo.
"Tatalo mai Isa ma Mele," said Rosa.
Isa confidently starts to lead the lotu:
"Fa'afetai mo le ola ma le malosi. Puipui mai i matou i lenei aso. Amene."

The switch between English and Samoan enabled children with varying proficiencies in either language to contribute confidently to the story while being exposed to the other language in a meaning-friendly way.

The switch between languages was not random. Three principles were at work in the example. First, the lotu (prayer) was in Samoan as is the custom at the A'oga Amata and within some families of the children listening to the story. It also created opportunities for children to recite prayers in other languages that may be used at home. Second, Samoan was used by the teacher in the story in ways that teachers frequently use Samoan in the center: "Tatalo mai Isa ma Mele," said Rosa. ("You say the prayer Isa and Mele," said Rosa.) Third, there were meaningful relationships between the sections of the text written in English and Samoan. In other words, the text in English provided clues for understanding the text in Samoan and vice versa: "because today" signals the reason for Isa . . . being in a happy mood. The two languages are not a paraphrase of each other but continue the story in an interconnected way (for further discussion of intrasentential translanguaging, see Seals, Pine, Ash, Olsen-Reeder, & Wallace, this volume).

2.4 Approach
We use a three-level approach to book experiences at the A'oga Amata (see Table 1).

Table 1. A three-level approach to a book experience

Level / focus	Sample questions relevant to the story (usually asked in Samoan)
1. Understanding the story	What is happening here? What is X feeling? What is Y doing? What is the problem?
2. Reasoning about the events in the story	"Why" questions about actions, motivations, characters, and feelings. Noticing consequences.
3. Appreciation of the story	Questions that encourage reflection. Questions that help children relate the story to personal experiences.

We read a story at least three times, giving progressive focus to each level of thinking in our talk about the story.

2.5 Transcripts
We transcribed the interactions of the children with the story as well as the conversations that developed with the teacher. From the transcripts, we have selected eight vignettes that indicate the impact of using two languages to shape the understanding of, reasoning about, and appreciation of the story.

3. Vignettes
3.1 Participation
All children participated at some point in the book experience without prompting by the teacher. The children initiated talk about the story and illustrations as well as responding to the teacher's questions or questions from other children.

Example 1
When a teacher (Feaua'i) sat down on a chair with the book, seven children gathered around her.

> **Moana:** [*speaking spontaneously*] Feaua'i, I like that book. Can you read it again, fa'amolemole [please].

On occasions, the conversations continued over several turns as the same child, or different children, contributed to the talk.

3.2 Translanguaging
For the most part, the children's talk involved utterances in either English or Samoan. Children who frequently used Samoan with family members at home appeared to feel justified in using Samoan to explore the meaning of the story and relate events to their own experiences.

Example 2
> **Eli:** Ou ke fiafia i le kusi, auā e fai e kamaiki le loku, pei o kakou. [I like the story, because the children do their lotu like us.]

> **Moana:** But I don't like children when they make silly faces and hit other children.

On occasions both Samoan and English appeared within the same utterance.

Example 3
> **Ahzaria:** Feaua'i, the children fai le lotu like us. I like it. [The children have the lotu like us.]

The teachers used Samoan and English in reading the story in accordance with the text. However, they always used Samoan in their talk about the story. Thus, they tended to enter into dual language conversations with children who preferred to use English. A teacher's use of Samoan in such situations resulted in more or less understanding for most children, but greater understanding for the Samoan-speaking children. In all, there was some evidence that alternating the language of the storytelling stimulated the use of Samoan by the children who used the language at home. This was to a degree not previously observed during book experiences.

3.3 Cognition

As a group, the children's reasoning about events in the story appeared to be helped by the use of the two languages in the text. The Samoan sections of the text washed over the children who preferred to use English. There was at least partial understanding due to the context and perhaps the repeated encounters with the story.

Example 4

Teacher: Aiseā Isa e fiafia tele? [Why was Isa very happy?]

Eli: E faia ia tatalo today fa'akasi ma Mele. [She will say prayers today together with Mele.]

Archie: Yes, the teacher chose her. She feels proud.

Teacher: Ioe, e filifili Isa ma Mele le tatalo ma amata le pese, pei o outou. Ua mimita o ia. [Yes, Isa and Mele will choose a prayer and start a hymn just like you do. She will feel proud.]

For children who prefer to use English, the understanding of Samoan is likely to precede a more active, spontaneous use of that language, an outcome similar to that seen in dual language conversations (De Houwer, 2015). The reverse is probably occurring with the Samoan-speaking children. Their English language proficiency is likely to be enhanced through processing the English portions of the text and the contributions of children using English. At the same time, their Samoan proficiency will be enhanced through expansions of their talk by the teachers in Samoan. Thus, alternating the language of the storytelling, and the interactions with the story, would seem to set up optimal conditions for language development (Cabell, Justice, McGinty, DeCoster, & Forston, 2015).

3.4 Appreciation
The ability of the children to relate the story to their own experiences appeared to be opened up through the choice of language in the text rather than closed off.

Example 5
Teacher: Aiseā, e te fiafia oe ile tala Eli? [Why do you like the story Eli?]

Eli: Ou ke fiafia i le kusi auā, e fai e kamaiki le loku, pei o kakou. [I like the story because the children do their lotu, like us.]

Moana: But I don't like the children when they make funny faces and hit other children.

Children were able to talk about practices at home related to themes in the story that were culturally nuanced through heritage backgrounds.

Example 6
Mason: Sometimes I say grace at home. Fa'afetai i le Atua

mo lenei mea 'ai lelei. [Thank you, God, for this
good food.] My mother says a different grace.

Such talk appeared to enable a smoother transition into
translanguaging in the conversations.

3.6 Teacher strategies

These are early days in reading a text of this kind with children from
diverse language and cultural backgrounds. At this stage, the teachers
tended to use each language separately rather than as a combined
competence. The teachers often extended a child's utterance spoken
in Samoan and opened up the talk for multiple turns. However,
when a child spoke in English, the teachers tended to reformulate
what the child had said into Samoan with minimal extension of the
thinking behind the child's utterances.

Example 7
Eli: E le fiafia tama. [The boys are not happy.]

Teacher: E sa'o Eli. E le fiafia tama i lē 'ote mai o le faia'oga.
[True Eli. The boys are not happy as they are being
growled at by the teacher.]

Example 8
Teacher: Fai mai e a James? [What did James say?]

Archie: I don't want to be your friend.

Teacher: Ioe, ua fai mai James e lē fia fai uō. [Yes, James says,
I don't want to be your friend.]

The need for the strategic appraisal of how the teacher and the children interact linguistically with texts of this kind is an important professional issue (for further discussion of teacher training, see also Busic & Sullivan, this volume).

4. Discussion

There were sufficient examples from reading the story on the various occasions to support the following observations:

a. Participation in each book experience was spread evenly among the children with little prompting by the teacher.
b. Samoan-speaking children appeared to respond to an expectation that using Samoan to discuss the story was acceptable even though there were children present in the group who preferred to use English.
c. The understanding of, reasoning about, and appreciation of the story was not compromised by the alternation of languages in the text or by the examples of translanguaging by the participants.
d. The teacher was able to extend the utterances of those children who preferred to speak in Samoan. In contrast, the teacher tended to reformulate English language contributions into Samoan.

Our current practice is to read picture books from three streams of children's literature on a daily basis: picture books in English, Samoan, and te reo Māori. We also add in picture books in the heritage languages of the children where these are available, and photo books based on the experiences that the children are having at the center or in the home. The captions in the photo books have usually been written in Samoan. Photo books would seem to be ideally suited to a translanguaging approach of the captions. Wherever possible, we should be using the words spoken by the children, teachers, family members, or other participants in the experience. If more than one language is being used, natural examples of translanguaging could occur in the photo stories.

Translanguaging offers a somewhat different model of multilingualism for literacy experiences at the A'oga Amata, one in which competence in Samoan and English combine in order to make sense of the story, reason about it, and appreciate the events. The model allows for the socialization of children into language-use choices more in keeping with the reality of their homes and the wider community.

Evidence of the efficacy of creating language alternating text for photo stories would lie in the greater spontaneous use of Samoan by both Samoan-speaking children and those who normally prefer to use English. Thus, the ubiquity of dual language conversations would be addressed. The strategic reading of stories that use alternating languages in the text will take time, reflection, and experience to develop. Moreover, the strategies will rest on a growing understanding of translanguaging developed through reading research articles, trialing procedures, and entering into the professional discussion of vignettes.

5. Conclusion

The stories developed in alternating languages by Dr. Corinne Seals and her team provided us with the opportunity to trial a new approach to the early multilingual development of children attending the A'oga Amata and who came from diverse language and cultural heritages. We were able to gather vignettes for professional discussion from the repeated reading of one of the stories. One noticeable feature of the transcriptions was the less frequent use of dual language interactions between the teacher and the children. In their talk, children were sometimes using Samoan – not usually the case during book experiences at the center. Utterances in Samoan were therefore being processed by the children from sources other than the teacher. In addition, there were examples where the understanding, reasoning about, and appreciation of the story by the group was helped through combining Samoan and English in telling the story.

References

Baker, C. (2011). Foundations of bilingual education and bilingualism (5th Ed.). Bristol: Multilingual Matters.

Cabell, S. Q., Justice, L. M., McGinty, A. S., DeCoster, J., & Forston, L. D. (2015). Teacher-child conversations in pre-school classrooms: Contributions to children's vocabulary development. *Early Childhood Research Quarterly, 30, 80–92.*

De Houwer, A. (2015). Harmonious bilingual development: Young families' well-being in language contact situations. *International Journal of Bilingualism, 19(2), 169-184.*

Garcia, O. & Sylvan, C. E. (2011). Pedagogies and practices in multilingual classrooms: Singularities and pluralities. *The Modern Language Journal, 95(3), 385–400.*

Ministry of Education (2017). *Te Whariki: He whariki matauranga mo nga mokopuna o Aotearoa - Early childhood curriculum. Wellington.*

Additional Bibliography

Gallagher, F. & Colohan, G. (2014). T(w)o and fro: Using the L1 as a language teaching tool in the CLIL classroom. *The Language Learning Journal, 45(4), 485–498.*

Ho, J. & Funk, S. (2018). Promoting young children's social and emotional health. *Young Children, 73(2), 73–79.*

Justice, L. M., McGinty, A. S., Zuker, T., Cabell, S. Q. & Piasta, S. G. (2013). Bi-directional dynamics underlie the complexity of talk in teacher-child play-based conversations in classrooms serving at-risk pupils. *Early Childhood Research Quarterly, 28(3), 496–508.*

Ritchie, W. C. & Bhatia, T. K. (2006). Social and psychological factors in language mixing. In T. K. Bhatia and W. C. Ritchie (eds.). *The handbook of bilingualism.* Oxford: Blackwell. 336–352.

Appendix A

Lotu Time – from O le Olaga A'oga[4]
(Samoan utterances translated and in bold)

Page 3
It was Lotu time, **Isa is very happy** because today, **she will say the prayer.**
"**You say the prayer Isa and Mele**," said Rosa.
Isa confidently starts to lead the lotu: "**Thanks for life and strength. Protect us today. Amen.**"

Page 4
When Isa opened her eyes, **she sees her friends James and Wei** who were giggling and pulling silly faces at each other.
Isa suddenly felt hurt **and angry. "Why are you playing during lotu?" yells Isa.**

Page 5
Isa walks to James and hits him on the back.
James immediately starts crying and says, "Ouch! **It hurts. Go away.** You are not my friend anymore."

Page 6
Isa feels sad about James's words. She only wanted him to listen and sit still during lotu time. Isa starts crying **and suddenly everybody was crying and feeling sad.**
"**That's enough!**" says Rosa. "**Stop crying everyone.**"
"Isa, remember, you must never hit another person, and

---

4   Written by Fabiefara Filo, Leitumalo Parsons, Honiara Salanoa, and Corinne
    Seals. Illustrated by Alex Hofmans.

when you are angry, **show love and respect to others**," Rosa gently reminds Isa.

Page 7
Rosa explains, "**People are different and have different beliefs. It is important to respect and love each other. James and Wei remember**, lotu time is very important, so playing games and pulling faces are not okay."

"Sorry." James, Wei and Isa apologise to each other, and then Rosa sends them to have morning tea.

Appendix B

Details of the 12 children who took part in the book experiences

Name, gender, and age[5]	Heritage language background	Languages used in the home
Freddy (m) 4 yrs 3 mths	Both parents are Pākehā NZers	English
Luisa* (f) 4 yrs 8 mths	Mother Samoan born Father Pākehā NZer	English (and Samoan)
Loimata (m) 4 yrs 10 mths	Mother Pākehā NZer Father Tongan, Samoan, Tokelauan	English (and Samoan)
Siaosi (m) 4 yrs 3 mths	Mother Tongan Father Tongan, Samoan, English	English (and Tongan)

5   Age at 27 March 2018

Name, gender, and age[5]	Heritage language background	Languages used in the home
Masina (f) 4 yrs 6 mths	Father Pākehā NZer Mother NZ-born Samoan	English (and Samoan)
Akenese (f)	Both parents are Pākehā NZers	English
Isaia (m) 4 yrs 3 mths	Father Pākehā NZer Mother NZ-born Samoan Family lives with Samoan grandparents	Samoan and English
Aliya* (f) 4 yrs	Both parents are NZ-born Samoans	English (and Samoan)
Tuki* (f) 4 yrs 5 mths	Father NZ-born Samoan Mother Pākehā NZer	English (and Samoan)
Teuila* (f) 4 yrs	Both parents are NZ-born Samoan	English (and Samoan)
Tupu* (m) 2 yrs 10 mths	Father NZ-born Tongan Mother NZ-born Tongan, Samoan, European	English (and Tongan)
Jamie* (m) 3 yrs 6 mths	Father NZ-born Samoan Mother Pākehā NZer	English (and Samoan)

* present at the second reading

CHAPTER 3

The use of translanguaging to bridge sociocultural knowledge in a puna reo

Corinne A. Seals, Russell Pine, Madeline Ash,
Vincent Ieni Olsen-Reeder, and Cereace Wallace[1]

1. Introduction

Aotearoa New Zealand (Aotearoa NZ) is a superdiverse country, with over 160 languages spoken by residents every day (Royal Society of New Zealand, 2013). Aotearoa NZ is proud of its superdiversity, which is regularly cited by the country's leaders, agencies, and societies as something that positively defines the character of the nation. Because of this embracing of superdiversity, there is a growing consciousness of the multicultural, multilingual landscape. At the core of Aotearoa NZ's rich sociolinguistic tapestry, both historically and politically, is the Indigenous Māori language (te reo Māori).

In Aotearoa NZ, it is imperative that translanguaging discussions include our Indigenous language, te reo Māori. Te reo Māori is Aotearoa NZ's first officially recognized language (since 1987), and it is the second most-spoken language in the country (Statistics New Zealand, 2013). It is recognized that "ko te reo te mauri o te mana Māori" [the language is the essence of Māori identity] (Ngaha,

1 Thank you to the puna reo whānau and the other members of the puna reo research team – Te Owaimotu Crawford and Sydney Kingstone. We also thank DVC Māori Professor Rawinia Higgins and the Victoria University of Wellington Mātauranga Māori Research Programme for supporting this research.

2005, p. 31). As such, Aotearoa NZ's government has made efforts in recent history to promote the preservation and revitalization of te reo Māori as an integral part of the country's multilingual and multicultural heritage (c.f. Seals & Olsen-Reeder, 2017). One of the government-sponsored teaching environments for te reo Māori is the puna reo, teaching children under five years old bilingually through te reo Māori and English. The puna reo is a place where multicultural, multilingual Aotearoa NZ is fostered, as well as being a place where translanguaging naturally occurs.

The present chapter presents research conducted in 2017 as part of the Wellington Translanguaging Project. We actively chose to conduct this research alongside the community at a local puna reo through the Kaupapa Māori approach of culturally embedded and responsive research (G. H. Smith, 1990; L. Smith, 1997; Pihama, 2001; Pohatu, 1996). Kaupapa Māori, and thus our research, is guided by the following eight principles:

1. **Tino rangatiratanga**: The research is to be governed and guided by Māori and to be for Māori.
2. **Taonga tuku iho**: Te reo Māori (language), tikanga (ways of being), and mātauranga Māori (Indigenous knowledge) are the guiding sources of understanding the world and are valid in and of themselves.
3. **Ako Māori**: Acknowledging ways of teaching and learning embedded in Māori knowledge and life.
4. **Kia piki ake i ngā raruraru o te kāinga**: Research must contribute positively to Māori communities and help relieve communities from disadvantage.
5. **Whānau**: Family is core to Māori communities, and it is the researcher's responsibility to embrace and care for these connections, including the researcher's position within the community.

6. **Kaupapa**: The research being undertaken must contribute to the larger collective aspirations of the Māori community.
7. **Te Tiriti o Waitangi**: The rights of Māori as guaranteed by the Treaty of Waitangi must at all times be affirmed and respected.
8. **Āta**: Relationships and well-being must be protected and nurtured in all work with Māori communities.

Guided by the above outlined Kaupapa Māori approach to research, this chapter looks at the puna reo teaching environment in Aotearoa NZ and asks, (1) what is the role of translanguaging in a puna reo, and (2) how does translanguaging connect to wider goals of te reo Māori revitalization and sustainability?

As evidenced and discussed below, our findings show the strong relationship between teacher–student and peer–peer socialization through translanguaging and investment in the multilingual, multicultural fabric of Aotearoa NZ. In particular, we focus on the ways in which translanguaging aids bridge building between students' acquisition of tikanga Māori and wider Aotearoa NZ cultural practices. Additionally, we discuss the ways in which translanguaging as modeled by teachers is then reproduced by students. This chapter concludes with a discussion of the role of translanguaging in acknowledging Aotearoa NZ's linguistic past and building a more inclusive future.

2. Review of literature
2.1 Translanguaging
Translanguaging, originally coined by Williams (1994, cited in Baker, 2006), is a theory, a pedagogy, and an analytical approach centered around rejecting the "monolingual bias." The monolingual bias is a persistent approach in linguistics and other fields that implicitly or explicitly considers monolingualism the norm (García & Wei, 2014). Monolingual bias manifests itself particularly through the concept of languages as named, separated, bounded entities, and the

assumption that people acquire and use those languages separately (García & Wei, 2014; Makoni & Pennycook, 2006).

Translanguaging therefore contrasts sharply with "code-switching", which is based on the idea that speakers "switch" from one language to another: that languages are separate and used separately (García & Wei, 2014). Instead, translanguaging takes the position that people have a linguistic repertoire with features that are socially constructed as belonging to a particular language. People use their repertoire flexibly and with sociocultural competency. However, because translanguaging opposes the monolingual bias, it conflicts with the dominant norms of linguistics and education, institutions (schools, governments, etc.), and wider societal beliefs. As a result, translanguaging is inherently political, and its critical nature is key (Canagarajah, 2013). Challenging the monolingual bias lifts up voices that otherwise may have been suppressed. Thus, translanguaging also inherently addresses issues of immigration, race, religion, and power imbalance.

The political nature of translanguaging often creates tension between established norms of talking about language(s) and natural translanguaging practices. People who translanguage negotiate the norms, catering to them or subverting them in accordance with their sociocultural competence. This tension is variously described as a push–pull between forces of fixity and fluidity and centripetal/centrifugal forces (Gutiérrez, Bien, Selland, & Pierce, 2011; Pennycook & Otsuji, 2015). This tension comes to the forefront with heritage languages or revitalizing languages, such as te reo Māori. How we can encourage translanguaging while also ensuring a space for heritage language or revitalizing languaging, without adopting a separatist monolingual viewpoint, therefore becomes a key question. Sustainable translanguaging practices (Cenoz & Gorter, 2017) explore precisely that. Additionally, as we argue in this chapter and through the Wellington Translanguaging Project, translanguaging and language revitalization efforts need not compete. Rather, then can support each other, adding flexibility to the approaches we take so that learners and speakers can make use of the processes that best work for them.

2.2 Language politics and tikanga

Translanguaging as pedagogy has implications for policy and practice within the global context as it poses new ways of conceptualizing language learning. Translanguaging challenges the assumption that languages need to be learned separated by subject, teacher, or periods of time, and instead examines how to best use students' linguistic and semiotic resources to help them to learn and engage with the material being acquired (Lasagabaster & García, 2014). Nevertheless, it is understandable that within language communities there are real and valid fears of language loss. Within many revitalization efforts, the focus has been on keeping domains exclusively for one socially recognized language or another (e.g. Māori or English) (Higgins & Rewi, 2014). We do not present a criticism of communities or of this approach. Rather, we are interested in opening a dialogue of how translanguaging can open up space for learners' full linguistic repertoire, no matter what that looks like, so that learners are encouraged to make use of their full repertoire and build across it.

As researchers have pointed out, translanguaging allows students to participate more in language lessons as they have access to their full linguistic repertoire (García, 2009) (see also, Burgess & Fiti, this volume). Moreover, when considering the role of translanguaging for te reo Māori and English, it can be argued that establishing a translanguaging space where teachers and students are able to move between and beyond socially constructed language ideologies and educational systems, structures and practices, will help generate new configurations of language and education practices (García, 2009). Furthermore, we find translanguaging already existing within the established immersion school settings, including kura kaupapa

Māori, a primary school level of education rich in Māori knowledge, traditions and cultural values communicated through the Māori language (Tocker, 2014) (see also, Tamati, this volume). Even in kura kaupapa Māori, the use of students' expanded repertoires is written into the founding Te Aho Matua charter document as a part of their operation. Therefore, translanguaging may already be a practice within an immersion schooling system that is being used more than we realize to move dynamically between te reo Māori and English to fulfil a variety of strategic and communicative functions (Te Rūnanga Nui, 2008).

Tension arises between translanguaging and traditional language revitalization because both are political. In particular, language revitalization efforts require careful control of linguistic domains, and that control is partly intended to restore mana (status) to a language like te reo. That means re-establishing language domains and establishing new immersion domains to speak it. The language comes first. However, translanguaging asks us to put the focus on settings in the background and to instead adopt a view that speakers come first. Speakers should access a full linguistic repertoire in order to communicate, even if that includes a more dominant language such as English.

In Indigenous language communities (including Māori) there is a real and valid fear of language loss or of letting English in. Professors Higgins and Rewi have likened this to a "Gollum" effect, wanting to protect what is precious by keeping it close and keeping domains as exclusively Māori-speaking ones (Higgins & Rewi, 2014). This is not a criticism. Rather, we seek to further open up dialogue about how a translanguaging design can work with language revitalization efforts on a larger scale, opening up space for English because all Māori speakers have English in their repertoire. Furthermore, as shown by Tamati (this volume), translanguaging with te reo Māori and English can have a positive effect across students' linguistic repertoires and educational achievement. Therefore, translanguaging does not mean replacing language revitalization efforts. Instead, the two approaches can work together to achieve more dynamic positive outcomes linguistically, socially, and educationally.

Furthermore, we also acknowledge that when working in a Māori space, it is important to first understand and acknowledge the values and beliefs that are an integral part of te ao Māori (the Māori world/worldview) when considering the context of translanguaging. This can be done be examining tikanga, which is derived from the Māori word tika, meaning "right or correct", and translates to "rule, plan, method," or more broadly, "the Māori way of doing things." Tikanga can be further understood as the ethical and common law issues that underpin the behavior of members of whānau (families), hapū (clans), and iwi (tribes) as they go about their lives, especially when they engage in the cultural, social, ritual, and economic ceremonies of Māori society (Mead, 2003). Such customs are commonly based on experience and learning that has been handed down through generations and constitute general behavior guidelines for daily life and interactions that occur within Māori culture (Durie, 1996).

Tikanga Māori is made up of a range of governing principles that are based on Māori world views and that influence Māori behavior (c.f. Mead 2003). The tikanga principles that were more essential throughout this research were whanaungatanga (belonging, inclusiveness, connectedness), manaakitanga (helping and supporting each other), kotahitanga (working as one, together), rangatiratanga (self-governance, being in control), mōhiotanga (sharing information, understanding), tuakana–teina (expert/novice relationships, helping each other), and kaitiakitanga (guardianship, to nurture, reciprocity). Within this chapter, we will be focusing on three tikanga principles that were highly prevalent in our findings and also play an important part in the preservation of te reo Māori: whanaungatanga, manaakitanga, and tuakana–teina. Whanaungatanga and manaakitanga are fundamental within the Māori culture, as the principles highlight the value of connections that people build together to promote a culture of inclusiveness and support (Bishop, 1996). Moreover, the tuakana–teina relationship plays an important role in facilitating and nurturing learning between two individuals who may have varying levels of competency in different domains (Mead, 2003). These three principles in particular connect to the linguistic and cultural socialization that occurred regularly alongside translanguaging at the puna reo.

2.3 Socialization

The effect of children's peers and siblings on language use and preference is well known (de la Piedra & Romo, 2003; Myers-Scotton, 1993; Seals, 2013, 2017). Siblings and peers can help co-construct meaning and socialize children into cultural knowledge and language use (de la Piedra & Romo, 2003). Older siblings even help socialize children into language preferences dictated to by older sibling's school peers (Seals, 2017). Furthermore, school peers in particular can influence language preferences, in conjunction with socialization through education (Seals, 2013).

Additionally, children's parents, teachers, and other adults in their lives also have an effect on language use and preference (Duff, 2003; Hwang, 2003; Kim, 2008; Schieffelin & Ochs, 1986). As a result, multiple actors influence how children are socialized into language use, to varying degrees and in different ways. A simple input–output of children being socialized into particular languages through school or home is not necessarily realistic (Kim, 2008). Rather, children absorb interactional expectations, made up of sociolinguistic and sociocultural practices, when interacting with their peers, siblings, and adults of regular influence in their lives.

To add to the complexity, children are also socialized into societal and cultural structures and expectations from birth, sometimes even competing structures (Butler, 1993; Dawson, 2019; Eckert & McConnell-Ginet, 2013; Seals, 2017). These include gender constructs, varying national or cultural identities, power inequalities, and more. Combined with socialization from teachers, peers, and family, socialization into language use and preference is complex and multifaceted. Yet, it is ever-present in home and educational practices. When investigating the use of translanguaging in a multilingual, multicultural context such as a puna reo in Aotearoa NZ, the dynamic and complex nature of socialization is a key element of interaction. As such, this topic repeatedly emerged from our data and became one of our key findings, as discussed further in the "Findings and analysis" section below.

3. Context and method
3.1 Context
The research for this chapter was conducted as part of the ongoing Wellington Translanguaging Project. This chapter focuses specifically on one of our research communities – a puna reo located in the greater Wellington region of Aotearoa NZ. A puna reo is an early childhood education center in Aotearoa NZ that is centered within a Māori community and often connected with a marae (sacred community grounds). Puna reo operate in both te reo Māori and English, but the exact linguistic practice varies from puna to puna. There is also an emphasis on child development and learning through tikanga. At least half of a puna reo's teaching staff are registered teachers, and the Aotearoa NZ government provides funding to support the running of the puna reo. Puna reo are open to children from all backgrounds, and the majority of children who attend have some connection to Māori descent.

3.2 Positionality

Regarding the research team – we come from a variety of sociocultural and linguistic backgrounds. The research team who worked on this part of the project consists of seven individuals. Three of the research team members identify as Māori and speak te reo Māori fluently. One of the research team members identifies as being of Māori descent but is often positioned as Pākehā (New Zealand European) in society. Another of the research team members is Pākehā but speaks beginning te reo Māori and is very invested in Māori well-being. The final two members of the research team are originally from overseas but now reside in Aotearoa NZ and are strongly committed to social justice for Indigenous peoples. All members of the research team are multilingual and are invested in promoting multilingual education. We also come from a variety of academic backgrounds. While we all trained in myriad disciplines, three team members maintain a primary focus on Māori Studies, two maintain a primary focus on Linguistics, one maintains a primary focus on Educational Psychology, and one maintains a primary focus on Law. We thus bring together a variety of backgrounds and perspectives, allowing for continuously rich, deep critical conversations.

3.3 Method

To conduct this research, we utilized an approach that merged Kaupapa Māori and school-based ethnography, always working with and alongside the community and the puna reo. We first approached the puna reo through an intermediary who is known to both the research team and the puna reo staff. Through this intermediary, we set up a time for a hui (social meeting) to all get to know one another. We were invited to have the hui at the puna reo, and there we met the teachers, as well as some of the children and parents. After spending time getting to know one another and discussing the project, it was decided that we would all move forward with this endeavor. We made arrangements for the parents to also have a chance to get information about the project and let us know of any questions or concerns.

When everyone was ready to proceed, the project leads (Corinne Seals and Vincent Ieni Olsen-Reeder), along with two research assistants (Russell Pine and Te Owaimotu Crawford), spent some time visiting the puna reo to understand the setting and participants better. After a few weeks, it was agreed by all parties that the data collection would begin. At this point, the decision was made for Russell and Te Owaimotu to attend the puna reo as participant observers twice per week for eight weeks, for three hours each time. During this time, they assisted the teachers whenever appropriate and observed the children's interactions and the workings of the puna reo. Simultaneously, three small video cameras and three hand-held audio recorders were set up in locations around the puna reo teaching space to gather a variety of perspectives and different levels of interactional detail. In total, approximately 250 hours of data was gathered.

We then allowed the data to "speak for itself," coding it emergently in NVivo10 and 11. All members of the research team received NVivo coding training, and all coding was normed across team members. We coded the data based on trends that we saw in the data, including anything to do with significant patterns in interaction, language use, mātauranga Māori, and connections to tikanga. At bi-weekly meetings, the research team reviewed the codes for consistency.

Once coding was completed, we ran "queries" looking for cross-code correlations to better understand the data. We then identified interactional patterns across the data and selected excerpts to transcribe and subject to interactional sociolinguistic discourse analysis (making use of our ethnographic knowledge in interpreting the discourse). The results presented below highlight three of our key findings: (1) the role of language use in socialization between children at the puna reo, as well as between children and the teachers; (2)

the interaction significance of translanguaging for bridge building between languages and cultures; and (3) student uptake and use of translanguaging as modeled by the teachers.

4. Findings and analysis
4.1 Language use and socialization
The first cross-code query that was meaningful in NVivo involved the intersections between coded nodes that described a "type of interaction" (i.e. questions, using agency, shifting attention, conflict) and coding to either the "Speaking English" or "Speaking te reo Māori" node. It is important to note here that while these labels identify individual socially constructed named languages, we coded by turn at interaction. That is to say, where translanguaging occurred in the turn, that turn was coded to both nodes. We did this to determine in part how often translanguaging was occurring in the data versus how often speakers were using one prescribed language or another. In the second query, NVivo was used to search for intersections between coding to nodes that described a particular activity (e.g. singing, painting, play, eating) and coding to either the "Speaking English" or "Speaking te reo Māori" node, or to both of these nodes.

Generally, as shown in figures 1 and 2, there was almost equal use of English and te reo across many different activities and types of interaction (differences were not statistically significant). Instances of "Speaking English" are shown to the left of each pair, while instances of "Speaking te reo Māori" are shown to the right of each pair. These figures show the relative frequency of te reo Māori and English in interaction at the puna reo. Regardless of the type of interaction or the specific activity (from high-frequency instances of children playing together and the use of directives to low-frequency instances of counting out loud and prompting), the use of English and te reo were relatively equal in the puna reo, which matches with the regular translanguaging that we observed in this space.

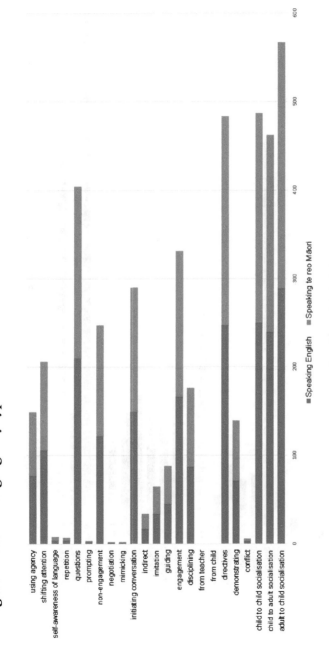

Figure 1. Use of "language" by type of interaction

Figure 2. Use of "language" by activity type

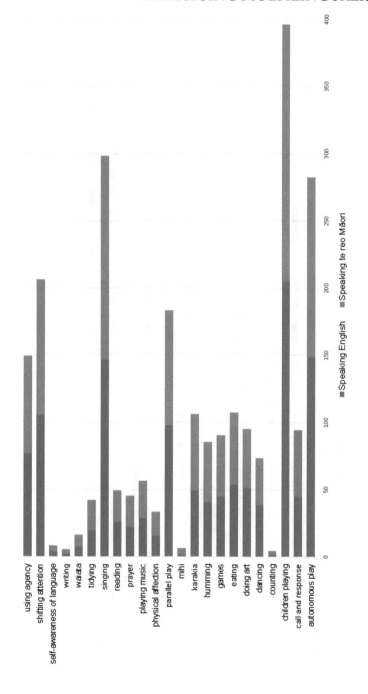

Further, the first query (type of interaction by "language") revealed high levels of socialization across both English and te reo. Table 1, below, displays the four most frequently occurring intersections between "type of interaction" nodes and English and te reo Māori nodes. Furthermore, of the top four categories, three were forms of socialization. This reveals that the socialization occurring was frequent and varied: both child- and adult-initiated, and both when interlocutors were children and adults. Adult-to-child socialization was coded 290 times as coinciding with English use and 279 times with te reo use. Child-to-child socialization was coded 251 times as coinciding with English use and 238 times with te reo use. Directives occurred 248 times in English and 237 times in te reo, and child-to-adult socialization occurred in 241 instances where English was used and 223 where te reo was used. Therefore, the data demonstrates no significant difference in the amount of socialization across languages, indicating that both te reo and English are crucial to the children's socialization at the puna reo.

Table 1. Type of interaction by "language"

Type of Interaction Node	Occurrences speaking English	Occurrences speaking te reo	Ratio of occurrences in English to te reo
child-to-adult socialisation	241	223	1.08 : 1
directives	248	237	1.05 : 1
child-to-child socialisation	251	238	1.05 : 1
adult-to-child socialisation	290	279	1.04 : 1

The second query (type of activity by "language") revealed that certain activities coincided with more translanguaging. The top five most frequently occurring intersections between activity nodes and English or te reo nodes are displayed in Table 2. Three different kinds of play frequently occurred with high uses of both languages (while translanguaging). Children playing together occurred 207 times coded with English use and 192 coded with te reo. Autonomous play was coded 149 times as coinciding with English use and 133 times with te reo use. Parallel play was coded 98 times as coinciding with English use and 85 times with te reo use. Moreover, when looking at structured activities, there were two in particular that occurred with high use of both languages: singing occurred 148 times in English and 152 times in te reo, and karakia (prayer) was coded 50 times as coinciding with English use and 56 times with te reo use. Like the findings related to type of interaction (Table 1), translanguaging occurred across all activities with an almost equal representation across English and te reo Māori.

Table 2. Type of activity by "language"

Activity Node:	Occurrences speaking English:	Occurrences speaking te reo:	Ratio of occurrences in English to te reo:
karakia	50	56	1 : 1.79
parallel play	98	85	1.15 : 1
autonomous play	149	133	1.12 : 1
singing	148	152	1 : 1.03
children playing	207	192	1.08 : 1

The findings discussed above were further evidenced in the discourse that we recorded and analyzed via interactional sociolinguistics. One of these extended representative excerpts is presented in the next section to show the richness of translanguaging that occurs in the puna reo.

4.2 Teachers' modeling of translanguaging and student uptake
The excerpt that follows is an extended example of the translanguaging interactions that we observed every day at the puna reo. The original spoken text is on the left, with the translation into English on the right. Any words associated with te reo Māori are in bold, while any words associated with English are not. As can be seen in Excerpt 1, translanguaging practices are a natural part of communication at the puna reo, with both teachers and children (tamariki) using translanguaging. Of particular interest in this section of the chapter are the ways in which the children provide updates to the teachers' translanguaging practices, and how the children then repeat the translanguaging practices into which they have been socialized.

Excerpt 1. Natural translanguaging in a puna reo

	Speaker	Original	Gloss
1	Teacher	**Ata mārie tamariki mā.**	**Morning children.**
2	Tamariki	**Ata mārie Whaea A--.**	**Morning Whaea A--.**
3	Teacher	**Kei te pēhea koutou i te rā nei?**	How are you today?
4	Tamariki	**Āe.**	Yes.
5	Teacher	**Kei te pai koutou?**	Are you well?
6	Tamariki	**Āe.**	Yes.

	Speaker	Original	Gloss
7	Teacher	I au ō koutou moe inapō?	Did you have a good sleep last night?
8		Did yous have a good sleep?	Did yous have a good sleep?
9		......	......
10		Kei te . . . R–	It is . . . R--
11		Tino pai tō tū i tō ringa he aha . . .	It's very good you putting your hand up, what is it . . .
12		He aha te āhua o te huarere ki waho?	What is the weather like outside?
13		What's the weather like outside?	What's the weather like outside?
14		Titiro ki waho.	Look outside.
15		Nā R-- te wā ki te kōrero i tū tana ringa.	It is R--'s time to talk, he put his hand up.
16 17		It's R--'s time to speak so me wahangū tātou.	It's R--'s time to speak so we need to be quiet.
18	Child 1	Raining.	Raining.
19	Teacher	Āe kei te ua, he aha atu?	Yes, it is raining, what else?
20		Tū mai to ringa Re---.	Put your hand up Re---.
21	Child 2	Wet.	Wet.
22	Teacher	Āe tino pai tō whakautu.	Yes very good answer.
23		K----.	K----.
24	Child 3	Cold.	Cold.

	Speaker	Original	Gloss
25 26	Teacher	**Āe kei te pupuhi te hau, kei te makariri, kei te ua hoki nē.**	**Yes, the wind is blowing, its cold, it is raining too.**
27 28		So **mehemea ka haere tātou ki waho me aha?**	So **if we go outside, what should we do?**
29		**P---.**	**P---.**
30	Child 1	Put your **pōtae** on or your **hū.**	Put your **hat** on or your **shoes.**
31	Teacher	**Ka pai, he aha atu?**	**Good, what else?**
32	Child 4	Umm…. Umm, put your jacket on.	Umm…. Umm, put your jacket on.
33 34	Teacher	**Āe me whakamau ō koti nē nō reira tino makariri ki waho.**	**Yes, you need to wear your jacket because it is cold outside.**
35		It's very cold outside.	It's very cold outside.
36 37 38		If we get a chance to go outside **me mau ō pōtae,** so **pōtae mahana,** your beanie **pērā ki a** Russell.	If we get a chance to go outside **you should wear your hat,** so **warm hat,** your beanie **like** Russell.
39		**Tītiro pērā ki a** Russell.	**Look, just like** Russell.
40		**Me mau ō koti me mau hoki i ō hū.**	**You should wear your jacket and you should also wear your shoes.**
41 42		We don't want to see anyone running outside with no **hū** on okay.	We don't want to see anyone running outside with no **shoes** on okay.
43 44		Okay **me whakamau ō hu i mua i tō puta i te kūaha** okay.	Okay **you need you put your shoes on before you exit the door** okay.

	Speaker	Original	Gloss
45	Teacher	**Nō reira i kite a Whaea**	**So Whaea J-- saw some**
46		**J-- i tētahi tamaiti e tino**	**children that were**
47		**kaha ana ki te whakapai**	**awesome at tidying up**
		i tēnei rā.	**today.**
48		So **Whaea** J-- saw	So **Whaea J--** saw
49		someone that was doing	someone that was doing
		awesome at tidying up.	awesome at tidying up.
50		**Ko ia anake.**	**He was the only one.**
51		He was the only one.	He was the only one.
52		The rest of you **i te noho**	The rest of you **just sat**
		noa.	**there.**
53		**Me whakapai tātou**	**We all need to tidy up**
		katoa nē i te wā	**when it is time to tidy**
54		**whakapai.**	**up.**
55		**Ehara noa mā tētahi**	**It's not a job for only**
		tamaiti.	**one person.**
56		We all need to help when	We all need to help when
		it's time to **whakapai.**	it's time to **tidy up.**
57		**Kaua e waiho noa iho**	**Don't just leave it for**
58		**mō tētahi tamaiti.**	**one child.**
59		Don't just leave it for one	Don't just leave it for one
		person.	person.
60		So **homai koa ō taramu**	So **give me a drumroll**
		mō te whetū o te	**please for the star of the**
61		**rangi...**	**day....**
62		**Ko R--!**	**It is R--!**
63		**Ka pai R--!**	**Good job R--!**
		Haere mai.	**Come over here.**

	Speaker	Original	Gloss
64	Teacher	**Tino pai tō mahi e hoa**	**Very good work my**
65		**me mahi tonu koe.**	**friend, keep up the good work.**
66		**I te rā katoa** we wanna see that – that **mahi** all	**Every day** we wanna see that – that work all
67		day okay, not just **i te ata.**	day okay, not just **in the morning.**
68		So **māu tō mātou karakia**	So **you lead our prayer**
69		(and then **ka kai mātou**).	(and then **we will eat**).
70		**Whakarongo** L-- 'kay?	**Listen** L--, 'kay?
71		**Nā R-- te wāhi ināianei ki te kōrero me wahangū**	**It is R--'s time to talk now so we need to be**
72		**me īnoi tātou.**	**quiet and say our prayer.**
73		Te whakamā koe?	Are you shy?
74		Are you shy?	Are you shy?
75		Mā Whaea e tīmata, okay?	Whaea will start, okay?

When the excerpt begins, the teacher, Whaea A ("Auntie A"), engages the students in the regular morning ritual of saying good morning and asking if they're well. (The rote sequence usually includes asking "are you well?" instead of "how are you?", which explains the children's answer of "yes" in lines 4 and 6.) Immediately after this opening sequence, Whaea A moves into one of the two most common types of pedagogical translanguaging that we found at the puna reo – she first speaks in te reo Māori and then repeats herself in English (lines 7–8 and 13–14). At first, it appeared that this was a simple self-translation to make sure all students were following along. However, our puna reo data holistically suggests that this type of translanguaging is more complex than that. Rather,

Whaea A is engaging in the type of self-repetition commonly found within child–caregiver interactions (Bost, Shin, McBride, Brown, Vaughn, Coppola, Veríssimo, Monteiro, & Korth, 2006; Girolametto & Weitzman, 2002; Thomason & La Paro, 2009), and she is translanguaging in the process. That is, instead of repeating herself twice in the same language as is commonly found in child–caregiver interactions, Whaea A is translanguaging midway through this interactional event. Thus, she is utilizing *translanguaging in self-repetition.*

As Whaea A's interactional turn continues, she moves into a second type of translanguaging – *continuous segmental translanguaging* (lines 17 and 18). Whaea A is translanguaging across grammatical segments of speech, as is common practice for multilinguals when not self-monitoring a strict adherence to a particular linguistic variety. Then, in line 20, Whaea A employs *cross-speaker interactional translanguaging*, building on the student's English utterance with te reo Māori, after first recasting the student's utterance into te reo. Whaea A utilizes cross-speaker interactional translanguaging again in the following turns, in lines 23 and again in lines 26–27, each time continuing the conversation while translanguaging interactionally. In line 28, we then see Whaea A again use continuous segmental translanguaging, first speaking a discourse marker of turn continuance ("so") before saying the content of the message in te reo Māori.

Whaea A's translanguaging strategies are regularly used at the puna reo, and her use of these strategies have socialized the children into the acceptance of translanguaging in this space. This becomes apparent when we see one of the students use continuous segmental translanguaging in line 30 to answer Whaea A's question from line 28. Whaea A then affirms the student's use of translanguaging in 31, saying "ka pai" [good], which likely affirms the student's participation, correct answer, and the acceptability of the student's use of translanguaging in answering. As evidenced by Whaea A's immediate continuance of the interaction, translanguaging practices are accepted as normal at the puna reo, not requiring any explicit reference to them.

Whaea A's use of translanguaging in self-repetition, continuous segmental translanguaging, and cross-speaker interactional translanguaging continue throughout the duration of the excerpt, and indeed throughout all of our observation data from the puna reo, speaking to its normalcy in practice. The children at the puna reo regularly participate in these verbal interactions with their teachers, utilising their linguistic resources as they see fit – sometimes relying on English, sometimes te reo Māori, and sometimes preferring translanguaging as modeled by Whaea A. In all cases, it is the children's active participation that is praised, as they develop the skills they need to be active learners at the puna reo.

5. Discussion: Translanguaging for inclusiveness

Translanguaging is a skill that can be developed for all learners, regardless of specific language background. This is important for the Aotearoa NZ educational environment, as learning spaces often include students who display varying degrees of multilingual competencies, including, for example, pupils with similar age-related competence in te reo Māori and English, students with competence in te reo Māori but who need to reinforce some aspects of their linguistic skills in English, and students with competence in English but who have not yet developed skills in te reo Māori (Harbott, 2017). In these rich and diverse linguistic environments, it is essential for teachers to support fluid multilingual development and to ensure that there is a space where students can coexist in order for them to have opportunities to translanguage in both pedagogic and non-pedagogic contexts. When translanguaging is modeled and used naturally, as in the puna reo where teachers were able to use English and te reo Māori with a high degree of flexibility, students' use of fluid multilingualism as a strategy for making meaning is supported and valued (Pacheco & Miller, 2015).

The teachers' natural use of translanguaging in the puna reo was skilfully implemented, as discussed in the section above. For students and teachers, the practice of intertwining languages to utilize their full linguistic repertoire was normal and was often embedded in tikanga principles, which comprise a strong foundation of the educational system and culture in Aotearoa NZ. By normalizing translanguaging and incorporating tikanga while doing so, knowledge of te reo is given status and encouraged among children, while continuously building upon their full linguistic repertoire. This not only enables children to develop a deeper and fuller understanding of te reo Māori, but also aligns with tikanga practices that are an essential part of children's development in Aotearoa NZ.

Furthermore, there are a number of educational advantages in translanguaging, including facilitating home-school links and helping the integration of fluent speakers with early learners (Baker, 2006). Such educational advantages integrate the practice of whanaungatanga as a sense of belonging and inclusiveness can be developed through establishing relationships with others. Likewise, manaakitanga is highlighted in this same passage when Whaea A emphasizes the importance of working together to support one another during clean up time. This is shown, for example, in Excerpt 1 when the teacher praises one of the students for helping care for the puna reo and reminds the other students that it is a job they all need to share and support each other in doing (lines 52–65). During this connection to tikanga, Whaea A utilizes both translanguaging in self-repetition and continuous segmental translanguaging throughout, therein communicating with children of varying linguistic backgrounds and making this connection accessible to all of them. Additionally, translanguaging further promotes whanaungatanga, as it enables the flexibility of different language repertoires, therein embodying belonging and inclusiveness.

Further, assumptions such as the need to be fully competent in the language before speaking it can be challenged when individuals are free to move in a "safe space" and shuttle between their unique linguistic repertoires. Challenging assumptions and using language to open up communication supports crucial connections while also integrating and promoting tikanga practices within educational settings. Furthermore, the processes of whanaungatanga and manaakitanga are associated with the enhancement of students' learning environments and well-being and can lead to positive student outcomes (Berryman, 2014).

Finally, the integration of fluent speakers and highly skilled translanguagers[2] with early learners connects the tikanga principle of tuakana–teina. The tuakana–teina relationship is an integral part of traditional Māori society and is used extensively in learning environments throughout Aotearoa NZ. This is because it provides a model for buddy systems where an older or more expert tuakana (brother, sister, or cousin) helps and guides a younger or less expert teina (Hemara, 2000). In the puna reo, this was a common and normal practice that involved children supporting each other, as well as teachers supporting the children, to enhance linguistic skills and understanding of te ao Māori.

Therefore, translanguaging not only promotes pedagogical practices that take into consideration multilingualism as a resource, but it also aids in embedding tikanga and making it accessible for children from a variety of linguistic backgrounds. Tikanga also becomes a part of the learning process, in and through translanguaging practices that provide an additional function for interactions. The potential benefits of creating such rich and diverse spaces for translanguaging to occur both in schooling environments and at home are pivotal for starting

2   Note: Fluency and skillful translanguaging are not the same thing. As we found in our data, the most fluent speakers are not always the most skillful translanguagers, and vice versa.

to move towards embracing new ways of thinking and preserving the important role tikanga plays in the culture of Aotearoa NZ. Education systems must start to move away from traditional views of bilingualism (where there is a focus on dividing and learning specified languages independently of each other) to a more flexible view that will foster the development of fluid, dynamic linguistic practices and the co-development of transcultural understandings therein.

6. Conclusion

As we have shown in this chapter, translanguaging is used strategically and regularly in the puna reo. Through translanguaging practices, children are socialized into fluid multilingualism practices and are encouraged to engage with te reo Māori however they feel comfortable – receptively (while actively responding in English), actively (using te reo), and/or via translanguaging practices. Furthermore, through the regular use of translanguaging, children are shown via linguistic modeling that translanguaging is an accepted practice at the puna reo and that the focus is more on participating in the interaction, regardless of what linguistic resources are used in the process. Additionally, the use of translanguaging during play, in particular, supports the research showing that translanguaging is a natural practice for multilingual speakers.

This chapter also discusses the interwovenness of translanguaging and transcultural practices. For example, both karakia and singing in te reo Māori occur frequently alongside translanguaging in the puna reo, underlining the cultural value of translanguaging practices alongside immersive te reo practices. Additionally, by normalizing translanguaging and incorporating tikanga, knowledge of te reo Māori and multilingual skills are given status and encouraged for the children at the puna reo, while simultaneously socializing children into te ao Māori. This co-occurrence of fluid multilingualism and traditional Māori practices signals the possibilities for utilising translanguaging while still making space for te reo Māori, as recommended by sustainable translanguaging advocates. As previously stated, translanguaging practices and revitalization efforts need not compete. Instead, they can work together to encourage a stronger presence for te reo Māori in children's present and future linguistic repertoires.

References

Baker, C. (2006). *Foundations of Bilingual Education and Bilingualism*, 4th edn. Bristol: Multilingual Matters.

Berryman, M. (2014). *Evaluation indicators for school reviews: A commentary on engaging parents, whanau and communities.* Background paper prepared for the review of the Education Review Office's Evaluation Indicators for School Reviews.

Bishop, R. (1996). Addressing issues of self-determination and legitimation on kaupapa Māori research. In B. Webber (Ed.) *He Paepae Korero, research perspectives in Māori education* (pp. 143–160). Wellington: New Zealand Council for Educational Research.

Bost, K. K., Shin, N., McBride, B. A., Brown, G. L., Vaughn, B. E., Coppola, G., Veríssimo, M., Monteiro, L., & Korth, B. (2006). Maternal secure base scripts, children's attachment security, and mother-child narrative styles. *Attachment & Human Development, 8*(3), 241–260.

Butler, J. (1993). *Bodies that matter: on the discursive limits of 'sex'.* London: Routledge.

Canagarajah, S. (2013). *Translingual practice: global Englishes and cosmopolitan relations.* New York: Routledge.

Cenoz, J., & Gorter, D. (2017). Minority languages and sustainable translanguaging: threat or opportunity? *Journal of Multilingual and Multicultural Development,* 1–12. doi:10.1080/01434632.2017.1284 855

Dawson, S. (2019). *Language Learner Identities: Moving between National Contexts.* Doctoral thesis. Victoria University of Wellington. New Zealand.

de la Piedra, M. & Romo, H. D. (2003). Collaborative literacy in a Mexican immigrant household: The role of sibling mediators in the socialization of pre-school learners. In R. Bayley & S. R. Schecter (Eds.), *Language Socialization in Bilingual and Multilingual Societies* (pp. 44–61). Buffalo, NY: Multilingual Matters.

Duff, P. A. (2003). New directions in second language socialization research. *Korean Journal of English Language and Linguistics, 3*, 309–339.

Durie, E. (1996). Will the settlers settle? Cultural conciliation and law. *Otago Law Review, 3(8), 449–465.*

Eckert, P. & McConnell-Ginet, S. (2013). *Language and Gender.* Cambridge: Cambridge University Press.

García, O. (2009). *Bilingual education in the 21st century: A global perspective.* Malden, MA: Wiley-Blackwell.

García, O., & Wei, L. (2014). *Translanguaging: Language, Bilingualism and Education.* Basingstoke: Palgrave Macmillan.

Girolametto, L. & Weitzman, E. (2002). Responsiveness of child care providers in interactions with toddlers and preschoolers. *Language, Speech, and Hearing Services in Schools, 33*(4), 268–281.

Gutiérrez, K. D., Bien, A. C., Selland, M. K., & Pierce, D. M. (2011). Polylingual and polycultural learning ecologies: Mediating emergent academic literacies for dual language learners. *Journal of Early Childhood Literacy, 11*(2), 232–261. doi:10.1177/1468798411399273

Harbott, N. (2017). Educating for diversity in New Zealand: Considerations of current practices and possible pathways? *Journal of Initial Teacher Inquiry, 3*, 20–23.

Hemara, W. (2000). Māori pedagogies: A view from the literature. Wellington, New Zealand: New Zealand Council for Educational Research.

Higgins, R. & Rewi, P. (2014). Right-shifting: Reorientation towards Normalisation.

Higgins, R., Rewi, P. and Olsen-Reeder, V. (eds.), *The Value of the Māori Language Te Hua o te Reo Māori, 2*, 7–32.

Hwang, H.S. (2003). *Constructing social identities and language socialization practices in an intermarried family with a transplanted Korean mother.* Unpublished PhD thesis. Tallahassee: Florida State University.

Kim, J. (2008). *Negotiating multiple investments in languages and identities:*

The language socialization of generation 1.5 Korean-Canadian university students. Unpublished PhD thesis. Vancouver: The University of British Columbia.

Lasagabaster, D. & García, O. (2014) *Translanguaging*: towards a dynamic model of bilingualism at school/Translanguaging: hacia un modelo dinámico de bilingüismo en la escuela, *Cultura y Educación 26*(3), 557–572.

Makoni, S. B. & Pennycook, A. (2006). *Disinventing and Reconstituting Languages*. Clevedon: Multilingual Matters.

Mead, H. M. (2003). *Tikanga Māori: Living by Māori values*. Wellington: Huia Publishers.

Myers-Scotton, C. (1993). *Social Motivations for Codeswitching: Evidence from Africa*. Oxford: Oxford University Press.

Ngaha, A. B. (2005). Language and Identity in the Māori Community. In J. Holmes, M. Maclagan, P. Kerswill, M. Paviour-Smith (Eds.), *Researching language use and language* (pp. 29–48). E-book of the 2004 Language and Society Conference. http://www.vuw.ac.nz/lals/about/NZLS/NZLingSoc.html#anchor1283518.

Pacheco, M. B., & Miller, M. E. (2016). Making Meaning Through Translanguaging in the Literacy Classroom. *The Reading Teacher, 69*(5), 533–537.

Pennycook, A., & Otsuji, E. (2015). *Metrolingualism: language in the city*. New York: Routledge.

Pihama, L. (2001). *Tihei mauri ora: Honouring our voices. Mana wahine as kaupapa Māori theoretical framework*. Unpublished PhD thesis. Auckland, NZ: The University of Auckland.

Pohatu, T. (1996). *I tipu ai tātou i ngā turi o o tatatau mātua tīpuna: Transmission and acquisition processes within kāwai whakapapa*. Unpublished Masters of Education thesis. Auckland, NZ: The University of Auckland.

Royal Society of New Zealand. (2013). *Languages in Aotearoa New Zealand*. Retrieved from http://royalsociety.org.nz/media/Languages-in-Aotearoa-New-Zealand.pdf

Schieffelin, B. B. & Ochs, E. (1986). Language socialization. In B.J. Siegel, A.R. Beals, & (eds.), Annual Review ofAnthropology (pp. 163–246).

S.A.T. (eds.) *Annual Review of Anthropology* (pp. 163–246). Palo Alto: Annual Reviews, Inc.

Seals, C. A. (2013). Te espero: Varying child bilingual abilities and the effects on dynamics in Mexican immigrant families. *Issues in Applied Linguistics, 16*(1), 119–142.

Seals, C. A. (2017). Dynamic Family Language Policy: Heritage Language Socialization and Strategic Accommodation in the Home. In J. Macalister & S. H. Mirvahedi (Eds.), *Family Language Policies in a Multilingual World: Opportunities, Challenges, and Consequences* (pp. 175–194). London: Routledge.

Seals, C. A. & Olsen-Reeder, V. (2017). Te Reo Māori, Samoan, and Ukrainian in New Zealand. In C. A. Seals & S. Shah, (Eds.) *Heritage Language Policies around the World* (pp. 221–236). London: Routledge.

Smith, G. H. (1997). *Kaupapa Māori: Theory and praxis.* Unpublished PhD thesis. Auckland, NZ: The University of Auckland.

Smith, L. T. (1997). *Ngā aho o te kākahu mātauranga: The multiple layers of struggle by Māori in education.* Unpublished PhD thesis. Auckland, NZ: The University of Auckland.

Statistics New Zealand. (2013). *2013 Census totals by topic.* Retrieved May 20, 2014, from http://www.stats.govt.nz/~/media/Statistics/Census/2013%20Census/data-tables/totals-by-topic/totals-by-topic-tables.xls

Te Rūnanga Nui (2008). *Evaluation Indicators for Kura Kaupapa Māori Reviews.* Wellington: Education Review Office. Available at http://www.ero.govt.nz/assets/Uploads/Evaluation-Indicators-March-2012.pdf

Thomason, A. C. & La Paro, K. M. (2009). Measuring the quality of teacher-child interactions in toddler child care. *Early Education and Development, 20*(2), 285–304.

Tocker, K. (2014). *Hei oranga Māori i te ao hurihuri nei. Living as Māori in the world today: An account of kura kaupapa Māori.* The University of Auckland. ResearchSpace@Auckland.

Williams, C. (1994). *Arfarniado Ddulliau Dysguac Addysguyng Nghyddestun Addysg Uwchradd Ddwyieithog.* Unpublished PhD thesis. Bangor: University of Wales.

CHAPTER 4

TransAcquisition Pedagogy with emergent bilinguals in Indigenous and minority groups for cultural and linguistic sustainability

Sophie Tauwehe Tamati

1. Introduction

This chapter focuses on the academic achievement of Māori students, in particular, a group of 24 Year 7 and 8 students enrolled in two kura kaupapa Māori schools. In kura, te reo Māori[1] is the main language of communication and curriculum instruction. Discussion in this chapter unpacks the TransAcquisition effect on the kura students' reading performance in English, which resulted in achievement levels well beyond what would be expected among similarly abled English-medium students. Kura kaupapa Māori schools were established in 1989 by the Education Amendment Act (1989, Section 155). The kura immersion model emerged out of a growing concern among kohanga reo[2] families that their children's fluency in te reo Māori would be lost if the Māori language immersion approach did not continue into their primary schooling (G. H. Smith, 1997) (for further discussion of Māori language education, see Seals, Pine, Ash, Olsen-Reeder, & Wallace, this volume). The Māori language

---

1   The Māori language
2   Māori immersion Early Childhood Education language nests

'immersion approach' was predicated on the belief that English would happen automatically since it pervaded every aspect of society. This resulted in the commonly held view that conversational English and academic English were one in the same thing and instruction in English wasn't needed (Hill, 2011).

However, following the turn of the century, Berryman and Glynn (2004) published an extensive list of issues associated with the provision of English instruction in kura. Their study identified the lack of evidence, resources, monitoring and evaluation information available for kura teachers to assist them in transitioning their students from "literacy in Māori to literacy in English" (Berryman & Glynn 2004, p. 144). It was clear that a change from the "English will happen automatically approach" (Tamati, 2011, p. 91) was required, and in 2005 that change came in the form of the "separate language approach" (ibid., p. 95). The separate language approach supports the practice of delineating English and Māori language zones and the assigning of different teachers for each language (Tākao, Grennell, McKegg, & Wehipeihana, 2010). This has prompted the view that English is competing against te reo Māori rather than complementing it, which has resulted in the practice of delaying English instruction, and, in some cases, "excluding it altogether" (Hill & May, 2014, p. 161).

Although English is the home language of most kura students (Bauer, 2008; May & Hill, 2004) their exposure to the academic language of English is limited. Schleppegrell (2012) describes academic language as a set of registers through which schooling activities are accomplished and by which children are expected to learn and use in their learning. Bernstein's (2000) research focused on the challenges of academic language for children unaccustomed to using it because of their social class. This is relevant because kura are situated in low socioeconomic communities (Office of the Auditor-General, 2010). Without explicit instruction in English, kura students are ill equipped to bridge what Bernstein (2000) terms as the "discursive gap" (p. 30) between the social English spoken at home and the academic English of leveled reading texts. This dilemma is evident in Hill's (2017, p. 49) study, which focused on the transition of five kura kaupapa Māori students to English secondary schooling:

> Fully participating in English-medium secondary school requires a confidence in the elements of academic English language that are not being sufficiently nurtured by either secondary schools or Māori-medium primary schools.

The aim of the study (Tamati, 2016) was to theorize, trial and evaluate the effectiveness of TransAcquisition Pedagogy in developing academic English literacy in 24 Year 7 and 8 students at two kura kaupapa Māori. If successful, TransAcquisition Pedagogy could provide an empirically validated approach to transition kura students from literacy in Māori to literacy in English.

2. TransAcquisition Pedagogy (TAP)

TransAcquisition Pedagogy (TAP) is theoretically justified by Cummins's (1981a, 1981b, 2001) idea of developmental language interdependence, which underpins his Common Underlying Proficiency (CUP) model. However, as an extension of Cummins's (ibid.) thinking, TAP uses the entwined roots of kahikatea trees to reconceptualize his idea of a centralized metalinguistic thinking system as an Interrelational Translingual Network (ITN). TAP is also an extension of Williams's (1994, 2002) translanguaging technique and aligns to García and Wei's (2014, p. 137) description of translanguaging as the "ways in which bilinguals use their complex semiotic repertoire to act, to know and to be." TAP draws on Hopewell's (2011, p. 604) research by assisting multilingual students to understand how to "draw on all their linguistic resources to accelerate their bilingual and biliterate development."

2.1 The TransAcquisition metaphor

TAP uses the metaphor of kahikatea trees, which normally grow in soft soil environments as groves where each tree entwines its buttressed roots with those of its neighbors to form a thick, matted footing that supports all the trees. The distinctive root system of the kahikatea trees is used to illustrate Cummins's (1981a, 1981b, 2001) idea of developmental language interdependence in his CUP model. The kahikatea metaphor characterizes languages as symbolic trees in the mind of the multilingual student that grow and develop individually and collectively in the language and literacy learning process. As a metaphoric representation of linguistic independence and interdependence, the entwined, entangled root system of the kahikatea trees symbolize the metacognitive web of linguistic and conceptual interrelationships between the languages of the multilingual student. In this way, the individual vitality of each language is enhanced when all the languages are utilized in the learning process.

2.2 The TransAcquisition cognitive linguistic principles

The TransAcquisition kahikatea metaphor naturally aligns to Hornberger's (2004) ecological linguistic framework which depicts language learning as an organic process, whereby one language and literacy develops in relation to one or more of the multilingual student's other languages and literacies. The transacquisitional language and literacy learning process is characterized as an organic process underpinned by three language and cognition principles. These principles engage multilingual students in flexible multilingualism (Creese & Blackledge, 2010) to use their languages interdependently in mutually supportive ways to acquire academic language through which academic knowledge is expressed. The TransAcquisition cognitive linguistic principles are *linguistic fluidity, relational transfer*, and *metashuttling*.

Linguistic fluidity is the natural, unconscious interflow of linguistic symbols and concepts between the languages of the multilingual student. This cognitive interflow represents the complex meanings associated with the academic knowledge taught in schools. Central to the TAP approach is the idea that this cognitive interflow remains untapped and under-utilized without explicit pedagogical intervention using transacquisitional tasking. The principle of linguistic fluidity aligns with what Creese and Blackledge (2010) describe as "permeable boundaries between languages" when multilingual students engage in flexible multilingualism.

The principle of *relational transfer* refers to what occurs when the multilingual student's metalinguistic processes are focused on interlingual relationships. It is synonymous with pedagogies that emphasize language fluidity and the overlapping of languages rather than the separation of languages (see Centeno-Cortés & Jiménez, 2004; García, 2011; García & Leiva, 2014). Relational transfer is activated when linguistic fluidity is pedagogically utilized in the transacquisitional Read-to-Retell-to-Revoice-to-Rewrite (R2R) tasking sequence. The transacquisitional tasking process is used to expand vocabulary, deepen reading comprehension and accelerate bilingual/biliterate development. The significance of relational transfer is justified by mounting evidence that confirms transfer between languages and literacies accelerates both primary language and target language development (see Cummins, 2008; Lowman, Fitzgerald, Rapira, & Clark, 2007; McCaffery, Villers, & Lowman, 2008). TAP uses the R2R tasking process to systematize the pedagogic use of linguistic fluidity and optimize relational transfer for accelerated bilingual and biliterate development.

The *metashuttling* principle describes the ability of multilingual students to consider their thinking while moving their thoughts back and forth between their languages. Metashuttling prompts students to focus on the reciprocal translingual interflow of concepts between their languages. While engaged in metashuttling, students use the intralingual and interlingual relationships in their linguistic repertoire to promote mutual language and literacy development. "Intralingual relationships" refers to the interconnected linguistic relationships *within* a language, while "interlingual relationships" refers to the interconnected linguistic relationships *between* languages. Not only does metashuttling enrich conceptual understanding, it also supports progressive conceptual development when students use it to compare, contrast, and clarify their conceptual understanding.

2.3 The Interrelational Translingual Network (ITN)

The kahikatea metaphor underpins the conceptualization of the multilingual student's ITN as the cognitive translingual facility by which the TAP principles are pedagogically utilized. The ITN conceptualization was inspired by the entwined entanglement of roots that girds the kahikatea trees together. As a refinement of Cummins's (2001) CUP model, the ITN is conceived as a web of linguistic and conceptual interrelationships between the syntactic instructions and semantic meanings that are intrinsic to each of the multilingual student's languages. The ITN is therefore conceptualized as an evolving organic web of complex interconnected linguistic and conceptual interrelationships that expands when a new language and literacy is being learned.

The ITN facility is activated when students engage in cross-linguistic analysis to identify linguistic and conceptual interrelationships at each stage of the R2R tasking sequence. This form of transacquisitional cross-linguistic analysis allows new knowledge to be integrated with previously acquired schemas to form new schemas in the biliterate learning process. The R2R tasking process provides multiple opportunities to engage the ITN facility and habitualizes the transacquisitional processing of schemas. Transacquisitional tasking maximizes the pedagogical value of engaging the student's

ITN to accelerate bilingual and biliterate development. It is via the ITN facility that the centralized processing system in Cummins's (2001) CUP model is pedagogically operationalized in the biliterate teaching of academic language and knowledge.

2.4 Transacquisitional tasking

Transacquisitional tasking is an example of epistemic ascent (Winch, 2013), whereby the sequential, structured tasking process ensures that the concepts already understood are brought into new relations of abstraction and generality, as further concepts are acquired and integrated into the student's understanding. TAP tasking provides multilingual students with opportunities to behave as "language users" to interpret, express and negotiate meaning through their languages. The tasking sequence involves the consecutive staging of the R2R process with a target language text that can be written, audio or audio-visual. The consecutive stages of the R2R tasking sequence form a systematized pedagogical scaffolding process to support the students in using their languages interdependently. This systematized sequential scaffolding process develops the students' academic registers in both instructional languages while improving reading comprehension and accuracy in the target language.

The tasking process activates the multilingual student's ITN in the use of *linguistic fluidity, relational transfer,* and *metashuttling* for multilingual and multiliterate development. TAP tasking reinforces the conceptual interrelationships *between the languages* by requiring the multilingual student to draw on all of their languages while engaging in the consecutive stages of the R2R process. By this means, TAP tasking engages students in cross-linguistic meaning making and conceptual knowledge building. This in turn promotes the reciprocal transfer of semantic knowledge *between the languages* to promote greater understanding of the meaning messages *in the languages.*

The sequenced arrangement of R2R stages denote ascending

layers of cognitive and linguistic complexity to promote Rata's (2015) theory of conceptual progression. In the tradition of Vygotsky (1962), conceptual progression (ibid.) ensures the explicit teaching of concepts from lower to higher order meanings. Throughout consecutive stages of the R2R tasking sequence, conceptual understanding is progressively developed as concepts are taught explicitly in an ordered, sequential way. Conceptual progression promotes the acquisition of academic language which students need to do their work at school. It is via academic language that academic knowledge is expressed. Characterized by specialist abstract terms, which cannot be "caught" and therefore must be "taught," Rata describes academic language as that which allows students to "think about what is not encountered in their experience by using concepts that *themselves* are not known in their experience" (Rata, 2015, p. 174).

3. Background

This study consisted of an eight-week intervention program using te reo Māori and English in mutually supportive ways to improve the kura students' reading accuracy in English. The TransAcquisition Intervention was carried out with 24 Year 7 and 8 students in two kura kaupapa Māori (hereafter referred to as Kura Kauri and Kura Tōtara). The intervention program involved eight weekly workshops between 1:30 pm and 3:00 pm on Thursday afternoons at Kura Kauri and Friday afternoons at Kura Tōtara. Both kura were low-decile schools with decile rankings of 1 and 2, respectively. These decile rankings placed each kura in the 10% of Aotearoa/NZ schools with the highest proportion of students from low socio-economic communities. By sheer coincidence, there were 12 participating students in each of the two kura. Kura Kauri had five boys and seven girls, while Kura Tōtara had six boys and six girls. The transacquisitional R2R tasking sequence was the teaching focus of the first two weeks of the intervention program. This allowed the kura students to become accustomed to using both their languages simultaneously and to become familiar with using graded reading material at their respective reading levels. In the remaining six weeks of the intervention, the students were able to select their own target texts from a range of graded readers at their respective reading levels to complete the tasking process independently, in pairs, or in small groups.

3.1 Mixed methods approach

A mixed methods approach was adopted using both quantitative and qualitative forms of data collection and analysis. This approach was chosen to integrate the benefits of both qualitative and quantitative approaches into the study (Creswell & Plano Clark, 2007). The data was analyzed using quantitative-dominant mixed analysis with the quantitative analysis conducted first and then used to inform the subsequent qualitative analysis component (Onwuegbuzie & Teddlie, 2003).

4. Qualitative analysis and findings

Throughout the eight-week TransAcquisition Intervention, I engaged in impromptu student conferences using open-ended questions and think-aloud protocols to digitally record the students' perceptions while they engaged in the sequential stages of the R2R tasking sequence. Sometimes I just listened to them as they expressed their reflections about the tasking process. Students also used digital recorders to record their reflections about their learning as individuals, in pairs, or in small groups.

4.1 The Reading-to stage

Urquhart and Weir (1998, p. 102) define skim reading as "reading for gist," where students focus *only* on the main ideas of the target text. The following comments from the kura students show how skim reading in the first R2R stage helped them to develop two significant abilities. First, it helped them to retain the main ideas and, second, it enabled them to retain the plot sequence of their leveled target text. Remembering the order of sequential events in a target text is an important cognitive function. It appears that skim reading plays an important role in developing sequential thinking. It does this by helping students to remove the "noise" of less important details while attending to the order of the main ideas, which are then stored in their long-term memory. For this reason, skim reading offers more than the ability to summarize – it also contributes to the cognitively important process of ordering information in sequence.

Te Ata

Te Ata was a confident, courteous, diligent Year 8 student. She was a natural leader and respected by all her peers. In her comment below, Te Ata instinctively recognizes that trying to remember too much information "clutters" the mind, which contributes to "cognitive overload" as a major barrier to learning.

> *Skim reading helps you to write the main things in order so you don't have to remember the whole story otherwise your head would get cluttered.*

Te Ata's description has prompted me to coin the term "cognitive clutter" to describe the irrelevant and unimportant information that can inhibit working memory and clutter the brain's storage capacity. According to Baddeley (1992, p. 556), working memory is "a brain system that provides temporary storage and manipulation of the information necessary for such complex cognitive tasks as language comprehension, learning and reasoning." For Te Ata and her peers, skim reading helped them to clear away cognitive clutter and, in doing so, reduced the cognitive load on their working memory to allow language and literacy learning to proceed with minimal effort. de Jong (2010, p. 105) defines cognitive load (sometimes referred to as 'learning burden') as:

> A theoretical notion . . . that cognitive capacity in working memory is limited, so that if a learning task requires too much capacity, learning will be hampered. The recommended remedy is to design instructional systems that optimize the use of working memory capacity and avoid cognitive overload.

4.2 The Retell-to stage

Retelling promotes the development of reading comprehension by requiring learners to focus their attention on the genre, language structures and meaning of the story while organizing their thoughts in the retelling process (Morrow, 2005). The following student comments focus on the retelling stage of transacquisitional tasking to show how the tasking process cognitively engaged the kura students and expanded their academic knowledge and language in English.

Aroha

Aroha was a self-motivated, self-managing Year 7 student. She was a natural leader, respected by all her peers as a deep thinker and articulate in both her languages. Although she was happy to work independently, she was a popular student in the class and often chosen by other girls in her class as their preferred group member. Aroha's comments confirm that the Retell-to pedagogical sequence was an effective strategy to strengthen the kura students' reading comprehension skills in English.

> *It's kinda hard but it's pretty cool telling it in your own words so you don't have to remember everything . . . I think it's easier doing my*

own words for the meaning 'cause you know what you're talking about ... I think I just need to remember the sequence . . . the raupapa[3] of it.

Aroha's comments shows that she enjoyed taking ownership of her learning. In her comment, it is evident that using 'her own words' not only made it easier for her to make meaning of the text, but it also made it possible for her to take charge of her learning journey. Retelling each target text in her own words allowed Aroha to take control of her language and literacy learning, which added to her self-efficacy.

In their study to investigate the relationship of self-efficacy beliefs, reading strategy use, and reading comprehension, Naseri and Zaferanieh (2012) found a significant correlation between self-efficacy beliefs and reading comprehension. Aroha's succinct comment below indicates a clear learning goal and a clear idea of how to achieve it. These dispositional attributes are indicative of high self-efficacy.

. . . you don't have to remember everything . . . I just need to remember the sequence . . .

Aroha intuitively recognized retelling as an effective strategy to eliminate cognitive clutter. Interestingly, she highlights the importance of remembering the sequence of events in the target text, which she uses as another self-invented strategy to clear cognitive clutter.

Mihi

Mihi was a straight-talking, no-nonsense, matter-of-fact Year 7 student. Her comment below reflects her holistic view of both her

3   Sequence

languages as being inextricably interconnected. Mihi's comment confirms that she accessed and used both her languages simultaneously in mutually supportive ways while engaged in the transacquisitional retelling of a target text.

> *To help me remember how to retell the story [in English] . . . I use Māori . . . so I can understand the story better.*

Mihi's reasoning is supported by Hopewell (2011), who makes the following claim:

> When language environments are planned so that all languages are understood to be resources that can be accessed and invoked strategically in the service of language and literacy acquisition, the learning burden is decreased resulting in an acceleration of the overall language and literacy acquisition. (p. 607)

Hopewell (2011) also recommends that "teachers must engage students in dialogues and learning activities that explicitly leverage cross-language connections to lighten students' learning burdens in ways that would accelerate the language and literacy development" (p. 606).

Mihi's reasoning is also substantiated by Bialystok, Craik, Klein, and Viswanathan (2004) who claim that "the two languages of a bilingual remain constantly active while processing is carried out in one of them" (p. 291). Mihi's ability to use both her languages simultaneously while engaged in the Retell-to stage is also supported by Kroll, Dussias, Bogulski, and Kroff (2012), who state that "the presence of activity among both languages when only one language is required, . . . suggests that proficient bilinguals have acquired not only linguistic proficiency but also the cognitive skill that allows them to juggle the two languages with ease" (p. 229).

The Retell-to stage in the transacquisitional tasking process prompted each student to take ownership of their English language and literacy learning. This resulted in students experiencing higher levels of self-efficacy, which was found to correlate with improved reading comprehension and higher academic achievement. The Retell-to stage helped them to eliminate cognitive clutter and thereby reduce the cognitive load or learning burden in order to optimize working memory to accelerate development of reading comprehension. Engaging in the Retell-to stage allowed the kura students to access and use both their languages simultaneously in mutually supportive ways. This enabled them to draw on all their metacognitive and metalinguistic resources to develop and refine their academic and linguistic skills in English.

4.3 The Revoice-to stage

"Revoicing"[4] is the focus of the third instructional stage of transacquisitional tasking. Revoicing describes a multilingual student's ability to produce a code-switched retell of their previous retelling of a target text. Revoicing engaged the kura students in producing a reo Māori revoice of their own English retell of an English target text at their reading level. The revoicing process builds new knowledge as the student uses both languages interdependently to enrich the understanding of the main concepts of each target text.

Revoicing encompasses the notion of cross-linguistic influence, which occurs in Second Language Acquisition when the influence of the student's other language(s) interacts in the acquisition process. This aligns to Vygotsky (1962), who attributes to the language learner the ability to transfer to a new language the system of meaning that they are already familiar with. The following student comments illustrate the pedagogical benefits of the Revoice-to stage. The comments show

4   Whakareo Anō

how revoicing acts as a conduit between the student's knowledge of words and their understanding of the meaning of those words across languages, one to the other.

Marama: "The book in my head"
Marama was a diligent, motivated Year 8. She liked to be organized and enjoyed working with others, preferring to take the lead rather than follow. The following is a transcript of my conversation with Marama in which she explains how she visualized the target text pages and the words to complete the Revoice-to stage. The transcript shows how detailed and complex the process was and how metacognitively aware she was of what she was doing.

> **Researcher:** I a koe e whakareo anō ana, pēhea tērā ki a koe? [What was it like revoicing?]

> **Marama:** I just keep on looking at the page and then remembering the picture and then go down to the words and the words I can remember I just put in my story.

> **Researcher:** But you didn't have the book in front of you when you were revoicing it.

> **Marama:** It was a flashback to the words.

> **Researcher:** So you're saying that you could see . . .

> **Marama:** . . . the book in my head.

Initially, I thought that Marama's visualizing strategy was her very own self-invented revoicing strategy. However, other students including

Hīria, Waiora, Tipene, and Hone reported using the same visualization strategy. This suggests that visualization is an important cognitive capability triggered by the code-switching function of the revoicing process. Marama's use of the phrase, "the book in my head" is a fascinating description of this cognitive strategy initiated and controlled by Marama. It is supported by Ness's (2011) study, which found reading comprehension "involves recalling information from text, extracting themes, engaging in higher order thinking skills, constructing a mental picture of text, and understanding text structure" (p. 98).

Hīria and Waiora

Hīria was a deep thinking, Year 7 quiet achiever, and Waiora was a self-motivated, self-monitoring, natural leader in Year 8. The following transcript of Hīria and Waiora's conversation shows how revoicing evokes considerable cognitive activity. Waiora used personal experience as her primary strategy to engage in the revoicing process. Like Marama, who talked about "the book in her head," Hīria referred to "pictures in her head" but went further to describe how she would place herself in the story as a character. These self-invented cognitive strategies to remember the sequence of events in the plot are examples of how revoicing triggered a flurry of complex cognitive processes.

> **Hīria:** How do you use your thinking processes in English and Māori to make meaning in revoicing?
>
> **Waiora:** I used personal experience to remember words. How do you use your thinking processes in English and Māori in revoicing?
>
> **Hīria:** I see pictures in my head that helps me remember the story . . . I wanted to be the character to help me remember how the story went.

The students' transcripts align with the literature that supports the use of code-switched story retelling to develop the bilingual students' critical biliteracy skills (Becker, 2001). The Revoice-to stage is the pivotal stage in the transacquisitional tasking sequence that promotes the development of critical biliteracy skills. The Revoice-to stage provided the kura students with opportunities to behave as "language users" rather than "language learners." Engaging in the Revoice-to stage accelerated the development of critical biliteracy skills by allowing the students to use their own experiences and all their linguistic resources (Soares & Wood, 2010). This deepened their reading comprehension in English and extended their knowledge about both their languages.

4.4 The Rewrite-to Stage
The students' productive efforts in creating their Māori and English texts in the Rewrite-to stage are not included here. This is because the focus of this chapter is the effect of the TransAcquisition process on the kura students' reading accuracy and reading comprehension skills in English.

5. Quantitative analysis and findings
5.1 Design
The three phases of the study design included a pre-intervention phase, an intervention phase and a post-intervention phase. During the pre-intervention phase, reading running records (Clay 1967, 1969) in English were used to establish the instructional reading age and reading level of each kura student. Reading running records are described by the Ministry of Education (2000) as "a standardised procedure that all New Zealand teachers can use for valid assessment and comparison of their students' emergent and early reading skills" (p. 3). A fiction text and a non-fiction text were used as the running record target texts to establish whether text type affected the reading

accuracy of the students. At the completion of the TransAcquisition Intervention, reading running records in English were again used to ascertain the reading age and reading level of each student.

5.2 Statistical significance, magnitude, and improvement rate in reading age

Using comparative quantitative analysis, the kura students' pre- and post-intervention running-record scores were then compared, as shown in Table 1.

Table 1. Frequency of levels of accuracy before and after the intervention.

Pre-intervention reading levels of accuracy (number of students)	Post-intervention level of those students (Tracked)		
	Low	Medium	High
Low (7)	3	1	3
Medium (5)	0	0	5
High (12)	0	0	12

Key findings: Shifts in reading accuracy scores

- Seven students scored low levels of accuracy before the TransAcquisition Intervention. Of those seven students, three remained in the low levels with improved scores at that level, one made an upward shift to the medium level of accuracy and three achieved high levels of accuracy after the intervention program.
- The students with low levels of accuracy before the intervention showed the greatest improvement of at least 10% in their accuracy scores after the intervention.

- The three students who scored low pre-intervention reading accuracy scores were boys who achieved medium reading accuracy scores after the intervention.
- Five students scored medium levels of accuracy before the intervention and they all improved by around 5% to high levels of accuracy after the intervention program.
- The twelve students who scored high levels of reading accuracy before the intervention maintained their performance at high levels of accuracy (well within ±5% in accuracy score) after the intervention.

In summary, a review of the individual shifts in reading accuracy levels suggests that the TransAcquisition Intervention had a larger effect on the students who initially scored low pre-intervention scores. Based on the analysis of shifts in reading accuracy by gender, transacquisition appears to have had a generally positive effect on all the boys who participated in the study, particularly the three boys who scored very low reading accuracy scores before the intervention.

Key findings: Shifts in self-correcting behavior

- A positive shift in self-correction scores occurred in all the kura students after the eight-week TransAcquisition Intervention.
- The lower quartile showed a shift in the kura students' use of self-correction strategies from 6% in the pre-intervention phase to 20% in the post-intervention phase. The median showed a shift from 17% to 31%, and the upper quartile showed a shift from 33% to 51%.
- The boys showed improvement in their use of self-correction strategies, shifting from 5% to 12%. In comparison, the girls showed greater improvement in their use of self-correction strategies, shifting from 31% to 63%.

- The Year 7 students showed significant improvement in their use of self-correction strategies, shifting from 36% to 60%. In comparison, the Year 8 students showed a greater improvement in the median, shifting from 12% to 29%.

Key findings: Shifts in the use of meaning, structure and visual reading cues

- A positive shift from 72.6% to 78.8% occurred in all the reading ability groups in the use of meaning, structure and visual cues (MSV) as the dominant self-correction collective cue.
- Overall, findings suggest that the kura students became more aware of textual and contextual features of words/phrases as a result of the TransAcquisition Intervention program, which enabled them to *recognize* their errors and then self-correct accordingly in their post-intervention reading assessment phase.
- Most of those students who were at low levels of accuracy before the intervention made positive changes in their self-correction scores after the intervention with an increase in their use of meaning, structure, and visual (MSV) cues.
- Students who were at medium levels of accuracy before the intervention all made positive changes in their self-correction scores by at least 15% after the intervention.
- Students who were at high levels of accuracy before the intervention maintained their high levels of self-correction scores after the intervention.

5.3 Summary of key findings in self-correction scores and use of reading cues

It can be concluded that the students began to use more metacognitive strategies while reading in English as a result of the TransAcquisition Intervention. The overall improvement in self-correction rates suggests that the kura students became more focused on textual features to read more accurately. Further to this, it appears that the intervention program prompted greater awareness in the kura students to *recognize* their errors and then correct those errors accordingly. This suggests that the students' decoding skills improved between pre- and post-reading running record assessments as they demonstrated greater perseverance, confidence and skill in risk-taking to improve their levels of reading accuracy in the post-intervention phase. Furthermore, the kura students not only demonstrated better decoding skills after the intervention, they also demonstrated gains in reading comprehension. These findings highlight the pedagogical effectiveness of TAP, which enabled the kura students to draw on all their linguistic resources to facilitate meaning making in their reading.

5.4 English-medium Comparison Group

It was considered ethically questionable to use one of the two kura as a true control group. This prompted the decision to use an English-medium school as a convenient sample of real students to form the Comparison Group. The advice of a School Advisor was sought and, after several meetings, six English-medium principals were recommended. Relevant information about the study was emailed to all the principals and one of the principals agreed to meet with me to discuss the research. After the meeting, the Term 1 and Term 4 reading running record scores of 22 students with similar reading ages to those of the kura Intervention Group were ascertained. This English-medium school (hereafter referred to as Putaatara School) was a full primary with a decile 10 ranking situated in a high socio-economic community. Although the English-medium Comparison Group was not a true control group, the use of the reading running record scores provided a real-life comparison of expected student gains over time. To this extent, the weekly gain in the reading age of the English-medium Comparison Group was estimated as 6.21

days improvement[5] in reading age per week. This is in contrast to the 5.20-week improvement in reading age per week of the Kura Kaupapa Māori Intervention Group. These findings show that the rate of change in reading age of the kura Intervention Group was 5.87[6] times faster than that of the Comparison Group in the decile 10 English-medium school.

6. Conclusion

In the kura kaupapa Māori context, TransAcquisition accelerated the students' biliterate development in the target majority language (i.e. English) while enhancing their pre-existing language/literacy in the instructional minority language (i.e. te reo Māori). As an exemplar of Lee and McCarty's (2017) Culturally Sustaining/Revitalizing Pedagogy, TransAcquisition is an effective pedagogical approach in contexts where cultural sustainability and language revitalization are a priority. TAP is therefore recommended for Māori-medium classrooms, Initial Teacher Education (ITE) programs, and Professional Learning and Development (PLD) teacher education programs. The findings of the study provide empirical evidence that TransAcquisition can assist kura teachers to assist them in transitioning their students from "literacy in Māori to literacy in English" (Berryman & Glynn, 2004, p. 144).

TAP is also recommended for English-medium teachers working with children who are speakers of languages other than English. Aotearoa New Zealand (Aotearoa NZ) is now ranked third among the 34 affiliate countries of the Organization for Economic Cooperation and Development (OECD) with the highest proportion of overseas born residents (OECD, 2017). Auckland is now identified as having one of the highest proportions of immigrants in the OECD

5   0.017 (years) x 365 (days) = 6.21 days improvement per week
6   5.2 (weeks) = 36.47 days; 36.47 ÷ 6.21 = 5.87

(ibid.). For many multilingual students in these groups, academic achievement is restricted by an education system that doesn't support their drawing on all their linguistic resources to accelerate their bilingual and biliterate development (Tamati, 2011, 2016). This problem is highlighted in a recent Education Review Office (ERO) report, which recommends that the education sector

> aim to build a diverse knowledge base for every teacher, with desired competencies in second language acquisition theory and development . . . to support Culturally and Linguistically Diverse learners to make both academic and language progress in all curriculum learning areas (ERO, 2018, p. 49).

In support of the ERO recommendations, it is now a matter of urgency that TAP be included in ITE programs and PLD initiatives for primary and secondary school teachers (for further discussion of the need for translingual teacher education, see Busic & Sullivan, this volume).

An additional problem faced by Māori and Pasifika students is "low teacher expectations" which, according to Mahuika, Berryman, and Bishop (2011), occurs when teachers problematize the lived experiences of Māori and Pasifika students in relation to assessment and learning. This is substantiated in the findings of a recent report by the UNICEF Office of Research (2018) in which Aotearoa NZ is identified as having one of the most unequal education systems in the world. The racialized undertone of low teacher expectation in Aotearoa NZ is evidenced in Turner's (2013) study, which shows that teachers not only had low achievement expectations of Māori students in particular, but also of Pasifika students. TAP offers real hope for Māori and Pasifika students in English-medium schooling to learn their own indigenous languages and literacies symbiotically with their language and literacy development in English.

The effect of TAP can be attributed to the cumulative influence of the R2R transacquisitional tasking process on the cognitive and linguistic processes associated with the students' Interrelational Translingual Network (ITN). I call this the "TAP effect," which enables multilingual students to use their languages in mutually supportive ways to accelerate their acquisition of academic language and deepen their understanding of academic knowledge. It is the "TAP effect" that reflects and embraces the dynamic manifestations of multilingualism. In this regard, TAP is a learning and teaching approach that is theoretically and pedagogically predicated on the dynamism of multilingualism. For these reasons, TAP has the potential to radically realign pedagogical approaches currently in place in the education of emergent multilingual students around the world.

References

Baddeley, A. (1992). Working memory. *Science, 255*(5044), 556–559.

Bauer, W. (2008). Is the health of te reo Māori improving? *Te Reo,* 51, 33–73.

Becker, R. (2001). Spanish-English code switching in a bilingual academic context. *Reading Horizons, 42*(2), 99–115.

Bernstein, B. (2000). *Pedagogy, symbolic control, and identity: Theory, research, critique.* Oxford, UK: Rowman and Littlefield.

Berryman, M. & Glynn, T. (2004). Whānau participation: Māori students' transition to English. *Proceedings of the Language Acquisition Research Forum* (pp. 143–158). Wellington, New Zealand: Ministry of Education.

Bialystok, E., Craik, F. I. M., Klein, R., & Viswanathan, M. (2004). Bilingualism, aging, and cognitive control: Evidence from the Simon Task. *Psychology and Aging, 19*(2), 290–303.

Centeno-Cortés, B. & Jiménez, A. (2004). Problem-solving tasks in a foreign language: The importance of the L1 in private verbal thinking. *International Journal of Applied Linguistics, 14*(1), 7–35.

Clay, M. M. (1967). The reading behaviour of five-year-old children: A research report. *New Zealand Journal of Educational Studies, 2*(1), 11–31.

Clay, M. M. (1969). Reading errors and self-correction behaviour. *British Journal of Educational Psychology, 39,* 47–56.

Creese, A. & Blackledge, A. J. (2010). Translanguaging in the bilingual classroom: A pedagogy for learning and teaching? *The Modern Language Journal, 94*(1), 103–115.

Creswell, J. W. & Plano Clark, V. L. (2007). *Designing and conducting mixed methods research.* Thousand Oaks, CA: SAGE.

Cummins, J. (1981a). *Bilingualism and minority language children.* Ontario, Canada: Ontario Institute for Studies in Education.

Cummins, J. (1981b). The role of primary language development in promoting educational success for language minority students. In P. Dolson (Ed.), *Schooling and language minority students: A theoretical framework* (pp. 16–62). Los Angeles, CA: State Department of Education, Office of Bilingual Bicultural Education.

Cummins, J. (2001). *Negotiating identities: Education for empowerment in a diverse society* (2nd ed.). Los Angeles, CA: California Association for Bilingual Education.

Cummins, J. (2007). Rethinking monolingual instructional strategies in multilingual classrooms. *The Canadian Journal of Applied Linguistics, 10*(2), 221–240.

Cummins, J. (2008). Teaching for transfer: challenging the two solitudes assumption in bilingual education. In J. Cummins & N. H. Hornberger (Eds.), *Encyclopedia of language and education* (2nd ed., Vol. 5., pp. 65–76). New York, NY: Springer.

ERO/Education Review Office. (2018). *Responding to language diversity in Auckland.* Wellington, New Zealand: New Zealand Government.

García, O. (2011). From language garden to sustainable languaging: Bilingual education in a global world. *NABE Perspectives,* 5–10.

García, O., & Leiva. C. (2014). Theorizing and enacting translanguaging for social justice. In A. Creese & A. Blackledge (Eds.), *Heteroglossia as practice and pedagogy* (pp. 199–216). New York, NY: Springer.

García, O., & Wei, L. (2014). *Translanguaging: Language, bilingualism and education*. New York, NY: Palgrave Macmillan.

Hill, R. K. (2011). Rethinking English in Māori-medium education. *International Journal of Bilingual Education and Bilingualism*, 14(6), 719–732.

Hill, R. (2017). Level 2 Māori Medium Programmes: What are the perceptions of parents and students on this form of education? *NZ Journal of Education Studies*, 52(2), 301–313.

Hill, R. K. & May, S. (2014). Balancing the languages in Māori-medium education in Aotearoa/New Zealand. In D. Gorter, V. Zenotz, & J. Cenoz. (Eds.), *Minority languages and multilingual education: Bridging the local and the global* (pp. 171–189). New York, NY: Springer.

Hopewell, S. (2011). Leveraging bilingualism to accelerate English reading comprehension. *International Journal of Bilingual Education and Bilingualism*, 14(5), 603–620.

Hornberger, N. H. (2004). The continua of biliteracy and the bilingual educator: Educational linguistics in practice. *International Journal of Bilingual Education and Bilingualism*, 7(2–3), 155–171.

Kroll, J. F., Dussias, P. E., Bogulski, C. A., & Kroff, J. R. V. (2012). Juggling two languages in one mind: What bilinguals tell us about language processing and its consequences for cognition. *Psychology of Learning and Motivation – Advances in Research and Theory*, 56, 229–262. doi:10.1016/B978-0-12-394393-4.00007-8

Lee, T. S. & McCarty, T. (2017). Upholding indigenous education sovereignty through critical culturally sustaining/revitalizing pedagogy. In D. Paris & H. S. Alim, (Eds.), *Culturally sustaining pedagogies: Teaching and learning for justice in a changing world* (pp. 61–82). New York: Teachers College Press.

Lowman, C., Fitzgerald, T., Rapira, P. & Clark, R. (2007). First language literacy skill transfer in a second language learning environment: Strategies for biliteracy. *Set*, 2, 24–28.

Mahuika, R., Berryman, M., & Bishop, R. (2011). Issues of culture and assessment in New Zealand education pertaining to Māori students. *Assessment Matters*, 3, 183–198.

May, S. & Hill, R. K. (2004). Māori-medium education: Current issues and future prospects. *Proceedings of the Language Acquisition Research*

Forum (pp. 5–37). Wellington, New Zealand: Ministry of Education.

McCaffery, J., Villers, H., & Lowman, C. (2008). Biliteracy: Finding the words to write in two languages within a diverse school setting. Paper presented at the *2nd Language Education and Diversity Conference*, Hamilton, New Zealand.

Ministry of Education. (2000). *Using running records: A resource for New Zealand classroom teachers.* Wellington, New Zealand: Learning Media.

Morrow, L. M. (2005). *Literacy development in the early years: Helping children read and write.* Boston, MA: Allyn and Bacon.

Naseri, M., & Zaferanieh, E. (2012). The relationship between reading self-efficacy beliefs, reading strategy use and reading comprehension level of Iranian EFL learners. *World Journal of Education, 2*(2), 64–75.

Ness, M. (2011). Explicit reading comprehension instruction in elementary classrooms: Teacher use of reading comprehension strategies. *Journal of Research in Childhood Education, 25*(1), 98–117.

Office of the Auditor-General. (2010). *Central government: Results of the 2009/10 audits.* Retrieved from http://www.oag.govt.nz/2010/2009-10/docs/central-govt-2009-10.pdf

OECD (2017), *International Migration Outlook 2017* (Summary), OECD Publishing, Paris. http://dx.doi.org/10.1787/f3a4fe3e-en

Onwuegbuzie, A. J., & Teddlie, C. (2003). A framework for analyzing data in mixed methods research. In A. Tashakkori & C. Teddlie (Eds.), *Handbook of mixed methods in social and behavioral research* (pp. 351–383). Thousand Oaks, CA: SAGE.

Rata, E. (2015). A pedagogy of conceptual progression and the case for academic knowledge. *British Educational Research Journal, 42*(1), 168–184. doi:10.1002/berj.3195

Schleppegrell, M. J. (2012). Academic language in teaching and learning: Introduction to the special issue. *The Elementary School Journal, 112*(3), 409–418.

Smith, G. H. (1997). *The development of kaupapa Maori: Theory and praxis* (Unpublished doctoral thesis). University of Auckland, Auckland, New Zealand.

Soares, L. B., & Wood, K. (2010). A critical literacy perspective for teaching and learning social studies. *The Reading Teacher, 63*(6), 486–494.

Tākao, N., Grennell, D., McKegg, K., & Wehipeihana, N. (2010). *Te Piko o te Māhuri: The key attributes of successful Kura Kaupapa Māori.* Retrieved on 28 February, 2019, from https://www.educationcounts. govt.nz/publications/maori/105966/80403/1.-the-nature-of-success

Tamati, S. T. (2011). The trans-acquisitional approach: A bridge to English in kura kaupapa Māori. *Pacific-Asian Education, 23*(1), 91–102.

Tamati, S. T. (2016). *Transacquisition pedagogy for bilingual education: A study in kura kaupapa Māori.* Unpublished PhD thesis. Auckland, NZ: University of Auckland.

Turner, H. B. (2013). *Teacher expectations, ethnicity and the achievement gap.* Unpublished Master of Education Thesis. Auckland, NZ: University of Auckland.

UNICEF Office of Research (2018). An Unfair Start: Inequality in Children's Education in Rich Countries. *Innocenti Report Card 15,* Innocenti Florence: UNICEF Office of Research.

Urquhart, S., & Weir, C. (1998). *Reading in a second language: Process, product and practice.* London, UK: Longman.

Vygotsky, L. S. (1962). *Thought and language.* Cambridge, MA: MIT Press.

Williams, C. (1994). *Arfarniad o Ddulliau Dysgu ac Addysgu yng Nghyddestun Addysg Uwchradd Ddwyieithog* [*An evaluation of teaching and learning methods in the context of bilingual secondary education*]. Unpublished PhD thesis. Bangor: University of Wales.

Williams, C. (2002). *Ennill iaith: Astudiaethau o sefyllfa drochi yn 11–16 oed = A language gained: A study of language immersion at 11–16 years of age.* Bangor, Wales: Ysgol Addysg Prifysgol Cymru.

Winch, C. (2013). Curriculum design and epistemic ascent. *Journal of Philosophy of Education, 47*(1), 128–146.

CHAPTER 5

Our way of multilingualism: Translanguaging to break a chain of colonialism

Madoka Hammine

1. Introduction

This chapter aims to conceptualize what "**our** way of multilingualism" means to us, by revisiting the translanguaging practices and pedagogy of elders living in the Ryukyus. I put emphasis on "our" to bring the knowledge of our elders forward. I focus on their way of practicing multilingualism, not the way of the outside, the west, or the Japanese mainland. I address the fact that there have already been translanguaging practices and pedagogy in the way of multilingualism in what the elders have experienced in the Ryukyus. Recognizing the translanguaging practices and pedagogy of our elders has the potential not only to revitalize indigenous languages but also to break the chain of colonialism.

The Ryukyuan language family consists of at least five distinct languages (Amamian, Kunigami, Uchinaaguchi/Okinawan, Miyakoan, Yaeyaman, Dunan)[1], traditionally spoken in the Ryukyu Islands, a chain of islands in the southwest region of Japan (see Figure 1). These islands were formerly part of the Ryukyu Kingdom (1479–1879) up until Japan took over and incorporated them into its

1   It is considered 5 to 6 languages depending on sources and definition. Please find further information on Ryukyuan languages in Pellard (2013), among others.

territory as Okinawa prefecture and Kagoshima prefecture. Ryukyuan languages have historically been treated in Japan as hōgen, or dialects of Japanese, and are still viewed as such by many Ryukyuan people[2]. This view of Ryukyuan languages as hōgen came from an ideology of Japan as a monolingual nation, which has been an obstacle to language preservation in the Ryukyus (Fija, 2016; Heinrich, 2012). According to the UNESCO expert of endangered languages, the use of the terminology "hōgen" encourages endangerment and delays revitalization (Arakaki, 2013; Fija, 2016, p.176). For Ryukyuan people, the ideology of Ryukyuan languages as a hōgen of Japanese made sense to align individuals to participate in social and linguistic change toward being Japanese (Arakaki, 2013; Heinrich, 2012) and strengthened the situation where Ryukyuan languages are to be seen as "less valuable" compared to Standard Japanese by its speakers (Takubo, 2015).

As the author and principal researcher of this study, I am situating myself as a cultural insider. I consider two of the Ryukyuan languages, Okinawan and Yaeyaman, as my heritage languages, which I did not have a chance to acquire completely in my childhood. My grandparents and some relatives are full speakers of Yaeyaman and Uchinaaguchi/Okinawan. A part of decolonizing work is to take back our place and our language through research process (e.g. Smith, 1999). The research process and this work are important to me and my family – and not only for purposes of academic research.

---

2   Ryukyuan people are defined differently in different fields, here Ryukyuan includes both Okinawan, Yaeyaman. However, later in this article, I use the term Yaeyaman to refer to people from Yaeyama Islands and Okinawan to refer to people from the Okinawa Island.

Figure 1. Map of the Ryukyu Islands and the Ryukyuan language[3] (Shimoji & Pellard, 2010)

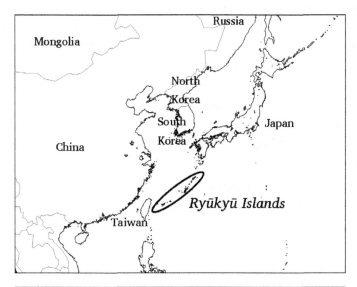

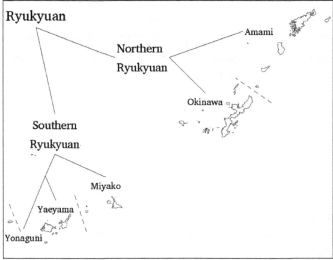

3 This figure posits five languages, but the UNESCO Atlas of World Languages in Danger defines Kunigami as an additional sixth language (Moseley, 2010).

I focus on one of my heritage languages: Yaeyaman. Yaeyaman is spoken on the Yaeyama Islands, lying more than 250 miles in the southwest of Okinawa Main Island (for a map, see Heinrich & Ishihara, 2017). The Yaeyaman language has several local varieties with varying degrees of mutual intelligibility (Pellard, 2013). Every island and every village of the Yaeyama Islands has its own variety of the Yaeyama language (see Figure 2).

The Yaeyama Islands have their own rich history as well as their own language, culture, and identity, which are different from the rest of the Ryukyu Islands (Matsuda, 2008; Miki, 2003). The Ryukyu Kingdom (1479–1879) brought the Yaeyama Islands under pressure for jintōzei (taxation based on the height of people), from Shuri, the capital city of the Ryukyu kingdom.[4] Kerr (2000, p. 436) notes, "By tradition Yaeyama was thought of as a place of harsh exile, where opportunities were too limited to be considered seriously by anyone who wished to improve his economic situation."[5] After the Kingdom was annexed in 1872 by Japan, Ryukyuan languages, including Yaeyaman, were assimilated into Standard Japanese by the national government, and identities of people who speak Ryukyuan languages have been simultaneously assimilated into Japanese (Clarke, 2015; Heinrich, 2012; Matsuda, 2008; Yokota, 2015).

4 Oyake Akahachi is known as a hero in Yaeyama who rebelled against the king of the Ryukyu Kingdom in 1500. He is known as a hero for the people who suffered from severe taxation. See more in (Nakata, 2004; Yoshida, 2015) for example.
5 Yaeyama Islanders' lives were significantly restricted by malaria. According to Matsuda (2008), until malaria was eradicated in 1960, Yaeyama was considered a backward and underdeveloped region.

Figure 2. Map of the Yaeyama Islands[6]

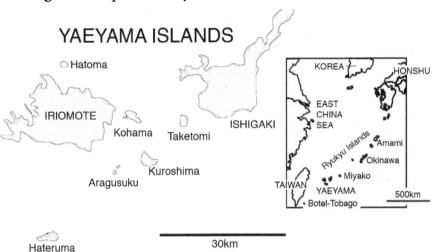

In the Miyara village on Ishigaki Island,[7] Miyara Yaeyaman (referred as Miyaran in this paper), a variety of the Yaeyaman language, is spoken (see Figure 2). The grammar has been studied by scholars both in Japanese and in English (e.g. Davis, 2014a, 2014b; Davis & Lau, 2015; Izuyama, 2003; Nakahara, 2003). The village has a population of around 1800 people, with about 763 households (Ishigaki, 2013). In Miyara, community members are aware that there used to be an older variety of Yaeyaman: what they call "mutu-meeramuni." The last full speaker of mutu-meeramuni has already passed away.

The village sustained substantial damage from a large Tsunami in 1771, resulting in over half of its population being killed. After the Tsunami, people on Kohama Island were forced to move to Miyara by the Ryukyu Kingdom. People from Kohama Island

6　Adapted from Anderson and Summerhayes (2008). I would like to thank the authors for the use of this resource.

7　Ishigaki Island is one of the Yaeyama islands (see Figure 2).

and people who are originally from Miyara have started using the linguistic variety known as "meeramuni"[8] (referred as Miyaran in this chapter). Yaeyaman is described as being critically endangered (Moseley, 2010), with approximately 350 native speakers of Miyaran (Davis, 2014a). This number represents the population who are bilingual in both Miyaran and Japanese, since there are no longer any monolingual speakers of Miyaran left. Currently, the population of the village also includes some people who moved from mainland Japan, some people from other islands of the Ryukyus, and some people from other villages on Ishigaki Island (i.e. women who are married to Miyaran men, or families who moved to the village). Thus, there are not only bilingual speakers of Miyaran and Japanese and monolingual speakers of Japanese, but also few speakers[9] of other Ryukyuan languages (e.g. Okinawan/ Uchinaaguchi), and few speakers of other varieties of the Yaeyaman language in the village.

2. Theory and methodology

In order to examine translanguaging practices in educational spaces in the village, I follow the framework of Hornberger (2005), "Opening and Filling Up Ideological and Implementational Spaces," focusing on the roles of individual teachers and community members. The concept refers to the act of filling teaching and learning activities in the classroom and in communities with multilingual educational practices. This concept emphasizes the importance of language

---

8   "Meeramuni" literally means the language of Miyara. Community members consider this variety as a combination of the older Miyaran language, mutu-meeramuni, and the one from Kohama. Here, I use Miyaran as a translation to differentiate it from different varieties of the Yaeyaman language.

9   Those speakers tend to be not the native speakers but semi-speakers of other Ryukyuan languages, since younger generations in the Ryukyus do not completely speak their languages.

educators and language users in filling up implementational spaces with multilingual educational spaces, whether with intent to occupy ideological spaces opened up by policies or to actively prod toward more favorable ideological spaces in the face of restrictive policies (Hornberger, 2005). Ideological spaces created by language-in-education policies can be carving out implementational ones at classroom and community levels, but implementational spaces can also serve as wedges to pry open ideological ones (Hornberger, 2002, 2005). I investigate the following research questions:

1. What kind of translanguaging practices exist in educational settings in the community?
2. How can translanguaging practices in educational settings open and fill up ideological and implementational spaces?

The study is based on nine months of ethnographic fieldwork in 2017, during which I observed the use of languages in formal and informal settings in multiple locations on the Yaeyama Islands as well as in the Miyaran community on Okinawa Island. I employ a participatory community-based research methodology within a framework of Indigenous Research Methodology (Smith, 1999). My experience forms part of this study, and I situate myself as a cultural insider. As an insider, I focus on the process of identifying and resisting the imposition of dominant values and knowledge systems that contribute to the subjugation of indigenous groups, as part of decolonization (Smith, 1999; Tuck & Yang, 2012).

During this fieldwork, I conducted some language lessons at Miyara Elementary School with local teachers and produced learning materials as a series of podcasts available on iTunes. I translated some stories from children's books (*The Gigantic Turnip* by Aleksey Nikolayevich Tolstoy and *Three Billy Goats Gruff*, a Norwegian folktale) into Miyara Yaeyaman.[10] I also participated in the sumamuni o hanasu taikai [island language speech contest] in July 2018 and published one bilingual essay in Miyara Yaeyaman and Japanese in 2017 (Hammine, 2017) (for further discussion on resource design, see Amosa Burgess & Fiti, this volume).

Data for this study included ethnographic observations of classroom instruction; individual interviews with school teachers, parents, and youth; document analysis (e.g. school curriculum, teachers' lesson plans, and language policy documents; language laws locally produced in the Ryukyus); and photographs intended to capture the linguistic landscape of how the local language was represented in schools and in the community. I used linguistic biographies to investigate how the teachers are experiencing language endangerment (Busch, Jardine, & Tjoutuku, 2006). Using video and audio recorders, interviews lasted from one to ten hours. Participants of interviews included regular school teachers, teachers who teach the Yaeyaman language voluntarily, and traditional speakers[11] and new speakers of the language in the community. Interviews were conducted using both Yaeyaman and Japanese, and transcribed, translated, and analyzed by the researcher. The following discussion summarizes the data and shows that teachers and community members (i.e. traditional speakers) use translanguaging pedagogy and practices to actively open more favorable ideological spaces in the face of restrictive monolingual policies in Japan.

10 The project is ongoing. In the year 2019, with the help of the Endangered Language Fund, I am planning to give books in Miyara Yaeyaman to the local elementary school.

11 I use the term "traditional speakers" when referring to people who have spoken the Yaeyaman language as their mother tongue, while the term "new speakers" refers to people who learned the Yaeyaman language as a second language (see also O'Rourke, Pujolar, & Ramallo, 2015).

3. Results and Discussion
3.1 Internalized colonialism

Due to the history of assimilation in the Ryukyus, teachers in the Ryukyus experienced the process of linguistic assimilation to teach Japanese throughout their own education (e.g. Kondo, 2008). It is the result of education reinforcing status differentials between home and school languages (i.e. Ryukyuan as a home language and Japanese as an official school language). As a result, students disengaged their identities from their home languages and the process of language loss was accelerated in the Ryukyus (e.g. Cummins, 1996). We can see the result of this language loss in traditional speakers' attitudes toward the indigenous languages of the Ryukyus (for further discussion of attitudes, see Pfeiffer, this volume). Traditional speakers still devalue their own language and culture due to the history of assimilation and discrimination in the past and they tend to speak "beautiful," "sophisticated" Japanese with people who are educated (Hammine, in press). I call the phenomenon of devaluing our own linguistic variety as linguistic self-orientalism (see Hammine, in press). Traditional speakers of Miyaran tend to have self-orientalism or internalized colonialism toward their own language, which often hinders new speakers from learning the language comfortably.

In addition to internalized colonialism among traditional speakers of Yaeyaman, we find the phenomenon of low self-esteem and a lack of self-confidence in the teachers of the Yaeyaman language. Teachers who teach their indigenous languages are trying to make implementational spaces in school by teaching indigenous languages. The language lessons are conducted regularly, once in every two months by the local women's association. However, the teachers who are teaching local languages are volunteers who have knowledge of the language but lack the official teaching qualifications and educational attainments considered prerequisite for being a "real" teacher in the Japanese school system. For instance, one teacher mentioned her profession is sometimes seen negatively by their own community. (The bolded text in interview extracts has been added for emphasis by the author.)

> *I am not a real teacher because **I do not have proper education.** Instead, you and for example, . . . have education from the University. I have only attended a high school. So, I am not a real teacher. You do not need to come to see my lessons.* (Interview with a Yaeyaman language teacher)

The above extract suggests that the local teachers tend to have negative self-esteem about their teaching professions. These teachers are volunteer teachers who often lack higher education at university level. Through educational policy based on dominant values, community members who are full speakers of Miyaran cannot pursue their higher education in Yaeyaman. This fact contributes to the phenomenon of teachers believing that our language is not sophisticated, and they lack confidence in teaching our languages without official educational qualification.

Due to the system of teacher circulation in the Japanese educational system, most of the official teachers with teaching qualifications in the village are usually from other parts of the prefecture (e.g. from other islands or other villages of the Yaeyama Islands). Official teachers get transferred to different schools every four to five years. None of the "real" teachers have the requisite knowledge of the language. The school system is based on dominant Japanese values, not leaving official space in the school curriculum for the Yaeyaman language or culture. This negatively influences volunteer teachers with sufficient knowledge of Yaeyaman: they lack confidence and positive self-esteem as teachers of indigenous language.

Another interview shows some volunteer teachers and younger speakers who attempt to create an implementational space in school and in the community, but it shows traditional speakers' internalized colonialism:

> *There are a couple of young men who learned the language by listening to the CD I made. Then they keep saying thank you to me. They say that is how they learned the language. You know, when you are alone in your car,* **you don't get embarrassed to speak the language***. For those who are embarrassed to say "miihai-yuu," [thank you in Yaeyaman] it is easier for them to say it while they are driving, and they can learn it naturally. It is the same in learning music. You learn it by ear.* **This is wonderful***.*
> (Interview with a Yaeyaman language teacher)

As shown above, some new speakers are motivated to learn the Yaeyaman language. However, since the traditional speakers often discourage the new speakers from learning the local language, new speakers tend to **get embarrassed** in learning the Yaeyaman language (see also Hammine, in press). The relationship between traditional speakers and new speakers is never neutral: in contexts of social inequality these interactions reinforce the devaluation of Indigenous group culture, language, and identity in the broader society. This corresponds to the fact that, without education based on understanding of indigenous knowledge, individuals fail to affirm their heritage and identities (Hornberger, 2014; Skutnabb-Kangas, 2010). In the case of Yaeyama, education is based on the Japanese school curriculum. When people go through official education, including elementary, middle school, high school, and universities, it is only in the Japanese language (Lee, 1996). As a result of educational policies completely based on Japanese values and in Japanese language, teachers or traditional speakers still view themselves as speakers of non-valuable language. These attitudes shared by traditional speakers often bring negative behavior toward learners who are learning indigenous languages; hence it makes it difficult to bring success to language revitalization.

The attributed values of the Ryukyuan languages as dirty, unsophisticated languages that do not suit education (i.e. educated people do not speak Ryukyuan languages) are the result of a history of assimilation and discrimination. It corresponds with the fact that minority group members may use assimilation strategies in their attempt to become members of the dominant group, not only by speaking the dominant language but also by identifying with the speakers of the dominant language (Liebkind, 2010). By speaking Japanese, and by identifying themselves with Japanese, Ryukyuan people have asked for certain social roles or resources (e.g. education or higher income).

3.2 Translanguaging pedagogy and practice

If we look at the translanguaging pedagogy and practices of traditional speakers, we find the multilingual reality of Ryukyuan islands and how traditional speakers naturally used to practice translanguaging. By recognizing their translanguaging practices, we could possibly break a chain of colonialism. The following is one example from one interview with a Yaeyaman language speaker and teacher. She speaks Yaeyaman with her children and grandchildren at home. As a member of the local women's association, she goes to school to teach the language.

> **MH:** How did you learn and speak Yaeyaman?
>
> **T:** Since I was born, I grew up listening to all the varieties of Yaeyaman language. Because my grandfather was a bakuro [a person who trades kettles], he was selling and buying cows with people from different parts of the islands. My grandfather. **That's why we had always guests from Hirae, Ohama, Ishigaki, Shiraho and Kabira . . . many places in the Yaeyama Islands. It is not a problem**

**to speak or mix different dialects of Yaeyaman.
It is natural for me.** That is why I am by myself
collecting 13 dialects of Yaeyaman. (Interview with a
Yaeyaman language teacher)

Previous research affirms the importance of affirming heritage
language learners' multilingual talent as a valued component of
their identities and hence as a part of what is called "empowering
education" (Cummins, 2014; Hornberger, 2005). We can see
differences in teachers' awareness of indigenous language as talents
of students and teachers themselves. I highlight the importance of
affirming heritage language learners' multilingual talents as a valued
component of their identities. When school contexts reinforce status
differentials between home and school languages, students disengage
their identities from their home languages and the process of language
loss is accelerated (Cummins, 1996). We can see the result of this in
traditional speakers' attitudes toward the Indigenous languages in the
Ryukyus, but they are using translanguaging in their everyday life.
It is important that heritage language learners are provided for and
choose to engage in bringing heritage languages forward.

Opening and filling up ideological spaces by the use of
translanguaging practices and pedagogy on the ground level could
possibly break a chain of internalized colonialism. In a local school,
we find translanguaging practices and pedagogy. Local school teachers
are trying to open implementational spaces by creating spaces for
indigenous languages in school. For example, in Miyara Elementary
School, teachers of the Yaeyaman language deliver lessons voluntarily
once in every two months. Volunteer teachers from the local women's
association[12] make posters of the Yaeyaman language to distribute in

12 The association consists of women who were born in the village or who are
   married to men in the village. This poster was a product of a larger group of
   women's associations of different villages on Yaeyama islands.

every elementary school on the island. This is an example of "bottom-up language policy" as a vehicle of cultural expression and door of opportunity for indigenous language speakers, and teachers' roles as policy-makers (Cummins, 2000; Hornberger, 2005).

Some aspects of the state educational policy make it difficult to keep indigenous languages. At the same school, official teachers come from different parts of the Ryukyus. Those teachers are not necessary from the local village since teachers are transferred to different schools every four to five years in Japanese public schools. However, the following example shows translanguaging, which is natural for older generations in the Ryukyus, could bring hope to language revitalization. The interview is with one teacher who teaches on Ishigaki Island. This teacher is from Okinawa Main Island and conducts lessons of Okinawan language, using translanguaging pedagogy. Although this lesson is conducted without official school curriculum support, he teaches classes using Okinawan, Japanese, and Yaeyaman.

> *When we use the story of momotaro [peach boy] in class, we teach both in Okinawan and in Japanese. This is originally a Japanese children's story, so Okinawan children do not know that what kibidango [a cake made of wheat] is, so I change it into saataa andaagii [Okinawan sweets] or kuruzaataa [brown sugar]. **I change it according to Okinawan knowledge. Children only know about Okinawa, you know**. So, we have to think, what we should do . . . I think about . . . what we have to do . . . then, I think that probably, **instead of teaching the language, we should make children who want to learn our language do so voluntarily**. I don't know, but I feel that it is not just . . . even if we teach and "Oh, we studied our language in school today." I don't know how it changes the situation.* (Interview with a teacher of elementary school on Ishigaki Island)

This example shows that, in school, teachers are trying to create a space for the local culture and knowledge by adapting teaching contents into the local context. This is also an example of translanguaging practice in school. By bringing their own local knowledge into dominant-value-based curriculum in school, local teachers are creating an implementational space for local languages. Considering that for empowering minority students, the instruction of teachers by using translanguaging practices challenges the devaluation of indigenous knowledge (Cummins, 2014). This example from one elementary school on Ishigaki Island shows the efforts of teachers in actual teaching practice to create an implementational space for local knowledge and local languages in school.

3.3 Ideological spaces: Colonialism within policies

Let us turn our eyes to the other side of the coin: ideological spaces. The following two extracts from language-in-education policies from the Ryukyus suggest educational policies made by themselves fail to create a space for indigenous language speakers. This goal of education to promote Okinawa prefecture to become the best in English language originates from the Okinawa Prefectural Board of Education.

> The Ministry of Education, April 2016, announced that Okinawa prefecture was ranked the worst in the score of English language exam for public high school students, compared with all the other prefectures in Japan. Okinawa prefecture has been trying to achieve the goal to be the best prefecture in English language amongst 47 prefectures in Japan and it has been putting a lot of efforts. **The Okinawa Prefectural Board of Education commented that this is a shocking result considering the efforts we have made.** (*Nihon Keizai Shimbun*, 2016)

Since Okinawa prefecture ranks the worst in English language of all the prefectures in Japan, teachers and the Board of Education are actively putting in an effort to solve "the problem." We can observe an ideology behind this policy, underlining that we have to be like Japanese, or better than Japanese. Ideologies gain power in the social and political world when they come to be accepted not as political constructions of that world but as descriptions of it, that is, when they become normalized as common-sense ways of thinking about the world (the notion of habitus by Bourdieu, 1980). Power is often invisible in that it frequently naturalizes events and practices in ways that come to be seen as "normal" to members of a community (Norton, 2012, p. 14). In the case of this example of language policy of Okinawa prefecture, teachers and policy makers themselves have made efforts to make "the best" prefecture in Japan.

The discourse of equality and social justice of equality rights and non-discrimination has desensitized many policy-makers and educators to the subtler forms of exclusion and discrimination that continue to operate in societal institutions, including schools (Cummins, 2014). Okinawa Prefecture remains the prefecture with the highest rate of child poverty and the lowest educational achievement among 47 prefectures in Japan (Kato, 2017; Uema, 2017), which are factors similarly observed among other indigenous minorities around the world. The academic achievement of a minority group is directly influenced by both the structures of schooling, which tend to reflect the values and priorities of the dominant group, and by the patterns of identity negotiation that students experience in their interaction with educators within the school.

The Japanese national policy of language education has rarely acknowledged the presence of indigenous people within the Japanese state (Fujita-Round & Maher, 2008; Gayman, 2011). Both the Ainu language (indigenous language in the north) and the Ryukyuan languages were assimilated into Japanese during the territorial expansion of Japan. Since the presence of indigenous groups in Japan represents a fundamental problem – because any recognition of an ethnic minority as an indigenous minority within Japan contests the understanding of Japan as a monoethnic nation and challenges fundamental discourse of nationhood within Japan (e.g. Siddle, 1996) – there has been little recognition of indigenous minorities in Japanese language or education policies and the status of groups as indigenous minorities has typically been downplayed (see also Gayman, 2011; Fujita-Round & Maher, 2008). The only policies that do acknowledge the Ryukyuan languages stem from the American administration[13] of the islands following the Second World War.

The following interview shows the language-in-education policy barriers to opening up ideological space for indigenous languages. It also shows the hierarchy of languages in Japan with Japanese and English as the first priorities in school.

You know, when we say that we, adults, should use the language. But there are many adults who don't know Yaeyaman. **So, we cannot say we should start using it.** *One way to incorporate it in school is to make a poster or to deliver language lessons. In this way, children see the local language in school. Delivering language lessons is absolutely one way. Look at how we are doing it at our kindergartens. However, due to the school curriculum, it is hard.* **Now we have English, then also we have to teach hiragana** *[Japanese alphabet] to the first-year students,* **then we have to teach English** *to the third-year students then now . . .* **here we have the Yaeyaman language**[14] *but it is too much. Too much to incorporate it in school.* (Interview with a teacher of elementary school)

13 Okinawa was under the administrative rule of the United States Civil Administration of the Ryukyu Islands after the Second World War, from 1950 until 1972.
14 Here I use the Yaeyaman language as a translation of sumamuni.

Looking at the extract above, teachers' descriptions explain the need to include indigenous viewpoints in the official school curriculum. This teacher comments that due to the official curriculum of teaching Japanese and then English, it is hard to include the Yaeyaman language. Language-in-education policies in Japan do not value the importance of bottom-up language planning as a "vehicle of cultural expression and door of opportunity for indigenous language speakers" (Hornberger, 2005, p. 4). Just as applied linguists increasingly foreground the role of the teacher as policy-maker in language teaching (e.g. Ricento & Hornberger, 1996), others emphasize the role of the teacher as policy-maker in heritage language teaching as well. The above example shows that although teachers in school recognize the importance of heritage language, the teachers who have higher university education themselves would like to promote English and Japanese languages over indigenous languages. On the other hand, teachers who voluntarily teach the Yaeyaman language lack confidence as teachers, because of lack of official institutional education.

In 2006, Okinawa Prefectural Government proclaimed September 18 as an island language day, by emphasizing the use of Ryukyuan language at an administrative level. Due to the recent changes in language policies at the prefectural government level, teachers are trying to open and fill up implementational spaces with multilingual practices, which is possible because of policy changes toward multilingualism in the Ryukyus (Heinrich & Ishihara, 2017). Language-in-education policy in the Ryukyus is not promoting real multilingualism, as the policy is promoting people to be more and more Japanese (e.g. by promoting Okinawa prefecture to be the best prefecture in English language). As noted by others the fact that constitutional and legislative instruments exist is of the greatest significance because they represent democratic space for the legal and effective promotion of multilingualism and mother tongue–based bilingual education, which open up ideological and implementational spaces for indigenous language education (e.g. Alexander, 2003; Hornberger & López, 1998).

4. Conclusion: Recognizing translanguaging, recognizing ourselves

This study of the Ryukyuan language shows that when a language is endangered, there are much bigger things at stake than the language itself. There is inequality, there is discrimination, there are different life chances, depending on which language people speak (see Romaine, 2008). The finding of my research suggests the need to investigate and re-evaluate the multilingualism in language-in-education policies. Research on endangered languages in Asia suggests that the ubiquity of the national official language, across all domains, including education, ensures its place as the language of social mobility, and also confers prestige on that language (e.g. Roche, 2017). This is consolidated by discourses that associate the national official language with progress, civilization, and human quality while denigrating minority and regional language as backward, unscientific and parochial, which is happening in the case of Ryukyuan languages. Indigenous languages are left and seen as languages of backwardness that are uneducated and ugly, while Standard Japanese is associated with beautiful, civilized, and sophisticated (see Hammine, in press). The oppressed minoritized languages are stigmatized through language-in-education policies in Japan, which value the dominant languages over minoritized Indigenous languages and keep assimilating indigenous languages and its speakers.

To implement and strengthen multilingualism in the Ryukyus, translanguaging could be a solution, and we need to revisit translanguaging practices of elders in educational contexts. In other words, policies supporting multilingualism and multiculturalism are necessary to change the situation. Japanese educational policies should consider including the indigenous perspective in education in order for the indigenous culture and traditions to be equal with the dominant culture, in a similar manner as in Nordic countries or in Australia or New Zealand (e.g. Huss, 2004).

The problem is bigger than language endangerment. What is shared among Ryukyuan language revitalization projects is a strongly held attitude of traditional speakers that our languages constitute invaluable repositories of distinctive knowledge, which affects the attitudes of teachers of indigenous languages. These attitudes, which I call internalized colonialism, do not promote the fact that children and teachers have a right and a need to express their multilingual talents both in school and at home. If we are not allowed to develop identities as Ryukyuans, it is not possible to achieve multilingualism, valuing our own languages in education. This fits well with Norton's notion:

> The question of "Who am I?" cannot be understood apart from the question, "What am I allowed to do?" And the question "What am I allowed to do?" cannot be understood apart from material conditions that structure opportunities for the realization of desires. (2012, p. 8)

Although each revitalization effort must be understood according to locally defined needs, goals, and available material and human resources (McCarty & Lee, 2014), the current language policies in the Ryukyus enhance "Japaneseness" and promote the devaluation of Ryukyuan languages. There is a vicious circle in the Ryukyus. In Sámi language contexts, for example, they have more choices to express their identity positively due to multilingual policy, whereas in the Ryukyus there is no choice to learn their language. Hence, it brings little self-esteem as Ryukyuan language speakers. Teachers often possess these attitudes themselves and they put it on new speakers, their students. Thus, language endangerment is also connected to educational underachievement in the Okinawa prefecture. In order to reverse underachievement among minority group students, classroom instruction must affirm students' identities and challenge patterns of power relations in the broader society (Cummins, 2014, p. 5).

Linguistically sustainable pedagogy goes beyond being responsive or relevant to the cultural experiences of minoritized group in that it "seeks to perpetuate and foster – to sustain – linguistic, literate, and cultural pluralism as part of the democratic project of schooling" (McCarty & Lee, 2014). Educational policies supporting culturally and linguistically sustainable pedagogy democratizes schooling by supporting both traditional and evolving ways of cultural connectedness for Indigenous groups. Cultural pluralism and tolerance in language-in-education policies might be the solution.

Indigenous language teaching in the Ryukyus has to be understood by comparing the Japanese situation with other parts of the world: local languages, local literacies, and local knowledges are increasingly foregrounded for attention in language education policy and planning all around the world, in a move which indexes precisely the heritage languages and cultures forward (e.g. Canagarajah, 2002, 2005; Lin & Martin, 2005; Omoniyi, 2003). By looking at the case of the Ryukyus, we can understand that to achieve successful language revitalization, it does not help to follow the way set by the Japanese national policy. We need to revisit our elders, who naturally used to practice translanguaging.

4.1 Another aspect of policy

Finally, festival, art, and music are part of our traditional education in the Ryukyus. In the traditional festivals, we are supposed to speak our languages, and that is where we learn the language. Educational policy usually focuses on "official" policies, but there are more things we should include. We learn, we speak, we dance, we sing in indigenous languages. Indigenous policies are there; they are just not visible (see also Canagarajah, 2005). Just as multilingualism of the Ryukyus has been brainwashed by the language policy based on monolingual ideology of the nation state, there is a need to revisit the concept of language policy once again by recognizing the translanguaging practices and pedagogy of elders in the Ryukyus.

Acknowledgements
The author wants to thank all of her family and relatives in the Ryukyus, and Dr. Christopher Davis, Dr. Patrick Heinrich, Dr. Masahide Ishihara and many other researchers who contributed to this research. The author wants to thank two anonymous reviewers and Ms. Jasmine Sargent for providing precise comments during the editorial process. This research was partially supported by University of Lapland research grant. Shikaittu miihaiyū.

References
Alexander, N. (2003). *Language Education Policy, National and Sub-National Identities in South Africa*. Strasbourg: Council of Europe (Reference Study).

Anderson, A. & Summerhayes, G. (2008). Edge-Ground and Waisted Axes in the Western Pacific Islands: Implications for an Example from the Yaeyama Islands, Southernmost Japan. *Asian Perspectives, 47*. 10.1353/asi.2008.0001.

Arakaki, T. (2013). Ryukyu ni okeru gengo kenkyu to kadai [Linguistics research and problems in the Ryukyus]. In Okinawa University Area Research Center (ed.) *Ryukyu shogo no fukkō [Revitalization of Ryukyuan Languages]* (pp. 13–29). Tokyo: Fuyoshobo.

Bourdieu, P. (1980). *The Logic of Practice*. Stanford: Stanford University Press.

Busch, B., Jardine, A., & Tjoutuku, A. (2006). Language biographies for multilingual learning. *PRAESA Occasional Papers No. 24, PRAESA Occ* (February), 5–100.

Canagarajah, S. (Ed.), (2002). Celebrating local knowledge on language and education. *Journal of Language, Identity, and Education, 1*(4) special issue.

Canagarajah, A. S. (2005). *Reclaiming the local in language policy and practice*. Mahwah, NJ: Erlbaum.

Clarke, H. (2015). Language and identity in Okinawa and Amami: Past, present and future. In P. Heinrich, S. Miyara, & M. Shimoji (Eds.), *Handbook of the Ryukyuan Languages*. Berlin: Mouton de Gruyter.

Cummins, J. (1996). *Negotiating identities: Education for empowerment in a diverse society*. Ontario, CA: California Association for Bilingual Education.

Cummins, J. (2014). Managing Diversity in Education. Languages, Policies, Pedagogies. In D. Little, C. Leung, & P. V. Avermeat (Eds.), *Managing Diversity in Education. Languages, Policies, Pedagogies*. Bristol: Multilingual Matters.

Davis, C. (2014a). Okinawaken Yaeyama Miyara hōgen [Okinawa prefecture Yaeyama Miyara Dialect. Research on endangered languages]. *Kikitekina jōkyō ni aru gengo ni kansuru chōsa kenkyuu [Field research on endangered languages and dialects]*. Nishihara: University of the Ryukyus Okinawa Research Center.

Davis, C. (2014b). Surface position and focus domain of the Ryukyuan focus particle du: Evidence from Miyara Yaeyaman. *International Journal of Okinawan Studies, 4*(1), 29–49.

Davis, C., & Lau, T. (2015). Tense, Aspect, and Mood in Miyara Yaeyaman. In P. Heinrich, S. Miyara, & M. Shimoji (Eds.), *Handbook of the Ryukyuan Languages* (pp. 1–41). Berlin: Mouton de Gruyter.

Fija, B. (2016). Attempt to revitalize the Ryukyuan languages by historical awareness, not by religious awareness. In R. Katsuragi & C. Maha, John (Eds.), *Gakushūin University: The Research Institute for Oriental Studies: Minority Language Revitalization: Contemporary Approaches* (pp. 174–199). Tokyo: Gakushūin University: The Research Institute for Oriental Studies.

Fujita-Round, S., & Maher, J. (2008). Language Education Policy in Japan. In N. Hornberger (Ed.), *Encyclopedia of Language and Education* (pp. 393–404). Boston: Springer.

Gayman, J. (2011). Ainu right to education and Ainu practice of "education": Current situation and imminent issues in light of Indigenous education rights and theory. *Intercultural Education, 22*(1), 15–27.

Hammine, M. (in press). Educated not to speak our language. *Journal of Identity, Language and Education.*

Heinrich, P. (2012). *The Making of Monolingual Japan: Language Ideology and Japanese Modernity.* Bristol: Multilingual Matters.

Heinrich, P & Ishihara, M. (2017). Ryukyuan Languages in Japan. In C. Seals & S. Shah (Eds.), *Heritage Language Policies around the World.* (pp.164–184). New York: Routledge.

Hornberger, N. H. (2002). Multilingual language policies and the continua of biliteracy: An ecological approach. *Language Policy,* 1, 27–51.

Hornberger, N. H. (2005). Opening and filling up implementational and ideological spaces in heritage language education. Modern Language Journal, 89(4), 605–609.

Hornberger, N. H. (2014). "Until I Became a Professional, I Was Not, Consciously, Indigenous": One Intercultural Bilingual Educator's Trajectory in Indigenous Language Revitalization. *Journal of Language, Identity and Education, 13*(4), 283–299.

Hornberger, N. H., & López, L. E. (1998). Policy, possibility and paradox: Indigenous multilingualism and education in peru and bolivia. In J. Cenoz & F. Genesee (Eds.), *Beyond bilingualism: Multilingualism and multilingual education* (pp. 206–242). Clevedon, England: Multilingual Matters

Huss, L. (2004). Revitalization through Indigenous Education: A Forlorn Hope? In N. Hornberger (Ed.), *Can Schools Save Indigenous Languages? Policy and Practice on Four Continents.* (pp. 125–135). New York: Palgrave Macmillan.

Ishigaki, S. (2013). *Meeramuni yōgo binran [Miyaran Language Vocabulary Book].* Naha: Nanyosha.

Izuyama, A. (2003). The grammar of the Ishigaki Miyara dialect in Luchuan. In A. Izuyama (Ed.), *Studies on Luchuan grammar.* (pp. 1–162). Kyoto: ELPR.

Kondo, K. (2008). *Hougenfuda – kotobatokarada [Dialect Tag – language and body].* Tokyo: Syakaihyouronsya.

Kerr, G. (2000). *Okinawa: The History of Island People* (Tuttle Pub). North Clarendon.

Lee, Y. (1996). *"Kokugo" toiu shiso: Kindai nihon no gengo ninshiki [The*

Ideology of Kokugo: Nationalizing Language in Modern Japan]. Tokyo: Iwanami Shoten.

Liebkind, K. (2010). Social Psychology. In J. A. Fishman & O. Garcia (Eds.), *Handbook of Language and Ethnic Identity* (pp. 18–31). New York: Oxford University Press.

Lin, A., & Martin, P. (Eds.), (2005). *Decolonization, globalization: Language-in-education policy and practice*. Clevedon, UK: Multilingual Matters.

Matsuda, H. (2008). Yaeyama: From periphery of the Ryūkyūs to frontier of Japan. *Japanese Studies, 28*(2), 149–164.

McCarty, T., & Lee, T. (2014). Critical Culturally Sustaining/ Revitalizing Pedagogy and Indigenous Education Sovereignty. *Harvard Educational Review, 84*(1)

Miki, T. (2003). *Yaeyama kenkyū no rekishi [History of Yaeyaman research]*. Ishigaki: Nanzansha.

Moseley, C. (Ed.) (2009). *Atlas of the World's Languages in Danger* (3rd edition). Paris: UNESCO. Retrieved from URL http://www.unesco. org/culture/en/endangeredlanguages/atlas

Nakahara, Y. (2003). Ishigakijima Miyara hōgen no oninkenkyuu jyosetsu [Intoroductory research on Phonetics for miyara dialect of Ishigaki Island]. Tokyo: Housei University Research Centre for Okinawan Culture.

Nakata, R. (2004). *Yaeyama rekishi dokuhon [Book of History of Yaeyama]*. Ishigaki: Nanzansya.

Nihon Keizai Shimbun, (2016). Eigo rikken Okinawa ga saikai? – koukousei no eigo hyoka ni gimon no koe [English prefecture, Okinawa ranks the worst? – rising questions about assessment of English skills among high school students]. Tokyo: Nihon Keizai Shimbun. (Accessed June 10th, 2019). Available online: https://www.nikkei.com/article/ DGXLZO04940850W6A710C1CC1000/

Norton, B. (2012). *Identity and Language Learning: Extending the Conversation*. Bristol: Multilingual Matters.

Omoniyi, T. (2003). Local policies and global forces: Multiliteracy and Africa's indigenous languages. Language Policy, 2, 133–152.

O'Rourke, B., Pujolar, J., & Ramallo, F. (2015). New speakers of minority languages:The challenging opportunity – Foreword. *International*

Journal of the Sociology of Language, 2015(231), 1–20. https://doi. org/10.1515/ijsl-2014-0029

Pellard, T. (2013). Nihon rettō no gengo no tayōsei – Ryuukyuushogo o chūshinni – [Linguistic Diversity of the Japanese Archipelago – focusing on Ryukyuan languages]. In Y. Takubo (Ed.), *Ryuukyuu rettō no gengo to bunka – sonokiroku to keishō – [Language and Culture of the Ryukyus – Documentation and Inheritance]* (pp. 81–92). Tokyo: Kuroshio shuppan.

Ricento, T. K., & Hornberger, N. H. (1996). Unpeeling the onion: Language planning and policy and the ELT professional. *TESOL Quarterly, 30*, 401–428.

Romaine, S. (2008). Linguistic Diversity, Sustainability, and the Future of the Past. In K. A. King., N. Schilling, L. W. Fogle., J. J. Lou., & B. Souku (Eds.), *Sustaining Linguistic Diversity: Endangered and Minority Languages and Language Varieties* (pp. 7–21). Washington: Georgetown University Press.

Shimoji, M., & Pellard, T. (Eds.) (2010). *An introduction to Ryukyuan languages*. Tokyo: ILCAA.

Siddle, R. (1996). *Race, Resistance, and the Ainu of Japan*. London: Routledge.

Skutnabb-Kangas, T. (2010). Education for Indigenous and Minority Children. In J. A. Fishman & O. Garcia (Eds.), *Handbook of Language and Ethnic Identity* (pp. 186–204). Oxford: Oxford University Press.

Smith, L. T. (1999). *Decolonizing Methodologies: Research and Indigenous Peoples*. New York: University of Otago Press.

Takubo, Y. (2015). *Ryukyushogo kenkyu no genzai – shōmetsu kiki gengo to mukaiau – Struggling with an Endangered Ryukyun Language: Creating a Disital Museum to Document Endangered Languages*. Tokyo: Rikkyo University College of Intercultural Communication.

Tuck, E., & Yang, K. W. (2012). Decolonization is not a metaphor. *Decolonization: Indigeneity, Education, & Society, 1*(1), 1–40.

Yokota, R. M. (2015). The Okinawan (Uchinanchu) Indigenous Movement and Its Implications for Intentional/International Action. *Amerasia Journal, 41*(1).

CHAPTER 5

Social network, dual identity, and agency in the implementation of indigenous language education in migration communities

Chun-Mei Chen

1. Introduction

This paper examines how social network, dual identity, and agency play a role in the implementation of indigenous language education for bilingual Paiwan-Mandarin children in urban migration communities, where Mandarin is the dominant language for communication and the Taiwanese dialect is the commercial language in the local marketplace. Taiwan is a linguistically diverse society, and 3% of the population are Austronesian descendants. Fieldwork in this study focused on linguistic forms, language choices, and language shift in the process of aboriginal language education among the urban Paiwan speakers. Dual or mixture pronunciation as communicative strategies in face-to-face conversation in Paiwan migration communities was examined. The survey on the language shift in the migration context enhances the understanding of social factors on minority language attrition, given the fact that second generations of the Paiwan aborigines have relatively less chance to speak their mother tongue. Multilingual education is linked to larger issues of indigenous linguistic human rights. In support of indigenous languages through multilingual models of education,

Paiwan children need to learn how to use their ancestral language outside of the classroom as a situated social practice, and how to reproduce, change, or mediate the Paiwan language in multilingual urban migration communities.

Paiwan is an indigenous language spoken in Southern Taiwan. The ethnic Paiwan people numbered around 101,400 in 2018. There are 16 indigenous languages recognized by the Council of the Indigenous Peoples supported by the government. Paiwan language has parallel palatal stops, which are rarely attested in the other Formosan languages (Austronesian languages spoken in Taiwan), and the merger of palatal stops also occurs in some varieties of Paiwan. Phonetic variation and accent patterns of the Paiwan language have been attested (Chen, 2009). Bilingual Paiwan-Mandarin children are able to read a Paiwan lexical word, as many second language learners can do, but the phonological variants and the placement of stress could distinguish them from their parents or other older native speakers in the same speech communities. Most Paiwan families in the urban communities did not have strict family language policies. Language use at home often varies across generations in Taiwan. Despite there being a difference in family language practices and backgrounds, bilingual Paiwan-Mandarin children negotiate and construct their Mandarin-dominant positions at home and in the communities through the use of the language. Speaking the Paiwan language at home often requires positive self-image and negotiation of the parent–child relationship.

Migration has been an inevitable issue among the indigenous Paiwan speakers. When the Paiwan speakers migrate from native villages to urban cities, their native words can be perceived as different in their new places of living. Many indigenous people live in urban areas, and the dominant discourses are reflected in the language policy and in educational policy. Government support constitutes a key component in minority language maintenance (Baker, 2003; Fishman, 1991).

Language shift from the Paiwan language to Mandarin or Taiwanese has been attested in many urban communities. Different languages and language varieties get their reputations through social status of their speakers in a speech community. Even if the linguistic choices are made in urban migration communities, Paiwan speakers in the communities will manage to make choices about how they sound. In addition to a description of language shift in urban migration communities, how to encourage Paiwan migrants use their native language or "family language" has become an issue between Paiwan parents and children. Sociocultural factors such as language identity come into play in the attrition of the minority language. Family language policy in the present study is examined through language use and language choice within the home among family members, which aims to understand how languages are managed, learned, and negotiated within the families (King, Fogle, & Logan-Terry, 2008). The study focused on daily interactions to see how the negotiations and challenges of language choice are made.

Fieldwork in urban migration communities was conducted to survey how social network, dual identity, and agency function in the implementation of indigenous language education in urban migration communities. More language-oriented approaches entail a shift in focus from attitudes within language maintenance processes, contexts, and experiences to viewing them as they emerge and are used as resources in interactions. Family face-to-face conversation in the urban migration communities was the main source for the investigation. Descriptions of the Paiwan migrants' linguistic behaviors and competencies do not always correspond to reality. Sociolinguistic phenomena such as language attrition and shift are best examined through triangulation of linguistic, observational, and interview data, rather than narratives only. In order to investigate language shift and the implementation of indigenous language education of the Paiwan speakers in urban migration communities, the present study pays attention to the conversation data and examines a range of linguistic devices, including elicitation, reported speech, interviews, and code-switching. The triangulation allows us to explain inconsistencies between content and forms.

There is an overt level of awareness regarding the use of the Paiwan language in the presence of Paiwan parents, grandparents, or close family members of the speakers, in urban migration communities. Many studies on bilingual socialization have worked with young adults and college students in a single setting. Findings from both Paiwan parents and bilingual Paiwan-Mandarin children in multiple sites may deepen our knowledge of Paiwan speakers' language choice and socialization in different linguistic and cultural contexts. Language use in native villages and urban migration communities can shed light on how the interplay between multiple memberships in diverse communities impact bilingual Paiwan-Mandarin speakers' socialization and language development.

All the courses are taught in Mandarin in public elementary schools in Taiwan. The government has formally allowed schools to teach local languages as optional classes since 1997, and the implementation of a mandatory local language curriculum began in 2001. However, some of the indigenous languages were not regularly taught in urban migration communities, depending on the number of indigenous children and qualified school teachers. Aboriginal children were occasionally forced to take another indigenous language as their local-language class due to the lack of standardized educational materials or qualified teachers. The indigenous language education in Taiwan has encountered challenges such as target population, syllabus, teacher supply, resources, and evaluation. Bilingual children in the present investigation were taking the Paiwan language as their local language in schools, and they had to learn appropriate language and behavior through activities and routines in formal educational contexts. They learned how to answer and how to participate in a sequence in the language course, and they constructed communicative competence, social relations, and identities.

The present study addresses roles of social network, dual identity, and agency in the implementation of indigenous language education by determining how bilingual Paiwan-Mandarin children in the migration communities negotiated their standing in the community context and at home and became the major force in determining language choice. Indigenous language researchers and educators have to frame their curriculum along with perceptions of shared values, and interactions of family and community forces. The study offers insights into the process of identity and agency formation through multilingual models of education.

2. Theoretical framework

Migration is an important factor in the erosion of traditional boundaries between languages, culture, and ethnic groups. The experiences of migrants have a particular focus on identity issues. Different evolving approaches to migration and diversity in the various Asian contexts raise significant questions about the identities of migrants and the position of future generations in society (Eng, Collins, & Yeoh, 2013). It has been observed that the identities of first generation immigrants do shift during the process of settlement, from close association with distant homelands to identities with less pre-migration affiliation. Focus group method is particularly useful in accessing social interactions with a minority group through elicitation and conversation (Hodges, 2009). In the present study, Paiwan parents migrated to urban communities in Central Taiwan at various ages but had ties to their native villages in Southern Taiwan. Their bilingual Paiwan-Mandarin children spoke the Paiwan language with their Paiwan family members or other Paiwan speakers in the urban migration communities. The use of the Paiwan language was also regulated by family language policy.

On the other hand, social network theory has played an important role in extending our understanding of language change (Milroy, 1992). Networks characterize the social relations contracted between individuals, whose groupings may in turn be characterized in terms of strong or weak ties, constituting dense or loose networks (Milroy & Gordon, 2003). Social network and age factors in the maintenance of an indigenous language in this study were examined as a case of supporting the argument that linguistic forms used by the minority language groups with different social relationships contrast in speech communities. Language change is linked to the nature of social network, and strong ties inhibit change while loose networks typically facilitate change. The interaction between linguistic features and social factors of the bilingual Paiwan-Mandarin children was examined to see how negotiations and transformations of language choice were implemented in creative and innovative ways.

Sociocultural theorists (Lantolf, 2000; Ricento, 2005) conceptualize identity "not as a fixed invariant attribute in the 'mind' of the individual learner" (Ricento, 2005, p. 895). Identity is theorized as a process involving dialectic relations between learners and the various experiences they inhabit. Learning one's ancestral language in an academic context and becoming engaged in a new culture involves adjusting one's sense of self and creating new identities to connect the known to the new (see also Hammine, this volume). Shaping new identities requires ongoing struggles and reconciliations. It was found that dual identity produced not only greater willingness to engage in contact but also greater social change motivation (Glasford & Dovidio, 2011). Members of ethnic minority groups are particularly concerned with respect within intergroup interactions (Bergsieker, Shelton, & Richeson, 2010). A dual identity can convey the respect while communicating shared values. Shared values and feelings of similarity promote positive intergroup expectancies and interaction (Mallett & Wilson, 2010). In the socio-constructionist approach

(Vygotsky, 1978), identity is seen as a product that is determined and learned by communicative practices. Language plays a central role in one's identity. Bilingual children in the urban migration communities perceive the ancestral language as it relates to them and at the same time re-examine their sense of identity in the light of the meanings perceived. They have a dual identity based on both the Paiwan and Mandarin speech and culture.

Agency starts with the belief that human beings have the ability to influence their lives and environment while they are also shaped by social and individual factors (e.g. Bourdieu, 1977; Giddens, 1984). Agency is defined as "the socioculturally mediated capacity to act" (Ahearn, 2001, p. 112). Children's agency is one of the important elements in the emerging field of family language policy (King, 2013). Language development is driven by learners' agency in investing language learning and using strategies to overcome problems (Flowerdew & Miller, 2008). Garrett and Baquedano-López (2002) argue that multilingual individuals, even young children, are agents with potential to renegotiate, challenge or transform social categories. Children become the major force in determining language choice (Fogle, 2012; Fogle & King, 2013). The exercise of children's agency is often mediated by social and cultural contexts. Ahearn's (2001) definition of agency states that agency is situated in a particular context. Lantolf and Thorne (2006, p. 142) argue that agency "is about more than voluntary control over behaviour." Agency, according to their explanation, can be exercised by individuals as well as by communities. Agency in the present study includes an awareness of the responsibility for the actions, and it mediates and is mediated by the sociocultural context (see also Tamati, this volume).

It is also important to address the issue of the development of indigenous language curriculum in Taiwan. The Ministry of Education and Council of Indigenous Peoples in Taiwan began to offer training camps for school teachers and members of aboriginal communities in

2001. The Council of Indigenous Peoples in Taiwan began to initiate "language nest" and cultural immersion programs in 2007. The Council of Indigenous Peoples began the administration of a proficiency examination system for aboriginal languages, and the Paiwan language was included in the system. Aboriginal students can obtain an extra 35% score on their university entrance examination by passing the aboriginal language proficiency examination. Dupré (2013) conducted an empirical study in Taiwan and found that ancestral languages in Taiwan constitute an important element of ethnic identities. Yet, the major issue in the implementation of the language education is the small amount of time devoted to indigenous language instruction. In the urban migration communities, the Paiwan language is used less and less at home, and the aboriginal languages are learned more as second languages. The effective implementation of indigenous language education represents linguistic human rights. The Paiwan migrants in bilingual Paiwan-Mandarin migration communities emerged to express ethnic identity and positive attitude toward Paiwan culture. The linguistic features of the bilingual Paiwan-Mandarin children have become a rise in a variety of the indigenous language.

The present study took place in an urban setting, and I worked most closely with Paiwan parents and bilingual children from indigenous families who were of ethnic minority backgrounds. I believe that indigenous language learning within communities must question the social dimensions of participation within communities. How migration communities sustain various social networks is important for understanding indigenous language education. The model to implement a socially situated stance of indigenous language education is achieved through the construct of identity and agency.

3. Methodology in migration communities

In the present study, the Paiwan families migrated to urban communities for various reasons. Some of the aboriginal urban migrants felt isolated or discriminated against in the urban communities. Urban Paiwan aborigines in this study lived in the same speech communities as their Paiwan relatives and did better in maintaining their cultural identities with a strong social network. Mandarin is the dominant language for communication, and the Taiwanese dialect is the commercial language in the local marketplace. The use of the Paiwan language in the migration communities was relatively restricted. The direct and person-to-person interaction between urban Paiwan migrants has an important role in the development of consciousness through interpersonal relations. Paiwan, as the home language, could not obtain equal status with the dominant language (Mandarin), because the language was used by a relatively small group of people. When the host language is the only language supported by the mainstream society, learning the home language may rely heavily on familial networks (Park, 2007). If parents value cultural maintenance and speak the indigenous language at home, this may increase the likelihood that their children are willing to learn the indigenous language. Not only pitch, but also vocabulary, pronunciation, and grammar can differentiate age groups in both Paiwan native villages (Chen, 2009) and migration communities. Social dialect research suggests relative frequency of vernacular forms in different age groups (see also Purkarthofer, this volume). Vernacular forms are high in childhood and adolescence. The case of bilingual children's language shift or code-switching therefore represents creative processes as the result of competence in two or more languages.

The study is based on a series of sociolinguistic interviews with Paiwan families, elicitation, and face-to-face conversation. Linguistic features presented in this paper draw from both quantitative and qualitative methods. Phonological varieties in Paiwan were verified by the number of tokens and checked with spectrograms in Praat. The triangulation of linguistic, observational, and interview data offered a basis to illustrate social workings of the indigenous language. There were 66 participants recruited during the fieldwork. Thirty middle-aged and elder Paiwan speakers in Southern Taiwan native villages were recruited as informants in the first investigation. Thirty-six Paiwan speakers from twelve Paiwan families in Central Taiwan migration communities participated in the second investigation. The duration of the data collection was 36 months. The researcher has been working with some Paiwan communities for more than 10 years, and some participants worked with the researchers in other projects prior to the investigations of this study. In order to ensure that participants felt as comfortable and confident as possible during the interviews, pre-existing family membership and friendship groups were recruited. The researcher was not a member of the Paiwan communities but lived in the neighborhood of the migration communities at the time of the investigations. A survey on demographic data was conducted in interactional conversation. Potential participants were asked about their date of arrival in the urban migration communities, age, Paiwan native villages, education, professional career, reason for migrating, their self-assessments of the Paiwan language on arrival and, as it is now, their attitudes toward the Paiwan culture, domains where the Paiwan language is used, frequency of visits to Paiwan hometowns, and family language policy.

The first investigation on the Paiwan language focused on phonological features and varieties in Paiwan native villages (in Pingtung County in Southern Taiwan). The native villages are the hometowns of the Paiwan parents in the urban migration communities. The major demographic difference between the Paiwan native villages and urban migration communities lies in the ethnic distribution of the residents. More than 90% of the residents in the native villages were Paiwan aborigines, and Paiwan was the primary communication language in the native villages among the middle-aged and elder residents. Young Paiwan residents in the native villages spoke Mandarin in public educational institutions and Taiwanese outside of the communities. Thirty middle-aged and elder Paiwan speakers in native villages were recruited as informants in the first investigation. The informants' pronunciation was considered representative in the native villages. Each informant in the native villages was asked to say 800 basic words in Paiwan for the compilation of phonological inventory and phonemes of Paiwan dialects and varieties.

In the second investigation, 360 minutes of family discourse and face-to-face conversation, and semi-structured interviews in workplace, schools, and community churches were recorded in the urban migration communities (Taichung City in Central Taiwan). The lexical word list for elicitation was divided into categories as follows: nature, plants, animals, people, body parts, culture, adjectives, time and existentials, numerals, pronouns, demonstratives, interrogatives, and locatives. Thirty-six Paiwan speakers in migration communities participated in the second investigation. They belonged to twelve families in two speech communities in Taichung City. The Paiwan speakers moved to the urban communities from Paiwan native villages, including Sandimen (Timur), Machia (Makazayazaya), Gulou (Kulalau), Danlin (Calasiv), Chunri (Kuabar), Mudan (Sinvaujan) in Southern Taiwan to Central Taiwan – more than 200 miles of migration. Participants in the migration communities include Paiwan parents and their bilingual Paiwan-Mandarin children. All parental participants in the second investigation were asked to report their indigenous language use at home, the Paiwan language proficiency of their children, their experience of using the Paiwan language in the communities, and their children's language choices. All participants reported no history of hearing impairments or speech disorders at the time of the investigation.

The number of bilingual speakers, the relative social status of the communities, and the duration of a contact situation are among the factors that are necessary to understand the linguistic outcomes of language contact in the migration communities. It has been noted that the major phonological change among the Paiwan dialects lies in palatal stops, palatal laterals, and uvular stops (Chen, 2009). There are twenty native consonant phonemes in Timur Paiwan and Makazayazaya Paiwan, and the glottal stop phoneme is the reflex of the uvular stop /q/. Twenty-three native consonant phonemes were attested in Kulalau Paiwan, Kuabar Paiwan, and Sinvaujan Paiwan dialects, and the glottal stop is somewhat marginal. In Calasiv Paiwan dialect, the palatal lateral consonantal phoneme was substituted by the interdental voiced fricative consonantal phoneme among young speakers, and the velar stop and the uvular stop were often pronounced as a glottal stop variant. In other words, phonological varieties were attested among the native villages. When the Paiwan speakers from different native villages with different Paiwan dialects migrated to the same community, mixture pronunciation with phonological alteration became a routine in their inner-circle conversation.

Twelve Paiwan mothers participated in all the sessions. They formed three strong "friendship" (inner-circle) groups in the investigation. The Paiwan fathers and bilingual children were bound to the Paiwan mothers' social network. All pairs of parents were living together. The Paiwan mothers were from six Paiwan native villages with different Paiwan varieties. All the participants felt that there was a lack of exposure to the Paiwan language in everyday context in the urban speech communities. Native speakers of Paiwan also need to understand the phonological variants among the dialects for better intelligibility in communication. Initial observations have revealed that Paiwan speakers in the urban speech communities "switched" to the Mandarin language in both formal and informal contexts, in workplace and family discourse or inner-circle church conversation. Yet, not all Paiwan parents and bilingual children "switched" between languages in the same way. Code-switching is a context-sensitive discourse strategy, and Paiwan parents and bilingual

Paiwan-Mandarin children have different language combinations, proficiency levels, and attitudes toward code-switching. The present study looks at the creative performance of bilingual children at home, in schools, and in community contexts.

Tailored elicitation questions were employed to elicit participants' personal experiences and remarks, avoiding direct questions. Separate sessions were conducted with the participant groups, lasting appropriately one hour per session. Natural topic shift was permitted to occur between informants, pertaining to less structured design to investigate the language shift in the urban speech communities. The settings for the data collection were for transactional or interactional conversation. All focus sessions began by familiarizing the investigator and participants through the lives in the urban communities. Recordings were transcribed and analyzed, drawing on the principles of constructing significant themes and patterns, exploring paralinguistic features. A list of about 30 broad themes was developed during the transcription-checking processes. Family language planning and indigenous language education will be understood not as separate phenomena. The triangulation of linguistic, observational, and interview data I used in the investigations proved well-suited in capturing the connections in the migration communities.

4. Dual identity and agency in the community social network
4.1 Social network and mixture pronunciation
Ferrell (1982) has noted that for centuries the Paiwan aborigines have been in contact with speakers of the other Austronesian languages such as Rukai and Puyuma to the north. He also noted that Paiwan dialect divisions involve notable differences in realizations of the voiceless velar, uvular and glottal stop, and of trill and retroflex. The first investigation in Paiwan native villages in Pingtung County (in Southern Taiwan) has found the various numbers of consonantal

phonemes. Uvular stop /q/ is absent in Sandimen (Timur) and
Machia (Makazayazaya) Paiwan dialects. Different dialectal varieties
have been classified into Northern Paiwan, Central Paiwan,
Southern Paiwan, and Eastern Paiwan dialects in the indigenous
language curriculum issued by the Council of Indigenous Peoples
and approved by the Ministry of Education in Taiwan. Although
some Paiwan aborigines do not agree with the classification, local
language curriculum is restricted to the major four Paiwan dialects.
Lexical differences among the Paiwan dialects were also found in the
local language curriculum. Examples in Table 1 illustrate the dialectal
varieties of the Paiwan language.

Table 1. **Examples of dialectal varieties of the Paiwan language
in the curriculum**

English Gloss	Northern Paiwan	Central Paiwan	Southern Paiwan	Eastern Paiwan
"mother"	kina	kina	ina	kina
"book"	sunatj	sunatj	hung	sunatj
"home"	tjumaq	umaq	tjumaq	umaq
"cloud"	qerpus	qarepus	qerepus	qurpus
"sleep"	taqed	kataqedan	taqedan	taqedan

When the Paiwan parents from different Paiwan native villages
migrated to the urban communities, they had to accommodate the
dialectal varieties within the social network, including phonological
variation and lexical differences. They also changed their versions
of pronunciation depending on the native villages of the Paiwan

recipients. The dominant languages outside the social network are Mandarin and Taiwanese. Mixture pronunciation in Paiwan helps in building the Paiwan ethnic identity within the Paiwan social network in the migration communities. Phonological varieties and alternation of variants were attested in the linguistic forms of the frequently used Paiwan lexicon. Paiwan parents were aware of the phonological variants in the migration communities, and the variants also represented the native villages of the Paiwan speakers.

When Paiwan parents implemented their native language policy at home, they had to be supported by their elder family members and other Paiwan speakers in the community social network. In Excerpt 1, the mother narrates how she used the social network support to normalize Paiwan use with her daughter. The excerpt was delivered in Mandarin and translated into English.

Excerpt 1. Interview excerpt of a Paiwan mother

On Friday I was talking about Saturday traditional feast in Paiwan and she [my daughter] said "It is very delicious?" in Paiwan because I was speaking to her vuvu [grandmother]. I am very strict with her speaking the Paiwan language at home with me and my mother. I asked her vuvu to visit us at least three months every year. Of course she liked to switch to Mandarin, but my mother and I would ignore what she said in Mandarin until she spoke Paiwan. I also asked my friends and relatives to speak Paiwan to my daughter when they visited me. If she [my daughter] answered in Mandarin, they would ignore her. When we have a traditional feast in our family, all the Paiwan elders spoke the Paiwan language only. Gradually, she [my daughter] liked to repeat what my mother said although my mother did not know how to write the language down. Her vuvu spoke Paiwan and understood a little Mandarin. She [my daughter] also went

*back to our native village every summer vacation and winter
break. She knew many Paiwan words and used more Paiwan
lexicon when she was in the native village. The Paiwan church
priest also taught the young Paiwan speakers in our [Taichung
migration] community how to type easy Paiwan texts. I asked my
daughter to go to the same church every Sunday to meet with other
Paiwan elders and the priest. She learned how to text me in the
Paiwan language and shared with me her activities in the church.*
[Laughter].

The Paiwan mother involved her daughter's Paiwan language
use in weekend activities. She also initiated social network at home
and in the community for the negotiation of indigenous language
education. Her arrangement of her daughter's trips back to the native
village enhanced the normalizing use of the Paiwan language. More
than half of the Paiwan families in the investigation socialized their
children in the migration communities, and the network and ties
to the native villages encouraged the children to speak the Paiwan
language. Through daily interactions and normalizing Paiwan use
with bilingual children, the Paiwan parents share an ethnic identity
and the proper status of the Paiwan language in the migration
communities.

The bilingual children frequently implemented mixture
pronunciation with other Paiwan family members and elder speakers
in the community network. The mixture pronunciation may be
different from their parents' linguistic features, depending on the
presence of family members or the themes of the conversation. It was
found that bilingual children alternated glottal stops with the uvular
stop /q/ in various contexts, regardless of the native villages of their
Paiwan parents. Most of the bilingual children learned the Paiwan
language from their family members. Two bilingual children, Tiuku
and Kaias (pseudonyms), learned the Paiwan language from their

caregivers, vuvu [grandmother] and auntie from different Paiwan native villages. They often alternated the mixture pronunciation of their parent's variety and the caregiver's varieties within the community network, depending on the recipients. If any Paiwan grandmother was present in the conversation, the bilingual children would choose the traditional pronunciation of the grandmother's hometowns. Terms of kinship, numerals, food, materials, and daily routines were more frequently used. Mixture pronunciation as communicative strategies in face-to-face conversation was attested in the urban migration communities. Parent–daughter conversation in the presence of a grandmother and the daughter's Paiwan friend in Excerpt 2 illustrates the adoption of mixture pronunciation. In the excerpt, Muni (pseudonym) is the daughter. The excerpt was delivered in Paiwan and transcribed in IPA fonts to show the phonetic distinction.

Excerpt 2. Mixture pronunciation in conversation

01 **Mother:** ini ja anan   nu-ʔan   ta   vɔɗɔvɔɗ
            not   yet   you-Nom-eat   Acc   banana
            "Haven't you eaten the banana?"

02 **Muni:** ini ja anan   ʔə-ʔan   ta   vɔɗɔvɔɗ
            not   yet   I-Nom-eat Acc   banana
            "I haven't eaten the banana."

03   [*toward her Paiwan friend*]   vələvəl
                                                banana
                                                "the banana."

The mother explained to the investigator that the word "banana" in the Paiwan friend's family was pronounced differently. Muni repeated her friend's version of "banana" to include the friend in their inner-circle conversation. Muni's dual pronunciation is associated with contexts and communicative strategy in face-to-face conversation. She played the role of a daughter, a granddaughter, and a friend in the situated turns. Bilingual Paiwan children in urban communities with multi-membership experience have a vital impact on the development of separate but connected language norms. The changes in the children's practices, depending on the context in the migration communities, have positive effects on the maintenance or use of the Paiwan language. Given that minority language issues in the urban communities have rarely been addressed, the results provide insights into underlying origins in the decline of the Paiwan speakers and family language maintenance among the urban Paiwan migrants. Bilingual children in the migration communities have less chance to use the indigenous language, and the social network initiated by language policy at home became essential for the negotiation of indigenous language education in the migration communities.

4.2 Dual identity in the migration community contexts

The use of the Paiwan language varied from child to child and over time in the urban migration communities. Parents established different language-use patterns with different children. One mother confessed that she used more Mandarin with her oldest child and more Paiwan with her younger child, especially after participating in the present investigation. The two children of the same family used both Paiwan and Mandarin at home. The younger sister spoke the Paiwan language more often. The Paiwan language used among the Paiwan siblings focused on daily activities. Excerpt 3 illustrates their interaction. In the context, the mother was preparing for dinner and the two daughters, Muakai and Tuku (pseudonyms), were doing their homework. Elder sister Muakai asked younger sister Tuku to take a shower first.

Excerpt 3. Language use between the sisters

01   **Muakai:** [*in Paiwan*] Sau pavanavu! [Go take a shower!]

02   **Tuku:**   [*in Paiwan*] Sau pavanavu! [Go take a shower!]

03   **Muakai:** [*in Mandarin*] Ni xian xizao zai chifan! [You go
        first take a shower and then eat dinner!]

04   **Tuku:**   [*in Mandarin*] Wo bu yao! [No, I don't want to
        do it!]

05   **Muakai:** [*in Mandarin*] Wo yao gen mama shuo. [I want to
        tell Mom.]

06   **Tuku:**   [*in Paiwan*] Malitsəŋ! [Be quiet!]

07   **Muakai:** [*in Mandarin and then Paiwan*] Wo yao gen mama
        shuo. Awta! [I want to tell Mom. Ouch!]

[*The mother entered the room and interrupted their conversation*]

08   **Mother:** [*in Paiwan*] kanu! [Go eat! (Meal time!)]

Eight bilingual children in the study were born and raised in Taichung,
the urban migration communities, and they identified themselves
as both Taichung (Mandarin-dominant community) residents and
ethnic Paiwan (community social network) speakers. Two pairs of
Paiwan parents relocated in the Taichung communities after one or
two migration trips to other cities. Paiwan parents faced the task of
negotiating language use at home ever since their children started
their school life. The pairs of the Paiwan parents in the interviews

encouraged their children to use the Paiwan language, including dual and mixture pronunciation in Paiwan and code-switching. Mandarin and Taiwanese words were widely borrowed into the Paiwan utterance by the Paiwan speakers, when referring to law, business, transportation, technology, and Chinese festivals. Mandarin is the dominant language in the urban migration communities, and a steady linear language shift from indigenous languages to Mandarin occurs over generations. Bilingual children produced and perceived the Paiwan language with shared values and shaped their identity in the communicative practices. They used Paiwan to refer to kinship terms, numerals, food, materials, and daily routines and replaced the Paiwan language with Mandarin in lexical items such as "night market," "convenience store," and technology products. They have a dual identity based on both the Paiwan and Mandarin speech and culture.

Excerpt 4 explained how a Paiwan mother explicitly encouraged her children to use the Paiwan language and Mandarin together. The mother narrated in Mandarin, and the excerpt was transcribed in English.

Excerpt 4. Paiwan mother's attitude toward her bilingual children

*I like my children to learn the Paiwan language at school, although the teacher at the school used different Paiwan dialects of teaching materials. When the pronunciation is different from mine, **I asked my children to follow the teacher's pronunciation.** I think being successful at school work is the priority. Mandarin is useful at school and in the future, but I like my children to speak the Paiwan language as well. As long as they speak Paiwan, their grandmother would be very happy. Vuvu [Grandmother] gave my children compliments. Here [in the urban migration* *communities], [children] speaking Mandarin would make more friends at school. There were few Paiwan kids in the neighborhood after all. My children knew when to switch to Mandarin.*

The Paiwan language curriculum at school did play an important role in shaping the mixture pronunciation and dual identity among the Paiwan children in the urban migration communities. The community-based Paiwan language classroom is characterized as the language teacher from Paiwan dialect S, adopting a textbook in Paiwan dialect S, with students from Paiwan dialect C, D, and G. The children learned their Paiwan language teacher's pronunciation at school and accommodated to their parents' pronunciation at home. They chose the Paiwan language as their local-language curriculum to disclose their Paiwan ethnic identity, and at the same time they socialized in schools with other Mandarin-speaking children in the academic context. They learned how to answer and how to participate in a predictable sequence in the language course.

It is suggested that Paiwan language programs should include extensive knowledge of the native language and mixture pronunciation among the Paiwan students. It may be necessary to develop from "user-input" and reinforce Paiwan students' motivation driven by the social environment. The results presented here indicate that implementation of indigenous language education as a social practice is a key to successful language maintenance in multilingual urban migration communities.

4.3 Bilingual children's agency in language use
Bilingual children spoke the Paiwan language to receive compliments or rewards from the elders or due to family language policies. There is a considerable shift toward Mandarin in the workplace and markets. Interviews with the Paiwan parents revealed that bilingual Paiwan children in the migration communities used mixture pronunciation

for negotiation and asking for favors. Most of the Paiwan parents held positive attitudes toward their children speaking the Paiwan language in the communities, regardless of their mixture pronunciation and code-switching. Code-switching is the alternation of different languages in the same episode of speech production, and it has been treated as an expressive and creative performance (Kharkhurin & Wei, 2015). Critical sociolinguistics claims that interactional and structural processes of language choice are never arbitrary but are linked to social ideologies and power relations (Heller, 1995, 2007). In the present study, I probed into the situated nature of code-switching and bilingual creativity of Paiwan children by showing the changes in the parent–children practices depending on the context and innovative capacity in the migration communities.

In the interview with Vigong (pseudonym), a bilingual son with Paiwan family policy, he confessed his frequent use of code-switching in the migration community. Excerpt 5 shows Vigong's experience of using the Paiwan language and code-switching to challenge his parents' power. The statement was delivered in Mandarin and translated in English.

Excerpt 5. Bilingual son's description of his language use

[Laughter] *When I spoke the Paiwan language to my friends at school in my Grade 1, they did not understand and laughed at me. But the elders in the communities liked me to speak Paiwan. One day, on my way back home, my friends and I heard the discussion of the elders in the Paiwan language about the upcoming Sunday feast. I replied to them in Paiwan that I would ask my mom to take me there to join the feast and thanked them. One vuvu [elder Paiwan relative] gave me 100 dollars and the other gave me candies. Suddenly, my friends admired me. I feel . . . it's cool to use Paiwan when talking to the elders. But Mandarin is more useful to make friends at school. So I use both languages. Sometimes I can't find the right Paiwan words . . . at home . . . when talking to my vuvu [grandmother]. I switched to Mandarin when my mom was not at home.* [Laughter] *I also mixed Paiwan and Mandarin on purpose and created new Paiwan words with my brother.* [Laughter] *My mom knew I was speaking some Mandarin words with vuvu, but vuvu would say I was a good child in front of my parents. My Paiwan language is much better than other kids. So, it's okay with my parents . . . when I speak Mandarin at home.*

Two patterns of code-switching were attested among the bilingual Paiwan children: code-switching from Mandarin to Paiwan in the form of "Mandarin main utterance, Paiwan ending particle" and overuse of the Paiwan particle "pai". Code-switching from Mandarin to Paiwan frequently occurred in insertions. The particle "pa-i" in Paiwan introduces suggestion to do something or makes commands less abrupt, and it can be used as a conjunction introducing new development in narrative (Ferrell, 1982). The Paiwan particle "pai" was preferred by bilingual children in their discourse with other family members. Some examples are illustrated in Excerpt 6.

Excerpt 6. **The use of Paiwan particle in bilingual children speech**

a. **pai** patsuni
   [**Let's** look at it!]
b. a **pai** maliceng
   [**Could you please** be quiet?]
c. galjuanan **pai** iljua lja u sengsengan
   [**Could you please** excuse me?]
d. djavadjavai balautunana'en **pai**
   [**Could you please** let me pass (the way)?]

e. **pai** e manu sa maqadi a pusalatj
   [**Could you please** help me?]
f. maliceng, **pai pai**!
   [Be quiet, **please. Please!**]
g. sau pavanavu **pai pai**!
   [Go take a shower, **please! Please!**]
h. OK. **pai pai**!
   [OK. Please! Please!]

Shown in (f), (g), and (h), the overuse of the particle was based on situational changes and innovative capacity. Repetitive use of the Paiwan particle was not found in their parents' talk. Most of the bilingual children agreed that their overuse of the particle triggered positive response from the Paiwan elders or family members. It was observed that bilingual children code-switched according to the situation and the topic or the setting. Positive responses were frequently received in face-to-face conversation, regardless of the age of the Paiwan recipients. Recipients' confirmation was a key factor in bilingual children's willingness to apply their Paiwan language. Overuse of the Paiwan particle "pai" among the bilingual children serves as one of the communicative strategies and creative linguistic forms in their face-to-face interaction. Bilingual children can become active and self-regulating as they develop familiarity and agency with the migration communities.

Bilingual children learn appropriate language and behavior through repetitive activities and routines in formal educational contexts and informal community social networks. They constructed not only communicative competence but also social relations and identities. Most Paiwan parents perceived the Paiwan language as more intimate than Mandarin. Bilingual children's agency can be seen in their negotiation of language choice at home through their flexible and mixed use of languages.

5. Discussion and conclusion

The present study investigated linguistic forms, language choices, and language shift among the bilingual children and their Paiwan parents. Semi-structured narrative interviews were conducted with 12 pairs of parents who had enrolled their children in Paiwan language education. Several findings of this study are noteworthy. The bilingual children achieved significantly more awareness on their Paiwan mixture pronunciation and Paiwan morphology. The overuse of the Paiwan particle also enhanced bilingual Paiwan-Mandarin children's linguistic awareness in Paiwan, which was their ethnic language. More encouraging in the findings is the positive attitude of the Paiwan parents toward their children's use of the minority language in the urban migration communities. Consequently, the language choices revealed context-based coding, function-oriented cooperation and integration, and situational changes such as settings or topic shifts.

The bilingual children played a wide range of speech roles in family discourse. School local-language curriculum, of course, held a leadership in establishing the "standard" of the Paiwan language learning, while at the same time shaping the bilingual children's dual identities and pronunciation. The significant contribution of the present study lies in its integration of social network, dual identity, and agency in the implementation of the Paiwan language in the migration communities. The study highlights the dynamic nature of the Paiwan language use in general in urban migration communities. Bilingual children's agency includes an awareness of the responsibility for their dual and mixture pronunciation, code-switching, overuse of the Paiwan particles, and innovation of Paiwan lexicon as mediated by the sociocultural context.

Indigenous Paiwan speakers migrated to urban communities for livelihood, and more and more young generations of the Paiwan speakers do not speak the Paiwan language, in both native villages and migration communities. Paiwan children in the migration communities have less chance to use the minority language, and the social network initiated by language policy at home became essential for the negotiation of indigenous language education in the urban migration communities. Mixture pronunciation is relevant in the analysis of Paiwan phonology, morphology, and everyday conversation. Situational changes may trigger code-switching in some multilinguals, while in others they may trigger inhibition of particular languages. The implementation of the indigenous language education in urban communities cannot be accomplished without the examination of family policy and interactions. Migrant Paiwan speakers need appropriate linguistic support for family language use, and adequate innovations of Paiwan lexicon and bilingual creativity could be resources for the perception of their own values as Paiwan individuals in the migration communities.

The findings in this study have implications for the Paiwan language pedagogy. The mixture pronunciation among Paiwan speakers in the urban communities should be taken into consideration in multilingual education. The natural use of the Paiwan language revealed advantages in creative thinking. Language teachers should develop strategies for encouraging the practices of the Paiwan language in their community-based classrooms. The creative forms as communicative strategies adopted by the bilingual Paiwan-Mandarin children could be strengthened by language choices and situational changes. Bilingual Paiwan children's preferences also seemed to weigh heavily when it came to determining which language was to be used in specific settings, and they had some space to negotiate with their parents regarding the family language policy and language choices in the urban communities. The purpose of encouraging children to speak the Paiwan language is to build their cultural identities. Through interactions in the community social network, bilingual children acquired multi-membership experience. The triangulation of the bilingual children, parents, and the community has a vital impact on the development of language norms. The study provides insights into the situated nature of code-switching by showing the changes in the children's practices depending on the context in the urban migration communities.

Bilingual children's agency had effects on the implementation of indigenous language education. Bilingual Paiwan-Mandarin children spoke the Paiwan language to receive compliments or rewards from the elders. The Paiwan language was used for negotiation and asking for favors. Paiwan language teachers encouraged the bilingual children to learn the language and to pass the language proficiency exam administered by the Council of Indigenous Peoples for practical reasons. Dialectal varieties among the Paiwan native villages became a minor issue in the migration communities. Language shift to Paiwan particle could be relevant for the bilingual children's identity and security in inner-circle communication in the migration communities. Community-based language curriculum should include comprehensive pronunciation choices and communicative tasks in assessing bilingual children's proficiency and accuracy. Bilingual children in urban migration communities with dual identity and agency have an impact on the implementation of indigenous language education.

References

Ahearn, L. M. (2001). Language and agency. *Annual Review of Anthropology, 30*, 109–137.

Baker, C. (2003). Biliteracy and transliteracy in Wales: Language planning and the Welsh National Curriculum. In N. H. Hornberger (Ed.), *Continua of biliteracy: An ecological framework for educational policy, research and practice in multilingual settings* (pp. 71–90). Celevedon: Multilingual Matters.

Bergsieker, H. B, Shelton, J. N., & Richeson, J. A. (2010). To be liked versus respected: divergent goals in interracial interactions. *Journal of Personality and Social Psychology, 99(2)*, 248–264.

Bourdieu, P. (1977). Cultural reproduction and social reproduction. In J. Karabel & A. H. Hasley (Eds.), *Power and ideology in education* (pp. 487–511). New York: Oxford University Press.

Chen, C.-M. (2009). Documenting the Paiwan phonology: issues in segments and non-stress prosodic features. *Concentric: Studies in Linguistics, 35(2)*, 193–223.

Dupré, J.-F. (2013). In search of linguistic identities in Taiwan: an empirical study. *Journal of Multilingual and Multicultural Development, 34(5)*, 431–444.

Eng, L. A, Collins F. L., & Yeoh, B. S. A. (Eds.) (2013). *Migration and Diversity in Asian Contexts*. Singapore: Institute of Southeast Asian Studies.

Ferrell, R. (1982). *Paiwan Dictionary*. Pacific Linguistics, Series C-No. 73. Canberra: The Australian National University.

Fishman, J. A. (1991). *Reversing language shift: Theoretical and empirical foundations of assistance to threatened languages*. Clevedon: Multilingual Matters.

Flowerdew, J. & Miller, L. (2008). Social structure and individual agency in second language learning: Evidence from three life histories. *Critical Inquiry in Language Studies, 5(4)*, 201–224.

Fogle, L. W. (2012). *Second Language Socialization and Learner Agency: Adoptive Family Talk*. Bristol: Multilingual Matters.

Fogle, L. W. & King, K. A. (2013). Child agency and language policy in transnational families. *Issues in Applied Linguistics, 19*, 1–25.

Giddens, A. (1984). *The Constitution of Society*. Berkeley, CA: University of California Press.

Glasford, D. E. & Dovidio, J. F. (2011). E pluribus unum: Dual identity and minority group members' motivation to engage in contact, as well as social change. *Journal of Experimental Social Psychology, 47*, 1021–1024.

Heller, M. (1995). Code-switching and the politics of language. In L. Milroy and P. Muysken (Eds.), *One Speaker, Two Languages*, (pp. 159–174). Cambridge: Cambridge University Press.

Heller, M. (2007). Bilingualism as ideology and practice. In M. Heller (Ed.), *Bilingualism: A Social Approach* (pp. 1–22). London, UK: Palgrave Macmillan.

Hodges, R. (2009). *Welsh language use among young people in the rhymney valley in contemporary Wales.* Cardiff: University of Wales Press.

Kharkhurin, A. V. & Wei, L. (2015). The role of code-switching in bilingual creativity. *International Journal of Bilingual Education and Bilingualism, 18(2),* 153–169.

King, K. A. (2013). A tale of three sisters: Language ideologies, identities, and negotiations in a bilingual transnational family. *International Multilingual Research Journal, 7(1),* 49–65.

King, K. A., Fogle, L., & Logan-Terry, A. (2008). Family Language Policy. *Language and Linguistics Compass, 2,* 907–922.

Lantolf, J. P. (2000). *Sociocultural theory and second language learning.* Oxford: Oxford University.

Lantolf, J. P. & Thorne, S. L. (2006). *Sociocultural Theory and the Genesis of Second Language Development.* Oxford: Oxford University Press.

Mallett, R. K. & Wilson, T. D. (2010). Increasing positive intergroup contact. *Journal of Experimental Social Psychology, 46(2),* 382–387.

Milroy, J. (1992). *Language Variation and Change.* Oxford: Basil Blackwell.

Park, I. J. K. (2007). Enculturation of Korean American Adolescents within Familial and Cultural Context: The Mediating Role of Ethnic Identity. *Family Relations: Interdisciplinary Journal of Applied Family Studies, 56(4),* 403–412.

Ricento, T. (2005). Considerations of identity in L2 learning. In E. Hinkel (Ed.), *Handbook of research in second language teaching and learning* (pp. 895–910). Mahwah, NJ: Lawrence Erlbaum.

Vygotsky, L. S. (1978). *Mind in society: The development of higher psychological processes.* Cambridge, MA: Harvard University Press.

CHAPTER 7

Austria's curriculum for heritage language education across languages: A case study in balancing speakers' needs on the local, national and international level

Judith Purkarthofer

1. Introduction

Heritage language education (HLE) is traditionally concerned with a limited number of named languages, thus seemingly opposed to ideas of translanguaging. At the same time, HLE happens by necessity in multilingual contexts, with students and teachers who use several languages in their daily life. This chapter sets out to investigate ideas of translanguaging that can be found in Austrian HLE, organized by the Austrian Ministry of Education (AMoE), and how they are supported or hindered by the existence of the joint *Curriculum for Mother Tongue Education* (*Curriculum für den Muttersprachlichen Unterricht*, BMB, 2011). I will analyze how the different needs of speakers on a local, national and international level are met by this policy document, which is valid across all HLE languages in Austrian schools. While the experiences in schools point to HLE as space of translanguaging, the focus on the curriculum contributes a perspective on meta-level translanguaging policy.

I will start with the theoretical framework and the methodology in section 2 before presenting the context of HLE and the HLE curriculum in Austria in section 3. To analyze ideas of translanguaging in Austrian HLE and how local, national, and international needs are met, I will present two examples in greater detail in section 4: (1) the history and present configuration of Bosnian-Croatian-Serbian HLE, as it serves one of the largest migrant groups in Austria and is among the oldest languages present in HLE and (2) the establishment of Somali HLE as the first African language in Austrian schools. In section 5 of the paper, I will discuss how the traditional understanding of HLE is challenged by complex multilingual repertoires of families and how accessibility of HLE needs to be adapted to multilingual speakers. In the concluding section, practical recommendations for educators and administrators are given based on the Austrian example.

2. Theoretical and methodological framework
2.1 Multilingual subjects and language as practice
Language is "very personal, unique and uncontrollable as it manifests the diversity of human beings" (Shohamy, 2006, p. 6), but at the same time "social, dynamic and changing as common features are shared, negotiated" (Shohamy, 2006, p. 7). In the midst of this very personal, yet inherently social phenomenon, multilingual speakers of heritage languages are challenged to navigate their worlds and organize the fulfillment of their needs. Languages as practices are not an end in themselves but rather part of a broader social world (Pennycook, 2010) and they are by no means neutral when used in social contexts and by real speakers. HLE is thus always concerned with languages but even more so with languages as social constructs, evaluated by the speakers and others around them (Bourdieu, 2001). However, with reference to Blackledge and Creese (2008, p. 535), it is necessary to highlight the very real effects of languages as social constructs:

If languages are invented, and languages and identities are socially constructed, we nevertheless need to account for the fact that at least some language users, at least some of the time, hold passionate beliefs about the importance and significance of a particular language to their sense of 'identity'.

Kramsch (2009), in her work on the multilingual subject, writes about the symbolic competence necessary to become a multilingual subject. As the overall goals of HLE consist of helping students to become multilingual subjects, the presence of these three abilities in the HLE curriculum is of special interest. According to Kramsch (2009, p. 201), this includes

- an ability to understand the symbolic value of symbolic forms and the different cultural memories evoked by different symbolic systems
- an ability to draw on the semiotic diversity afforded by multiple languages to reframe ways of seeing familiar events, create alternative realities, and find an appropriate subject position "between languages," so to speak
- an ability to look both *at* and *through* language and to understand the challenges to the autonomy and integrity of the subject that come from unitary ideologies and a totalizing networked culture.

This chapter is concerned with experiences and organizational aspects of multilingual education – and how the curriculum as a policy measure can be linked to translanguaging. Li Wei (2011) states that the

act of translanguaging then is transformative in nature; it creates a social space for the multilingual language user by bringing together different dimensions of their personal history, experience and environment, their attitude, belief and ideology, their cognitive and physical capacity into one coordinated and meaningful performance, and making it into a lived experience. (p. 1223)

Experiences of speakers, forming over time complex linguistic repertoires (Busch, 2013), are important to understand conditions of learning and motivations to take up certain resources. Beliefs about (the use of) languages form language ideologies that value some languages over others or sanction the use of e.g. minoritized languages in school. These ideologies, together with polities (or social structures) and identities (or social actors) are significant in the creation of language regimes (Kroskrity, 2000). However, there is a complex and sometimes contradictory array of ideologies present in language communities, forming *language ideological assemblages* (Kroskrity, 2018).

2.2 Methodology: Long-term ethnography

The research process behind this contribution can be described as a long-term ethnography of HLE in Austria, in which I had several different roles. Between 2008 and 2016, I worked repeatedly with the AMoE, gaining insight into the organization of HLE. In different research projects since 2007, I encountered HLE and HLE teachers in several schools. Finally, I was asked to teach in the joint teacher training of teachers of heritage languages and, since 2012, I have worked with three groups of teachers to whom I owe some moments of irritation when I started being interested in the needs and opportunities of a joint HLE curriculum.

Educated as a sociolinguist with a strong interest in policy and practice, writing a paper that analyses *translanguaging policy* is thus equally motivated by my academic interest and my own position as an advocate of multilingual education. This general belief in multilingual education is not hindering a critical stance toward the forms it might take and the power relations it can reproduce.

In terms of data collection, my aim is to give a thick description of HLE in two specific cases. I therefore make use of published research papers (Busch, 2006; Rienzner, 2013) as well as collaborations and conversations with both researchers and policy documents – both the HLE curriculum and the yearly reports on enrollment in HLE published by the AMoE (Garnitschnig, 2018). Another source of data is multimodal group activities in teacher training with HLE teachers, encompassing designs for the ideal school, short autobiographical writings on lived language experience, and photo elicitations on important aspects of teaching in HLE. Given the sometimes precarious position of HLE teachers, I am hesitant to publish from these sources, but draw on the field notes I took during the week-long courses.

Field notes are but one means of recalling (or recording) research data (Heller, 2008), but in contrast to recording audio, the social practice of note-taking is generally perceived as less frightening (Purkarthofer, 2019). I am also drawing on notes, following Creese's suggestion to use them "as an analytical process which reveals the dialogic of small and large phenomena" (2011, p. 43), in this way serving my aim to combine the perspective of different scales.

For the analysis of this diverse set of data, I will use the notion of language ideologies and ideological assemblages to analyze the policy texts and possible effects of the curriculum by drawing on the example of two cases. By categorizing all information I was able to gather from my sources, I arrived at representations of ideological assemblages relevant for different scales (Blommaert, Collins & Slembrouck, 2005). While experiences are happening in a continuum, I am distinguishing three scales in this research. The *local* scale is linked to individual speakers and their lived language experience and to the small groups of immediate language communities in Austrian schools. The *national* scale draws its importance in this study mainly from the organization of schooling in Austria and is thus linked to the school authority, the national political context and other legal constructs.

The *international* scale has proven to be important to understand the links between Austrian HLE and other places, be it the countries of origin or else connections to extended family networks.

Analyzing the curriculum (3.2) has given first insights into the scope and scales touched by HLE. This was combined with the research papers, which gave both international context and insights into local practices. Autobiographical writings of the teachers mainly contributed to an understanding over time, both on a national and local scale. The "ideal school activity" brought imaginations, wishes and ideologies to light and the photos from the photo elicitations provided very concrete moments to exchange about practices. For each case study (4.1 and 4.2), I attempt to give a "translation of experience into textual form" (Clifford, 1988, p. 25) that should enable the reader to draw conclusions and to make my observations and interpretations meaningful for other national and local contexts.

To rephrase, these are the research questions that this chapter sets out to answer: (1) How is HLE in Austria, despite being organized along the lines of separate languages, compatible with ideas of translanguaging, in particular when it comes to a joint curriculum for HLE? (2) How are the needs of multilingual speakers met on local, national, and international scales by the curriculum and (2a) by HLE more broadly, if one considers the case of multivariety HLE Bosnian-Croatian-Serbian? And finally, (3) how can the joint curriculum contribute to the integration of more (and new) languages and how has this happened in the case of Somali?

3. Heritage language education in Austria: Context and curriculum

3.1 Research and present situation

HLE is one of many potential terms to describe the situation of multilingual speakers whose language of schooling is not their (only) family language and who decide to pursue education in more than one language. While HLE is organized as private initiative in many parts of the world, in other parts it is included in mainstream schooling, albeit often as a voluntary subject.

In Austria, HLE is considered a voluntary subject but is organized in mainstream public schools, under the authority of the AMoE. Children can claim one or up to three languages (including German) as their home or heritage languages at school entrance level. They are then entitled to attend HLE classes under the condition that a sufficient number of students are present in the same school or region. Groups are often heterogeneous in age, as children from primary school to upper secondary school (thus from age 6 to 18) are entitled to HLE. For some of the larger languages (i.e. Turkish and Bosnian-Croatian-Serbian), HLE teachers are present in mainstream classes in team teaching with the mainstream teacher for up to 12 hours a week. For most of the smaller languages, the groups gather for two hours a week in the afternoon.

Given the different biographical trajectories of the students, the use of the home language alongside German in the family and complex linguistic situations, the language competence as well as the motivation of the students vary enormously between children in the same language groups. While it is theoretically possible to attend more than one HLE class, for practical reasons it is very unlikely. The opening numbers of 5 to 12 students per region per language (depending on the federal state) leave some children, speakers of rather infrequent languages, without adequate resources – HLE is thus not really an individual right but rather tight to sufficient group size.

Teachers in HLE are hired for their language skills and they are not required to hold a pedagogical degree. However, most of the teachers are highly educated, but many have gained their qualifications in countries other than Austria. Since 2012, a joint course of 30 ECTS (equaling six months of full time study) was organized four times to enhance the HLE teachers' qualifications, their knowledge in pedagogy, language teaching and learning as well as culturally and linguistically reflective methods of teaching. Completing the course led to better work contracts for most of the teachers.

In the school year 2016/2017 about 220,000 pupils in Austria claimed a language other than or in addition to German, which equals about 27% of the total school population (Garnitschnig, 2018). These multilingual children account for more than 50% in the capital city of Vienna but less than 10% in the rural federal states. About 33,000 children are enrolled in HLE, thus reaching about one sixth of the students, and they are taught by 425 teachers in more than 800 schools. Currently, 26 languages are on offer: Albanian, Arabic, Armenian, Bosnian-Croatian-Serbian, Bulgarian, Chechen, Chinese, Czech, English, French, Hungarian, Italian, Kurmanci (Kurdish), Macedonian, Pashto, Farsi, Polish, Portuguese, Romani, Romanian, Russian, Slovak, Slovene, Somali, Spanish, Turkish, Zazaki (Kurdish). The main languages by number of learners are Turkish, Bosnian-Croatian-Serbian and Arabic, with the latter growing rapidly since 2015, replacing Albanian among the top three. The list of languages changed slightly over the years, depending on numbers of enrollment, but, due to the joint curriculum for all languages, it is relatively easy to add new languages to the list. In section 4.2, I will demonstrate this process in the case of one of the latest additions, the Somali language.

For the last 20 years, a yearly report on HLE, including statistics of teachers and students, has provided an overview about the main developments (Garnitschnig, 2018). Earlier research on HLE in Austria was mainly organized by the AMoE and produced largely unpublished reports serving the development of HLE and HLE teacher training. However, some publications have appeared in German (e.g. Çınar, 1998; Fleck, 2010, 2013), but only little research has been done on didactics, implications of the curriculum or the multilingual nature of the learner groups (i.e. Busch, 2006). More recently, a growing interest in MA students is documented by an increasing number of theses on the topic that will hopefully be followed by extended publications.

On an international level, Doerr and Lee (2013, pp. 3–4) give an overview on existing literature, distinguishing two main strands of research: one strand, named linguistic proficiency approach, takes a stronger interest in an individual's proficiency and focuses on pedagogies to support language learners when they are neither native speakers nor foreign language learners. An example of such an approach can be found in Sevinç and Backus (2017) who analyze interviews with members of three generations of Turkish immigrants in the Netherlands, talking about their feelings of anxiety in relation to their heritage language but also the majority language in their country of residence.

The second strand, that the authors rename the self-esteem approach, has its focus on the social conditions of learning, the power issues related to minority and majority speakers (e.g. Blackledge & Creese, 2008; De Korne, 2017; Purkarthofer, 2016; Valdés, 2017). Apart from purely linguistic skills, HLE can support multilingual speakers as it can contest social hierarchies and inequalities both within and beyond the classroom (see also, Rosén, Straszer, & Wedin, this volume). Schools and teachers have acted as agents of monolingualization, but they also hold the potential to promote inclusivity and multilingualism by addressing multiple social groups, helping them to develop plurilingual capacities, or to reclaim marginalized heritage languages (Purkarthofer & De Korne, in press; Reath Warren, 2017). Situated on a meso level, schools and other educational initiatives connect the individual and the state level and might act as spaces "where circulating discourses are recontextualized and potentially renegotiated by agents, such as teachers and pupils"(Musk, 2010, p. 45).

3.2 History of HLE and the HLE curriculum

Austrian HLE underwent three stages in the past decades. Firstly, early private initiatives started to teach the children of migrant workers in the 1970s. Teaching children in "their" language, with teachers sent from the countries of origin, was seen as a means to enable them to continue their education in their home countries upon their return. We have however learned since then, that most of the children and their parents stayed and have become at least bilingual and rather multilingual in the years that followed.

In a second stage, mainly motivated by a relevant number of child refugees from the former Yugoslavian countries that fled the war(s) in the 1990s, private initiatives reached the end of their capacities and the teaching was taken up by the Austrian school authorities and the AMoE. Since the early 1990s, HLE is offered in several languages and its teachers are employed by the Austrian school boards organized on a federal state level.

In a third phase, since the early 2000s, the number of languages has gone up from 12 in 1998 to 26 in 2016. The percentage of children in HLE increased. Generally speaking, the awareness of teachers and school leaders increased during the third phase, and HLE is now considered more favorably in many places. Apart from the HLE curriculum that will be discussed in detail below, a website was established by the AMoE that serves as a platform for teachers across federal states and makes information available to schools and parents in several languages[1].

The HLE curriculum (in its current version BMB, 2011, translated by the author) was developed to set a framework for teaching that is meaningful to the students, teachers, and parents. It has three main aims:

---

1 https://www.schule-mehrsprachig.at

1. Development of the first language / mother tongue as a basis for education and the learning of other languages
2. Teaching about the country/countries of origin (culture, literature, society, politics)
3. Spaces for debates about bicultural and multilingual processes (living in more than one language, migrant culture, mobility and integration, social and psychological conflicts, etc.)

Analysis of the curriculum text shows that the first aim is closely linked to the *local scale*, enabling individual young speakers to develop their home language and build on this knowledge throughout their education. This formulation draws on a language ideology that highlights the first language as a necessary basis for further learning: mainstream teachers and HLE teachers consider this argument especially effective to support children's enrollment into HLE.

When analyzing HLE in practice in Austrian schools on a *local* scale, HLE is linked to very concrete and specific people, teachers and children, who grow up in a certain context at a certain time. For them, the language of schooling is often their stronger language, while their home language or "mother tongue" holds emotional and practical value in the family and with relatives. Depending on the language in question, speakers might be met with favorable language ideologies (of beautiful languages, being the bearers of culture) while others might be confronted with devaluing ideologies of "dialects, tribal or even unknown languages" (Busch, 2014). For children and teachers, being associated with heritage languages can also carry the risk of being seen as a learner of German, an outsider etc. (Purkarthofer, in press). Kramsch's *subject position between languages* thus needs to be developed in HLE.

The feeling of being an outsider can also be enhanced when *national* links (to countries of origin) are assumed, or else when the country of residence, in this case Austria, fosters a monolingual language ideology or contributes to monolingual German language regimes in schools. School communities and other teachers might be very welcoming, but they might also express their feeling that certain languages and their teachers do not belong (even less so, if they are paid by different schemes etc.). Notions of culture that foster monolithic understanding may leave very little room for minoritized languages and their speakers.

Finally, and on an *international* scale, languages and their speakers may be situated along the lines of international conflict. This was visible in the Balkan wars, but it is still an important topic as a number of children arrive in Austria as refugees from Chechnya, Syria, Afghanistan, or Somalia. Language as a marker of belonging is thus highly loaded with meaning: HLE teachers feel that they have to be careful about their own position while parents might be hesitant to reveal their languages or political stances. In this case, the ability to look *at and through* languages is also asked of the teachers and administrators whose goal it is to find the adequate resources for each student.

4. Local, national and international scales: Analyzing multilingual subjects in ideological assemblages

4.1 Multilingual HLE: The example of Bosnian-Croatian-Serbian and Romani

With the first case study, I am focusing on (2) How are the needs of multilingual speakers met on local, national, and international scales by the curriculum and (2a) by HLE more broadly, if one considers the case of multivariety HLE Bosnian-Croatian-Serbian? I will discuss the history and present configuration of Bosnian-Croatian-Serbian HLE, as it serves some of the largest migrant groups in Austria and has been continuously present since the beginning of HLE. Busch (2006) has published one of the rare papers on practices in Bosnian-Croatian-Serbian HLE in Austria.

Migrant workers from former Yugoslavia came to Austria already in the 1960s and the children of these families were among the first to attend HLE in then "Serbocroatian." In 1992, the last bilateral agreements ended and the Austrian school authorities took the organization of HLE in their hands: not least because of the many children that came among the more than 110,000 refugees from former Yugoslavian countries, especially Bosnia, Croatia and the Kosovo. Given the heterogeneity of the group of students, and the ongoing tendencies of differentiation of the former "Serbocroatian" language into several languages, decisions on teaching were needed. In fierce discussions, with linguists and educators involved, it was decided to opt for multi-variety teaching in the case of the South slavic languages, now called Bosnian-Croatian-Serbian. Members of the "Serbocroatian" diaspora in Austria and families who lived with several varieties were among the strongest defenders of such a joint HLE: even today, more than 25 years later, the issue was brought up in teacher training and the necessity to counter nationalist tendencies among the students was voiced by teachers.

HLE teachers have to accommodate the different varieties that the children bring to the group, including reading and writing in the Latin and Cyrillic alphabet. Busch (2006) gives an extensive list of possible cases of "multilingual" children who might take part in Bosnian-Croatian-Serbian HLE, but would bring very different preconditions to class. Her conclusion in 2006, that teachers would opt for a laissez-faire approach due to the complex heteroglossic situation, still holds true today according to the teachers in teacher training. And, as she already stated then, this is equally true for many of the languages in Austrian HLE: the Arabic HLE regroups children from Morocco to Syria, some with other minority languages as family languages; Albanian regroups speakers of at least the two main varieties and in the Turkish HLE, at least Kurdish and Arabic are often among the other resources that children bring to class. The

Farsi teaching includes third-generation heritage learners as well as very recent immigrants from Afghanistan; and French or English HLE have to be considered multi-variety classes with speakers from very different parts of the world.

Over the years, it was obvious that even this multi-variety approach in Bosnian-Croatian-Serbian was challenged when children from Serbia signed up for the classes, who were also Romani-speaking (but did either use Serbian more or were ashamed of being associated with a language of lesser status). In the meantime, Romani is taught as HLE as well, but from talks with the teachers, it is still obvious that communicating in three or even more languages is part of the students' everyday reality and all of them at least trilingual in Romani, German and Serbian/Slovak/Czech etc. The HLE teaching is happening in at least two, rather three languages.

For all teachers, the choice of languages is thus a sensible topic where there is much to learn about the children and their family background. Especially in languages that had to be hidden, were repressed, or are associated with little prestige, it is not an easy task for the teachers to establish spaces where learning can occur.

Analyzing this case on a *local* scale, the heterogeneous nature of the group of learners becomes very obvious: given the long history of migration, the complex and changing political landscape of the countries of origin, and the individual family biographies, teachers are challenged to work with the students in their class, taking their specific needs and abilities into account (see also, Rosén, Straszer, & Wedin, this volume). The number of students and teachers however, makes it rather easy to establish HLE for Bosnian-Croatian-Serbian and it is (together with Turkish) among the languages that are now used for trilingual alphabetization in mainstream classes in a small number of Viennese schools.

On a *national* scale, the support for Bosnian-Croatian-Serbian is relatively good as the communities are well established. However, the employment of the teachers by the state and their alignment with the Austrian school instead of the (national) language communities can be seen as an important precondition to overcome prejudices from parents and community members. Discussions about the varieties in question and the "correct" or "pure" forms of certain varieties are still ongoing, but at least the teachers in the trainings were rather optimistic about countering these tendencies or else diverting them to more linguistic discussions of variation in languages.

On an *international* scale, Austria's connections to the Balkans have traditionally been strong. As such, Bosnian-Croatian-Serbian is among the languages that members of the German-speaking population are interested in learning – even more so as Croatia especially is one of the major holiday destinations for Austrian tourists. These experiences are also strengthening the interest of non-heritage learners (Purkarthofer & Mossakowski, 2012) and enhance the status of the languages in schools.

4.2 Making space: The example of Somali HLE

In the second case study, I will use the example of Somali to address my research question (3) How can the joint curriculum contribute to the integration of more (and new) languages and how has this happened in the case of Somali? This case study also gives insight into how it is possible for teachers and parents to work toward a recognized HLE in their environment.

Research has been done by Rienzner (2013) and I am drawing on her work as well as my own involvement with this case. In the course of a research project on multilingual speakers encountering monolingual institutions in Austria, a health professional drew attention to the fact that Somali mothers and their teenage daughters reported difficulties when it came to discussing bodily changes, health issues, or contraception during puberty. The mothers could speak German, but they had not necessarily discussed health topics in their language classes, especially as they are traditionally surrounded by taboo and can hardly be addressed in mixed classrooms. The daughters (and sons, obviously) had had their health education in the Austrian school system and were thus more proficient in these topics in German. Their Somali, while being adequate for family interactions, did reportedly not cover technical terms like specific body parts and biological functions.

Motivated by this reported example, the researchers together with a Somali women's association, invited parents to inform them about the option of HLE in Austrian schools. During the meeting, about 60 enrollment forms were collected that were later handed to the school board for the city of Vienna. Given that the Somali community of about 8000 speakers is mainly present in two districts of Vienna, two schools were identified that could host groups of learners. Among the women of the association, one person volunteered to become the teacher. Once the school board confirmed the sufficient number of students, the availability of a teacher and the cooperation of the schools, the teaching could start about half a year after the initial meeting. Support from the researchers was not officially necessary but it proved useful when interacting with the administration and it was also helpful to overcome hesitations from the local schools.

The rather low threshold to introduce a new language for HLE is in practice often met with resistance (or perceived lack of resources) and the institutional challenges are present for students as well as teachers. One main point of concern is the ad-hoc nature of the HLE: parents have to sign the enrollment forms each year within the first days of schooling and HLE teachers are often forced to spend hours collecting those papers and reminding parents to sign in time. As the number of students is not determined earlier, the teachers' contracts and, for example, the number of hours they can teach are only fixed at the beginning of the school year.

Analyzing the different scales that are relevant for this case, the *local* scale is well represented, with the involved parents eager to join a university-hosted information meeting far from their areas of residence. Gaining access to the resources of officially recognized HLE in their own language was evaluated very positively by the parents, most of whom have come to Vienna rather recently, in the last 15 years. The conditions for teaching were rather favorable on a local scale as the number of children with Somali as their home language was rather high (due to the relatively homogeneous group of migrants) and most were living relatively close to only few schools. The necessary number to open a group was thus reached more easily than for languages of more dispersed communities. While it is possible for HLE to regroup children from the same school across age groups, students from different schools can also learn together, and, theoretically, groups could be formed from schools all over one county. This last case, however, is very impractical for students and parents and is rarely met with long-term success. Age-heterogeneous groups on the other hand are very common across most languages (Fleck, 2013).

On a *national* scale, Somali was the first "African" language to enter the Austrian HLE. In terms of recognition this presented a novel situation for its speakers. Again, in connection with the research project and the Somali women's organization, a second initiative was started: the local branch of the municipal library in the district with a large proportion of the Somali speakers opened a small section with books for children and adults in Somali. The small collection was opened with a reading and festive event, inviting the students and HLE teacher as well as the parents.

On an *international* scale, Somali is recognized as the official language of Somalia. Conflicts between different Somali groups do also influence language use, but have been less of an issue in the first years of teaching and learning in Austrian HLE. (They were more pronounced in other cases, as, for example, in the case presented earlier.) Importing books directly from Somalia is, however, rather complicated, and resources for HLE in Austria are mainly coming from the UK and Sweden, where larger Somali-speaking communities exist.

4.3. A shared HLE curriculum: Responses on the local, national and global level

In the final part of the analysis, I will summarize findings in response to my research question (2) about how the needs of multilingual speakers are met on local, national, and international scales by the curriculum and HLE more broadly. I will re-read the findings from the perspective that the very same curriculum is valid for all languages in question and can thus be read as a form of *translanguaging policy*. On an organizational level, I was able to respond to research question (3) by demonstrating with the case of Somali how a shared curriculum can facilitate the integration of more (and new) languages. In the case of Bosnian-Croatian-Serbian, the shared curriculum can be read as a unifying force: it brings the same teaching goals to teachers and students of different backgrounds and can enable dialogue instead of separation.

The specific benefit of a joint HLE curriculum, valid for all languages in the same way, lies in strengthening each language as it can draw on the validity of the first-language-as-a-basis ideology *on a local scale*. The link between the home language(s) and the languages of schooling is highlighted and the children are constructed as multilingual speakers. In the case of new languages, no extra recognition of a new curriculum has to take place – a process that could easily take years – until all relevant actors are involved. As the case of Somali demonstrated, with a sufficient number of enrollment forms, a qualified teacher and some organizational details solved, the teaching could start with the following school year.

The contents of the curriculum, detailed further by the AMoE, ensures that all children in HLE are met with relevant teaching content and can develop their multilingual competencies. The specific focus of the HLE curriculum helps HLE teachers to plan their teaching but also to stand their ground vis-à-vis parents and other teachers who would prefer to have the resources of HLE merged into German-language teaching. Both HLE teachers and administration reported that some parents and teachers tried to reduce HLE to supporting the learning of German. Despite formal clarifications on that matter, even sent out to all schools in Austria in the form of an official decree, the teachers still sometimes have to defend their teaching hours and claim spaces for their languages. The shared curriculum can in this case strengthen solidarity at least among the HLE teachers of different languages.

The second aim is closely linked to the *national and international scale*, meant to facilitate children's orientation in the cultures and countries of their parents or grandparents. In teacher training, several teachers reported the children's lack of knowledge about the countries that are often constructed as their home countries or at least countries of origin. However, for many the country of their parents and grandparents is more closely linked to holidays than to everyday life. At the same time, one teacher of Turkish reported that some children in her group felt insecure when visiting family abroad as they were not able to navigate in a society that was supposedly using "their language." Knowledge about the country acquired through HLE was helping those children. This part of the curriculum carries the assumption that children with more than one language in their life do automatically connect the use of this language to places or, more precisely, countries. Others have problematized the connection between languages and states at length (e.g. Lane, Costa & De Korne, 2017), and I will only get to one aspect of this in the final discussion in section 5.

A different aspect of the national scale is the curriculum's effect on the teachers in HLE. While the first teachers in the 1970s were employed by foreign states and sent to Austria to teach, HLE teachers are now employed by the Austrian school authority and hence part of the Austrian school system. They are required to follow Austrian rules and regulations regarding teaching and they can rely on some support systems if they encounter problems with parents or students.

At least officially, their role in the school is well defined and they are not meant to act as translators or spokespeople of the school leaders and other teachers. In reality, however, the teachers take on quite a few additional tasks in what could be termed cultural mediation, from informing parents in several languages to acting on behalf of "their" students if they feel that their potential is not seen by the German-speaking teachers. One teacher even reported that parents would call her with all kinds of questions, including to ask for translations of letters that they had received from the municipality. While most teachers report a feeling of responsibility and try to help if possible, most also feel that these extracurricular activities are in a way undermining their position as a teacher.

Regarding the recognition of HLE teachers, the shared curriculum definitely made self-representation and training easier: in the last six years, four rounds of year-long continuous education classes have taken place, each consisting of six very intensive weeks of training as well as assignments and project work. These courses have reached more than 100 HLE teachers so far and are continuing in 2020. Among the great yet unexpected outcomes of the course was the formation of an HLE teacher association. For the teachers, the exchange with colleagues, often neglected in daily school life, proved to be very important and they felt generally strengthened in their activities.

Finally, the third aim of the curriculum is most obviously linked to the position of speakers and learners as they are learning more than one language. The majority of teachers in HLE have themselves migrated to Austria or else have grown up as children of immigrants: their role is thus not only of teachers but also of multilingual and usually multicultural role models who are thought to be well equipped to help students in finding their multilayered and fluid subject positions. Usually, teachers have been in Austria longer than their students, and they also play an important role in being multilingual role models. On an *international* scale, teachers are positioned as representatives of the Austrian state, they can act as such and are thus less likely to be associated with conflicting parties in the countries of origin. Within the communities, however, teachers reported that their being identified with ethnic or religious groups or language varieties is commented upon, and they are sometimes met with prejudices. Teachers of languages with highly precarious status (e.g. Kurdish varieties, Romani, and others) are more likely to experience such reactions – in times of changing language regimes and shifting standards (as in the case of Bosnian-Croatian-Serbian at a certain point), no neutral variety exists and teachers develop different strategies to deal with the social consequences.

The results of this analysis align with the five generalizations that Tollefson and Tsui (2014, pp. 208–209) found in their analysis of global cases of access and equity in language education. While their work is concerned with the medium of instruction policies, I find the generalizations apply just as well to HLE. I thus rephrase slightly their generalizations that can help to achieve greater access and equity in education:

1. The importance of self-determination in school administration and policy making
2. The value of ideology and discourse to support HLE and translanguaging
3. The importance of using the legal context to promote HLE policies for access and equity
4. The value of historical context and precedents
5. The importance of HLE (and more general education) policies that fill specific, identifiable needs

In the first generalization, Tollefson and Tsui (2014) highlight the need of self-determination on school administration and policy making, and in their fifth generalization, they talk about the importance of policies that fill specific, identifiable needs. As can be seen from the Austrian cases, the identification of local needs is a precondition to successful organization of teaching and learning, be it the identifiable need for intergenerational communication in the Somali community or the unifying instruction in an ethnically and linguistically complex group of (former) migrants from the Balkans that enables students to keep in touch with their extended families in different successor states of former Yugoslavia. In the second and fourth generalization, the value of HLE needs to be seen and understood: on the one hand as a part of the biographical repertoire of families and speakers, and thus as the historical language repertoire of communities, but also as a prospective tool and means of expression. Meetings one's family language outside of the home and in contexts of education gives ideological credit but also demonstrates the possibility of using languages to access knowledge and literature. On a national scale, the third generalization about using the legal context for the promotion of HLE is visible in the attempts to address groups that have not yet gained access to HLE but might fulfil the necessary preconditions. Especially in the case of minoritized languages, the legal right to HLE needs to be accompanied by actions that support the de-facto access to the necessary steps. As in the case of Somali HLE, the organizational support of the researchers help to navigate the administrative steps and get parents and students in contact with the administration.

Despite these generally favorable conditions, heritage languages and their speakers are still under pressure and, in the next part of this chapter, I will address challenges of terminology, on the policy level as well as in observed practice in local class rooms.

5. HLE and translanguaging: Contradictory ideologies?

In the final section of the paper, I will discuss how the traditional understanding of HLE is challenged by complex multilingual repertoires of families and how notions like translanguaging question traditional accessibility and organization. This discussion is linked to (1) how HLE in Austria, despite being organized along the lines of separate languages, is compatible with ideas of translanguaging, in particular when it comes to a joint curriculum for HLE.

The assumption in the early years of HLE in Austria (as in many other places) was that students would enter school with one home language other than German. This language was the language of both parents and the language of the country of origin (to which the students would return within few years' time). The students were expected to have a relatively high competence in their home/heritage language and without explicitly mentioning it, they were expected to behave like monolingual speakers in many ways.

Research in multilingual language acquisition has shown how patterns of acquisition are neither parallel nor independent – and school reality has shown that ideas of accessibility to HLE need to be adapted to multilingual speakers that no longer only bring their "one" heritage language to school. Multilingual families are diverse (and have always been that way) and apart from different experiences depending on the generation, the age of onset, or previous experience with schooling in another language, there are large differences in competence and experiences in all languages spoken in a given group.

Furthermore, there are situations where heritage language is not so easy to define: how is it if one's parents are speakers of Bosnian, but have never used the language at home? What if the stepfather speaks Turkish and it has thus become a very relevant language for the child, but one that only entered when it was already in pre-school? What if mother and father each have a different first language, bringing Spanish and Czech, in addition to German, into a child's repertoire?

What if Arabic is a very relevant language for a best friend, but not for my own family?

The Austrian school authorities have addressed the first issue about more than one home language by allowing the registration of up to three languages of daily relevance for each child. HLE teachers report however that practice in schools differs with the school leaders as they are encouraging parents to include more or fewer languages for their children.

Brizić (2006) has shown in a large study that especially parents with minoritized home languages (e.g. Kurdish or Romani) are unlikely to report these languages for fear of social stigmatization. Depending on the perceived climate at a school, parents with German and an additional language might feel forced to drop the second language, especially if their child is believed to have strong German skills. While the curriculum does not state that the heritage language should only be taught to strengthen German, it is sometimes interpreted in this way by teachers or parents.

The mis- or under-identification is socially motivated and understandable, but it is risky in that it contributes to the creation of new hierarchies. By reducing speakers to one or the other language, this practice ignores elements of the diverse linguistic repertoires of speakers in multilingual areas (Blackledge & Creese, 2010). Social and biological lineage might not align, and may marginalize children even further by denying them "proper" status as heritage language speakers. Criteria to assign teachers and teaching materials, as well as other resources, are in themselves problematic, as students might be forced to choose what to learn based on essentialist and excluding criteria (i.e. choosing one line of heritage over another, one dialect over another) (Busch, 2013). Additionally, minority language initiatives run the risk of reproducing and/or commodifying tokens of culture and language and making stereotypical use of linguistic resources (i.e. in traditional songs and dances), while potentially over-looking contemporary culture and multiple belonging (Heller & Duchêne, 2012).

I argue that a shared curriculum can act as a translanguaging space in Li Wei's sense, "a space for the act of translanguaging as well as a space created through translanguaging" (2011, p. 1223), and that it can also in this case serve as an adaptable tool to take the multilingual realities of children, parents, and teachers into account. Thinking of HLE as something that is not happening behind closed doors for each language alone, but as a shared practice established across language borders, can hopefully help to unite students and teachers. The experiences with shared teacher training are very promising. Exchanges between the teachers underline not only their challenges but also how shared strategies can help to strengthen the position of HLE and HLE teachers in schools if approached together. It can however hardly solve the larger issue of HLE, which is who decides who has the right or obligation to attend HLE in the first place. As long as family of origin is weighed as the main criteria, HLE can also be used as an instrument of exclusion, between heritage language speakers and those who only speak the language of schooling. Thinking about HLE as a tool in schools that helps students to develop languages that they find relevant in their life would ask for changes in access and enhanced support. It could however help to resolve other issues, linked to languages and stigmatization. Researchers can help to clarify ideologies and power relations, language hierarchies and regimes and it is up to them, alongside educators, parents, and students to bring their lived realities to the tables of policy makers to demand changes.

6. Conclusions

HLE in Austrian schools looks back at a rather successful history and its potential is increasingly recognized by school authorities, teachers and parents. In a language ecology with German, it is however still under pressure and risks being abandoned with the next assimilationist turn in politics. A lot could be said about the political climate of multilingual education, but this chapter's aim was to show how HLE and translanguaging can be combined but can also be perceived as contradictory ideologies. In the case of the Austrian HLE, the analysis of speakers' needs on different scales, from the very local to the international, demonstrated the manifold challenges of HLE aiming to be relevant for speakers.

For educators, this means having to include reflective elements into their teaching to enable their students (and themselves) to understand the complex position of the multilingual subject. Exchange across HLE groups, as was the case in the joint teacher training, can serve as a very good lens to reveal language ideological assemblages present in schools and in society at large.

Administrators are asked to ensure some degree of flexibility to adapt to changing political landscapes as well as new language needs. Low thresholds for new teachers, accompanied by continued education, can answer to demands in even rural areas with smaller speech communities for certain languages. At the same time, the institutionalization of HLE in Austria can serve as an example of how continuity can be reached by integrating HLE into mainstream schools and by making HLE teachers a part of the national teaching scheme.

Acknowledgements
The author wants to thank Elfie Fleck, heart and soul of the Austrian HLE for many years, and all teachers and researchers who contributed to different stages of this ongoing research. This work was partly supported by the Research Council of Norway through its Centres of Excellence funding scheme (project number 223265).

References
Blackledge, A. & Creese, A. (2008). Contesting 'language' as 'heritage': Negotiation of identities in late modernity. *Applied Linguistics, 29*(4), 533–554.

Blackledge, A. & Creese, A. (2010). *Multilingualism*. London, UK: Continuum.

BMB/Austrian Ministry of Education. (2011). *Fachlehrpläne für den muttersprachlichen Unterricht.* Informationsblätter zum Thema Migration und Schule Nr. 6/2016–17. http://www.schule-mehrsprachig. at/fileadmin/schule_mehrsprachig/redaktion/hintergrundinfo/info6-16-17.pdf [accessed 28.1.2019]

Bourdieu, P. (2001). *Language et pouvoir symbolique*. Paris, FR: Seuil.

Blommaert, J., Collins, J., & Slembrouck, S. (2005). Spaces of multilingualism. *Language & Communication, 25*(3), 197–216.

Brizić, K. (2006). The secret life of languages. Origin-specific differences in L1/L2 acquisition by immigrant children. *International Journal of Applied Linguistics 16*(3), 339–362.

Busch, B. (2006) Bosnisch, Kroatisch, Serbokroatisch, Jugoslawisch, Romani oder Vlachisch? Heteroglossie und 'muttersprachlicher' Unterricht in Österreich. In P. Chichon (Ed.), *Gelebte Mehrsprachigkeit* (pp. 12–28). Vienna, AT: Praesens Verlag.

Busch, B. (2013). *Mehrsprachigkeit*. Vienna, AT: UTB.

Busch, B. (2014) "Sonstige (einschließlich unbekannt)": les notions désignant les langues associées à l'immigration en Autriche. In J. Busquets, S. Platon, & A. Viaut (Eds.), *Identifier et catégoriser les langues minoritaires en Europe occidentale* (pp. 309–328). Pessac, FR: Maison des sciences de l'homme d'Aquitaine.

Çınar, D. (Ed.) (1998). *Gleichwertige Sprachen? Muttersprachlicher Unterricht für die Kinder von Einwanderern.* Innsbruck, AT: Studien Verlag.

Clifford, J. (1988). *The Predicament of culture. Twentieth century ethnography, literature, and art.* Cambridge, MA: Harvard University Press.

Creese, A. (2011). Making Local Practices Globally Relevant in Researching Multilingual Education. In F. M. Hult & K. A. King (Eds.), *Educational Linguistics in Practice. Applying the Local Globally and the Global Locally* (pp. 41–55). Bristol, UK: Multilingual Matters.

De Korne, H. (2017). "A treasure" and "a legacy": Individual and communal (re)valuing of Isthmus Zapotec in multilingual Mexico. In M. Flubacher & A. Del Percio (Eds.), *Language, Education and Neoliberalism: Critical*

Studies in Sociolinguistics (pp. 37–61). Bristol, UK: Multilingual Matters.

Doerr, N. M. & Lee, K. (2013). *Constructing the Heritage Language Learner. Knowledge, Power, and New Subjectivities.* Berlin, DE: De Gruyter.

Fleck, E. (2010). Migration und Sprachförderung an österreichischen Schulen. In R. Muhr & G. Biffl (Eds.), *Sprache-Bildung-Bildungsstandards-Migration:Chancen und Risiken der Neuorientierung des österreichischen Bildungssystems* (pp. 139–156). Frankfurt, DE: Peter Lang.

Fleck, E. (2013). Zur Situation von lebensweltlich mehrsprachigen SchülerInnen: aktuelle Lage und neuere Entwicklungen in der Bildungspolitik. In R. de Cillia & E. Vetter (Eds.), *Sprachenpolitik in Österreich* (pp. 9–28). Frankfurt am Main, DE: Peter Lang.

Garnitschnig, I. (2018). Der muttersprachliche Unterricht in Österreich. Statistische Auswertung für das Schuljahr 2016/17. Informationsblätter zum Thema Migration und Schule Nr. 5/2018–19. http://www.schule-mehrsprachig.at/fileadmin/schule_mehrsprachig/redaktion/hintergrundinfo/info5_09-2018.pdf [accessed 28.1.2019]

Heller, M. (2008). Doing ethnograpy. In L. Wei & M. G. Moyer (Eds.), *Blackwell Guide to research methods in bilingualism and multilingualism research* (pp. 249–262). Malden, MA: Blackwell.

Heller, M. & Duchêne, A. (2012). Pride and profit: Changing discourses of language, capital and nation-state. In A. Duchêne & M. Heller (Eds.), *Language in Late Capitalism: Pride and Profit* (pp. 1–42). New York, NY: Routledge.

Kramsch, C. (2009). *The Multilingual Subject.* Cambridge: Cambridge University Press.

Kroskrity, P. V. (2000). Regimenting languages: Language ideological perspectives. In P. V. Kroskrity (Ed.), *Regimes of Language: Ideologies, Polities, and Identities* (pp. 1–34). Santa Fe, NM: School of American Research Press.

Kroskrity, P. V. (2018). On recognizing persistence in the Indigenous language ideologies of multilingualism in two Native American Communities. *Language & Communication, 62*(B), 133–144.

Lane P., Costa J. & De Korne H. (Eds.) (2017). *Standardizing Minority Languages. Competing Ideologies of Authority and Authenticity in the*

Global Periphery. New York, NY: Routledge.

Musk, N. (2010). Bilingualism-in-practice at the meso level: an example from a bilingual school in Wales. *International Journal of the Sociology of Language 202*, 41–62.

Pennycook, A. (2010). *Language as a Local Practice.* London, UK: Routledge.

Purkarthofer, J. (2016). *Sprachort Schule. Zur Konstruktion von mehrsprachigen sozialen Räumen und Praktiken in einer zweisprachigen Volksschule.* Klagenfurt, AT: Drava

Purkarthofer, J. (2019). Using Mobile Phones as a Social and Spatial Practice in Multilingualism and Family Research [45 paragraphs]. *Forum Qualitative Sozialforschung / Forum: Qualitative Social Research 20*(1), Art. 20, http://dx.doi.org/10.17169/fqs-20.1.3110.

Purkarthofer, J. (in press). Lines of exclusion and possibilities of inclusion – A tale of two schools in Austria. In A.-B. Krüger, L. Mary & A. S. Young (Eds.), *Migration, multilingualism and education: Critical perspectives on inclusion.* Bristol, UK: Multilingual Matters.

Purkarthofer, J. & De Korne, H. (in press). Learning Language Regimes. Children's representations of minority language education. *Journal of Sociolinguistics.*

Purkarthofer, J. & Mossakowski, J. (2012). Bilingual teaching for multilingual students? Innovative dual medium models at Slovene-German schools in Austria. *International Review of Education, 57*(5). 551–565.

Reath Warren, A. (2017). *Developing multilingual literacies in Sweden and Australia: Opportunities and challenges in mother tongue instruction and multilingual study guidance in Sweden and community language education in Australia.* Stockholm, SE: University of Stockholm, PhD thesis. http://su.diva-portal.org/smash/get/diva2:1116085/FULLTEXT01. pdf

Rienzner, M. (2013). "Platz machen" und Schule (mit)gestalten. Muttersprachlicher Unterricht in Somali. In J. Purkarthofer & B. Busch (Eds.), *Schulsprachen – Sprachen in und um und durch die Schule.* Schulheft 151 (pp. 28–42). Innsbruck: Studienverlag.

Sevinç, Y. & Backus, A. (2017). Anxiety, language use and linguistic competence in an immigrant context: a vicious circle? *International Journal of Bilingual Education and Bilingualism,* 1–19. DOI 10.1080/13670050.2017.1306021

Tollefson, J. W. & Tsui, A. B.M. (2014). Language diversity and language policy in educational access and equity. *Review of Research in Education, 38,* 189–214.

Valdés, G. (2017). From language maintenance and intergenerational transmission to language survivance: will "language" education help or hinder? *International Journal of the Sociology of Language, 243,* 67–95.

Wei, L. (2011). Moment Analysis and translanguaging space: Discursive construction of identities by multilingual Chinese youth in Britain. *Journal of Pragmatics, 43,* 1222–1235.

CHAPTER 8

Maintaining, developing, and revitalizing: Language ideologies in national education policy and home language instruction in compulsory school in Sweden

Jenny Rosén, Boglárka Straszer, and Åsa Wedin

1. Introduction

The focus in this chapter is the goals and content of home language instruction in Sweden. Sweden has a long tradition of offering instruction in the home language of students, both for national minority languages and for immigrant languages. Since the home language reform in the mid-1970s, home language instruction (which in 1997 was named Mother Tongue Tuition [MTT]) has been an elective subject offered in compulsory school and regulated in the national curriculum. However, in regard to multilingual education, Sweden has a rather juxtaposed position: on the one hand, Sweden is historically stereotyped as a rather homogenous country in terms of its linguistic and cultural diversity; while on the other hand, Sweden is seen as a country with a progressive policy where the right to home language instruction is regulated in the Education Act and organized through the national education system. The aim of this chapter is to illuminate policies regarding MTT in Sweden by exploring the development of the subject in Swedish compulsory schools from a historical perspective and in relation to the attitudes of teachers toward the subject. From the perspective of translanguaging as language ideology (Mazak, 2017; Paulsrud & Rosén, 2019), we investigated how perceptions of language in general and mother tongue specifically are constructed in policy documents as well as among practitioners in contemporary Swedish schools. Further, we are interested in the ideological dimension of translanguaging as it challenges a monolingual bias in education as well as the different forms and functions of languages that are perceived as more prestigious than others. The following research questions have guided the analysis: (1) Which shifts in the MTT curriculum can be identified during the period 1970–2018? (2) How has the MTT subject been legitimized in policy during the period? And (3) How do primary school teachers in a Swedish compulsory school perceive MTT? Hence, the analysis brings into focus both a historical and a contemporary perspective on MTT in order to critically discuss if and how MTT as a school subject contributes to a language ideology that embraces multilingualism.

The right to home language instruction is regulated in the Swedish Education Act, which stipulates that "a student with a guardian with a mother tongue other than Swedish should be offered mother tongue tuition in this language if 1) the language is used on a daily basis at home, 2) the student has basic knowledge in the language" (Swedish Education Act, 2010, p. 800, chapter 10, 7 §, translated by the authors) (see also Busic & Sullivan, this volume). Further conditions in terms of the number of students requesting MTT in a specific language is stated in the Education Ordinance (2018). The restrictions stated above (1–3) do not apply to speakers of the five recognized minority languages: Finnish, Yiddish, Meänkieli (Tornedal Finnish), Romani Chib (all varieties), and Saami (all varieties). The Swedish Language Act from 2009 (SFS, 2009, p. 600) aims to specify the position and usage of Swedish and other languages in Swedish society and is also "intended to protect the Swedish language and language diversity in Sweden, and the individual's access to language." Through this act,

Swedish is recognized as the common language in Swedish society, a language which every resident should have access to and the right to learn, develop and use, while it is stated to be the right of all individuals to use and develop his/her language.

Hence, state-mandated policies with regard to language and education could be seen as supportive of linguistic diversity. However, research has highlighted the fact that, despite strong support in policy, its implementation has been less successful (Hyltenstam & Milani, 2012; Spetz, 2014). State-mandated education policies always include questions of language, both explicitly through regulations regarding the languages that should be taught and given academic credits, and also implicitly through unspoken language norms. Formal education is usually a central institution for standardization (Blommaert & Rampton, 2011), often with a monolingual bias, and as Hélot (2012) argues, "[c]oncieved as linguistically and culturally homogenous spaces, our schools find it difficult to question their monolingual habitus, and to imagine that multilingual practices could become the norm in education as well" (p. 214).

Moreover, languages are often regulated in terms of time and space between subjects, such as English or Swedish, and also through concepts such as mother tongue, home language, and foreign languages[1] (Rosén, 2017). Thus, education is an essential field with regard to the negotiation of language ideologies, which can be defined as "beliefs, feelings, and conceptions about language structure and use which often index the political economic interests of individual speakers, ethnic and other interest groups, and nation states" (Kroskrity, 2010, p. 192). During the last ten years, translanguaging has emerged as both a theoretical and a pedagogical concept, especially in the field of bilingual and multilingual education (see for

---

1   Which in the Swedish school context are called modern languages (see also Rosén, 2017; Bagga-Gupta, 2012).

example Paulsrud et al., 2017; Mazak, 2017). Translanguaging also includes an ideological perspective as it "challenges a monolingual bias in education, especially the assumed appropriate forms and functions, as well as the understanding of language prevailing it" (Paulsrud & Rosén, 2019, p. 5) (see also Chen, this volume). In the Swedish context, MTT has developed as part of the state-mandated school system regulated by national acts and curricula, and as such is an important field for negotiations of language ideologies.

This chapter starts with the theoretical framework and a brief overview of previous research on MTT in Sweden, followed by the design of the study and the empirical material. In the section *Findings*, the analysis of the national policy document and the interviews is presented, and finally the chapter wraps up with some conclusions.

2. Theoretical framework

The theoretical framework in this chapter includes the language ideological perspective of translanguaging and ethnography of language policy (McCarty, 2011; Hornberger & Johnson, 2007), which "should include both critical analyses of local, state, and national policy texts and discourses as well as data collection on how such policy texts and discourses are interpreted and appropriated by agents in a local context" (Johnson, 2009, p. 142). Therefore, studies of language policy need to both critically analyze and go beyond the formal and declared policies in order to examine the situated contexts where language policies are constituted, negotiated, and practiced (Bonacina, 2010; Menken & García, 2010; Rosén & Bagga-Gupta, 2015). From this perspective, language and education policy should not be understood only as an object but rather as a process with a focus on what policy *does* rather than what it *is* (McCarty, 2011, p. 2). Hornberger and Jonsson (2007) suggest that "[h]istorical and intertextual analyses of policy texts can capture the confluence of histories, attitudes, and ideologies that engender a language policy but, alone, cannot account for how the creation is interpreted and implemented in the various contextual layers through which a language policy must pass" (p. 511). Hence, including the voices of teachers in the analysis should not be understood from a top-down perspective, where teachers are expected to implement a policy, but rather as a process where "teachers can transform classrooms, thereby promoting institutional change that can lead to political and, ultimately, broader social change" (Ricento & Hornberger, 1996, p. 418).

2.1 Research about MTT in the Swedish context

In the Swedish context, MTT is a subject that students in elementary school and high school may study if they choose, and if they fulfil the requirements (see above). MTT is usually 30 to 60 minutes per week, which may be included in the ordinary schedule, or positioned outside the ordinary school day. In some contexts, the MTT teacher is included in the team of teachers at a particular school, but more commonly he or she travels between schools. It may also be the case that students have to go to another school than their ordinary one to receive MTT. In 2017–2018, 27% of all students in Swedish compulsory schools had the right to MTT and, of them, 59% participated in MTT classes (SNAE, 2018).

With regard to the historical development of MTT in the Swedish context, Cabau (2014) identified three phases. The first phase was characterized by a laissez-faire policy, where children were offered MTT generously in order to implement the intentions of the home language reforms. In the second phase, from the mid-1980s, several restrictions on MTT were introduced; in order to be entitled to MTT, children needed to already have basic knowledge of the language in question and at least five children had to enroll in MTT in order for the municipality to be required to organize it. Moreover, municipalities were not beholden to provide MTT for more than seven years. The third phase, from the late 1990s onward, was characterized by a stronger position for the five recognized national minority languages compared to other languages. For example, students were not obliged to have basic skills in the minority language or use it daily. The position of the national minority languages vis-à-vis other languages has, since the examination by Cabau (2014), become even stronger, as will be further elaborated on below. Other scholars, such as Hyltenstam (1986), Nauclér (1997), and Huss (2003), have suggested different phases or added new phases with regard to MTT in the Swedish context. Hyltenstam (1986) suggests a first period until the 1970s was characterized by assimilation, with an assumption that children with an immigrant background need special support in Swedish due to their expected deficiencies in the language. The second period was characterized by the home language reform, emphasizing the importance of the first language for the development and well-being of the child.

With regard to Swedish immigration policy in general, Borevi (2002) identifies three phases: establishment (1968–1975), evaluation during the 1980s, and reevaluation during the 1990s. During the period of establishment, special political actions were aimed at immigrants as a group. In the 1980s, politicians started to question policies addressing immigrants as a homogenous group, further suggesting that actions for cultural maintenance among immigrants did not advance integration. In the 1990s, the previous immigrant policy was re-evaluated by introducing a new politics of integration (Borevi, 2002).

Despite a long tradition of MTT in Sweden, the number of research studies is limited and mainly focused on policy. Still, a number of researchers highlight the fact that, despite strong support in Swedish policies on varied levels for MTT, its implementation and practice has been less successful (Hyltenstam & Milani, 2012; Lainio, 2012; Spetz, 2014; Norberg Brorsson & Lainio, 2015). Lainio (2012) uses the concept *ambiguity* when referring to the official discourse of support in policies, rhetoric and research that is not implemented in practice. A similar point is made by Cabau (2014), in distinguishing between language-in-education policy (decision-taking), language-in-education planning (decision-implementation) and the challenges facing MTT. Cabau (2014) highlights several explanations for the implementation problems of MTT, such as a lack of teacher education and the status of languages other than English in the Swedish school system as well as in society at large. Other scholars have demonstrated the marginalized position of MTT in Swedish schools due to the subject's often poor conditions and status (Lainio, 2012; Ganuza & Hedman, 2015; Reath Warren, 2017).

Studies have brought attention to the challenges of MTT teachers, such as the non-mandatory status of MTT, disjuncture from other subjects in school, issues of legitimacy and the limited time allocated to the subject. Despite problems with its implementation, Ganuza and Hedman's study (2018) showed that MTT had a positive effect on students' literacy development both in Swedish and the home language.

Salö, Ganuza, Hedman, and Karrebaeck (2018) have analyzed MTT in Sweden and Denmark using a historical, comparative perspective. The analysis shows that relations between agents from the academic and the political fields can explain the differences between the two countries. In the Swedish case, the strong position of agents from the academic field in relation to political stakeholders has influenced policy making, while the question of MTT in Denmark has mainly been political with less influence from the academic field.

3. The design of the study

The empirical material analyzed here consists of policy material such as curricula and syllabi, inquiries, and reports covering the period 1970 to 2018 (see Table 1) and interviews with primary school teachers during a three-year ethnographic study.[2] The policy material analyzed was produced by the Swedish government, including political inquiries and propositions, or by the Swedish National Agency of Education (SNAE), as well as national curricula, syllabi, and commentary material. In total, new state-mandated curricula for compulsory schooling were published in 1980, 1994, and 2011, but adjustments and revisions were also made in between the various publications and are thus included in the analysis. Moreover, commentary materials published by the SNAE on certain issues of the curriculum have also been included if they were somehow related to MTT. The syllabi for home language in the curriculum from 1980 (ME, 1980), the curriculum from 1994 (SNAE, 1994), the curriculum from 2011 (SNAE, 2011), and the current curriculum from 2018 have been analyzed, focusing on the subject that was initially called Home Language and would later, in 1997, be renamed Mother Tongue Tuition (MTT). Other policy material such as inquiries and propositions have been used to contextualize and bring a deeper understanding of the political framework in which the subject of MTT has developed. An overview of the policy material can be found in Table 1.

Moreover, semi-structured interviews have been conducted with six primary school teachers from three compulsory schools in two municipalities in Sweden. All teachers worked in schools with a high number of students with mother tongues other than Swedish, and also a high number of newly arrived students. During the interviews, the teachers were asked among other things about the organization and aim of MTT, MTT's role for the students' learning, and cooperation with MTT teachers. Here, we have focused only on teachers' views expressed about the aim of MTT and its importance

2   Mother Tongue and Study Guidance in Compulsory School (financed by Dalarna Centre for Educational Development, 2015–2017).

Table 1. Overview of policy material used.

Type of material	Publisher	Year
Curriculum and commentary material		
Curriculum for compulsory school. Generic part. Additions and revisions from 1st of July 1987.	Swedish National Board of Education	1978
National curriculum for compulsory school. Introduction, goals and guidance.	Swedish Ministry of Education	1980
Students with linguistic and cultural backgrounds from other countries. Commentary material to the curriculum.	Swedish National Board of Education	1986
Home language classes and composed classes. Commentary material to the curriculum.	Swedish National Board of Education	1988
Curriculum for compulsory school, preschool class and Recreation Centre.	Swedish National Agency of Education	1994
Compulsory school. Comment to syllabi and grading criteria.	Swedish National Agency of Education	2000
Curriculum for the Compulsory School, Preschool Class and the Recreation Centre.	Swedish National Agency of Education	2011

Type of material	Publisher	Year
Commentary material to the syllabi in mother tongue tuition besides the national minority languages.	Swedish National Agency of Education	2016
Curriculum for the Compulsory School, Preschool Class and the Recreation Centre. (revised 2018)	Swedish National Agency of Education	2018
Public inquiries, political propositions and reports		
The Royal Commission on Immigration 3. The Immigrants and the Minorities. Report from the Royal Commission on Immigration.	Swedish Ministry of Interior	1974
The government proposition about guidelines for the politics concerning immigrants and minorities.	Swedish Government	1975
The home language reform. A summary.	Swedish National Board of Immigration	1977
Government proposition regarding the curriculum for compulsory school.	Swedish Government	1979
Government proposition. Sweden, the future and diversity – from immigrant policy to integration policy.	Swedish Government	1998
More Languages – More Possibilities. The development of mother tongue support and mother tongue tuition. Report to the Government.	Swedish National Agency of Education	2002
National Minorities in preschool, preschool class, and school.	Swedish National Agency of Education	2015
National minority languages in school. Improved conditions for instruction and revitalization.	Public inquiry	2017

for their students. The interviews were conducted in Swedish, and transcribed, but they are presented here in translated form (our own translation). Citations from the policy documents have also been translated by the authors, except the 2011 curriculum.

The main focus of the analysis of the curricula, syllabi, inquiries and interviews have been on the expressed aim and goals of the MTT subject. The texts have been analyzed using a qualitative analysis of how the concepts were used in order to identify discursive shifts across time as well as between different documents. Accordingly, the analysis has focused on not only what is communicated in the texts but also how it is expressed.

Transcriptions from interviews have been analyzed through qualitative content analysis, in a first stage with examples where they expressed their views of MTT, its organization, the role of MTT for students' learning and their own cooperation with MTT teachers. The aims they expressed were categorized by trying to find common themes. First, we will present the findings of the policy material analysis and then of the teachers' views.

4. Findings and analysis

In this section, we will start by giving a short history of the introduction and development of home language education in Sweden, followed by an analysis of the position of MTT as a school subject. We then analyze the particular position of languages defined as minority languages in the Language Act, before we turn to the voices of the teachers, where we focus on their views on the aims of MTT.

4.1 Home language instruction: Developing a new school subject

During the 1960s, students with a migrant background were given the opportunity to participate in home language instruction in compulsory schools. However, even though the state allocated money for such instruction, municipalities were not obliged to organize it. Still, the home language reform in 1977 became a landmark for the development of Home Language (and later MTT) as an eligible subject in Swedish compulsory schools, as municipalities were required to organize home language instruction for all children using a language[3] other than Swedish at home (e.g. Hyltenstam & Tuomela, 1996; SNAE, 2002).

Although both migrants and indigenous linguistic minorities have always resided in Sweden, the increase in migration beginning in 1940s until the mid-1970s gave way to a political and public debate regarding the status and situation of immigrants. A commission on immigration was set up, which later on presented a new immigrant policy based on the principles of equality, freedom of choice and partnership (ML, 1974). In terms of education, equality meant equal opportunities for students despite their linguistic background. The principle of freedom of choice emphasized the right of immigrants to choose to maintain their cultural and linguistic identity (see also Cabau, 2014; Hyltenstam & Tuomela, 1996; Runblom, 1995). The need for an immigrant policy was motivated by the perceived difficulties of immigrants to adjust to Swedish society. In the commission report, the term "linguistic minorities" included both immigrants to Sweden and indigenous minorities since both faced similar issues with regard to cultural and linguistic integration (Prop, 1975, p. 26). In order to implement the goals of the immigration policy, home language instruction as well as support in Swedish was to be organized by schools. In 1976, the Swedish Parliament

3 Although we are aware of the problematic perspective on categorizing students' linguistic repertoires into different named languages as well as first and second language, we use language in the singular when we refer to policy documents using such categorizations in the chapter. MTT was designed based on an understanding of *one* home language in relation to *one* dominant language in society and school, and hence such a perspective is reflected in citations and references to the policy documents.

decided to organize home language instruction for what were called immigrant children and children of linguistic minorities. It was not children's migration status per se that conditioned the right to home language instruction but "that the instruction was estimated necessary for the student's development and persistent education" (NBI, 1977, p. 3).

A change in the national curriculum for compulsory schools was made in 1978 in accordance with the home language reform, stating that "students should be given the possibility to keep and develop their home language, and take charge of their cultural heritage and in the future be able to freely choose in which society they want to reside" (NBE, 1978, p. 24). It is important to note that students in official documents are expected to have *one* home language expressed as *their* language. Home language instruction was further motivated by the importance of language for students in developing their personalities and belonging to more than one culture (NBE, 1978, p. 24). In the political proposition for a new curriculum, home language instruction was also mentioned with regard to internationalization, stating that expanded home language instruction would provide Sweden with individuals that had multilingual competence.

In 1980, a new curriculum was introduced for compulsory schools including Home Language as a separate subject, stating that "the aim of home language instruction should be to keep and to develop knowledge in the language, used by the child in their daily environment. Doing so will promote the emotional, linguistic and intellectual development of the child" (ME, 1980, p. 58). A further argument was that knowledge of a first language ("or your own language," as it was stated) is a precondition for development. Furthermore, the aim of the instruction was for the students to later become bilingual and belong to two cultures, as they thereby get the possibility to enact and feel belonging to the cultural background of their parents and their home country.

The importance of cultural identity is also emphasized in commentary material to the curriculum (NBE, 1988) concerning home language classes in relation to mixed classes, stating that "good knowledge in the home language and Swedish is essential for identity development" (p. 11). In the commentary material to the curriculum, produced by SNAE, the aim and motivation of home language instruction was further developed, and the goal of active bilingualism added (NBE, 1985, p. 7). The document also highlighted the heterogeneity among students taking part in home language instruction with regard to competence both in the home language and in Swedish, and also with regard to the possibility of using the languages outside the school setting, thus distinguishing between Swedish environments and home language environments.

To sum up, the introduction of home language instruction in the Swedish school system was part of a larger shift in immigrant policy dominated by the principles of equality, freedom of choice, and partnership. Emphasizing the right of immigrants to choose their cultural identity, including their linguistic identity, motived the right to home language instruction. The stated goal for the school was to promote active bilingualism and to enable the students to belong to two cultures. Thus, cultural belonging in relation to identity as well as emotional and cognitive development were tied to questions of home language in the policy documents.

4.2 Regulation and a new curriculum

During the late 1980s, a number of restrictions were introduced regarding both the language skills of the students and the organization by the municipality. Children could only participate in MTT in one language that was used in daily interaction in the home. A new national curriculum for compulsory schools was introduced in 1994, including a new syllabus for MTT, still called Home Language Instruction (SNAE, 1994). The concepts *immigrant student* or *minority student* were replaced by the concept *student with a home language other than Swedish*. The aim of the subject stated for these students became to develop their language in order to achieve a strong self-esteem and a clear perception of themselves and their situation in life. The instruction was that it "should promote the students' development towards bilingualism and double cultural identity" (ME, 1994, p. 24). Hence, there was a change from *active bilingualism* to *bilingualism*, and from *belonging to cultures and languages* to *double cultural identity*. The concepts *double cultural identity* and *bilingualism* manifest a discourse of double bilingualism (Creese & Blackledge, 2010; Jørgensen, 2008), where the linguistic and cultural repertoires of the students are viewed as separate entities. The discourse of double bilingualism is also manifested in the syllabi stating that the student should compare the home language with the Swedish language and through that develop their bilingualism. Moreover, students should acquire knowledge about history, traditions, and society in "their native culture" and compare this with Swedish conditions (SNAE, 1994, p. 24). Hence, students participating in MTT became positioned as belonging to a different cultural background from others. With regard to the structure and character of the subject, it was stated that "the reading of literature, writing and conversation about the students' experiences and participation in two cultures should be the basis for working with the language development in the subject" (SNAE, 1994, p. 24).

After 1994, no further changes were introduced regarding MTT until 1997, when the term "home language" was replaced with "mother tongue," changing the name of the school subject to Mother Tongue Tuition. The reason behind this shift was that the concept of home language instruction had been misinterpreted as a language used only in the home domain and not suitable for school practices or as a school subject. Still however, the requirement for attending MTT was that the language children choose to study as their mother tongue was used on a daily basis at home with at least one of the parents (SNAE, 2002; see also Straszer, 2010).

During the 1990s, a general shift in immigrant policy in Sweden was made, moving beyond policies directed at immigrants as a group and, instead, toward policies of integration (Prop, 1997/1998, p. 16). The point of departure for the reform was the idea that questions regarding immigrants should be integrated into other political areas, and that policies directed toward immigrants as a group should be reduced (Prop, 1997/1998, p. 16; see also Borevi, 2002). The goals of the new integration policy were equal rights and possibilities regardless of ethnic and cultural background, diversity as a foundation of society and development characterized by mutual respect and tolerance, which everyone despite their background should be part of and responsible for (Prop, 1997/1998, p. 16). Although it was stated that the new policy should not influence MTT, the shift from a focus on cultural belonging and identity toward a more language-focused subject could be perceived in the light of the new integration policy in general.

4.3 A language subject

Home language and later mother tongue continued to be framed in the singular, as one language, between 1994 and 2011, marking a monolingual norm and a presumption that a person has one mother tongue. In 2000, revisions of the syllabus for MTT made it more similar to other subject syllabi such as Swedish (SNAE, 2000). In the commentaries regarding the revisions published by the SNAE, it was stated that the point of departure for the syllabi was that students with a double cultural belonging construct their identity through language, in both the mother tongue and Swedish (SNAE, 2000, p. 46). A foundation in the so-called native culture was regarded as a presumption for positive integration and, therefore, it became the responsibility of the subject to teach the culture of the area where the language was used. Similar to previous syllabi, a contrastive perspective between the mother tongue and Swedish, and between aspects of the native culture and Swedish culture, was emphasized (SNAE, 2000, pp. 46–48). An important addition in the revision was that students that did not have basic competence in the language and/or did not use the language on a daily basis at home could not study MTT but were allowed to study the specific language as a foreign language, called "modern language" in the syllabi (SNAE, 2000, p. 48).

In 2001, the Swedish government gave SNAE a mission regarding MTT in order to improve the situation for children and youths with a foreign background, suggesting that MTT was one means to strengthen their personal and cultural identity and development into multilingual individuals (SNAE, 2002, pp. 14–15). In the light of the new integration policy, it is important to highlight that the extent of MTT in Swedish schools had decreased during the 1990s and that MTT had not been integrated into regular school activities (SNAE, 2002). Three aspects of MTT were identified in the mission: (1) the importance of the mother tongue for the development of identity, (2) the mother tongue as one of the students' languages, and (3) the mother tongue as a tool for learning (SNAE, 2002, pp. 21–22).

In 2011, a new national curriculum for compulsory schools was presented. With regard to MTT, different functions were assigned in the syllabi, as (1) a tool for learning, (2) skills for comparing Swedish and the mother tongue, and (3) knowledge of texts and culture from areas where the mother tongue is spoken. The aim of MTT for students was stated as to develop knowledge in and about their mother tongue, and teaching was to provide students with abilities to develop their cultural identity and become multilingual (SNAE, 2011). Similar to other language-focused subjects, the MTT syllabi started out by stating that language "is the primary tool human beings use for thinking, communicating and learning. Through language people develop their identity, express their feelings and thoughts, and understand how others feel and think" and, further, that "having access to their mother tongue also facilitates language development and learning in different areas" (SNAE, 2011, p. 83). The aim of the MTT subject is for the students to develop knowledge in and about the mother tongue, developing their spoken and written language skills as well as reading literature. Compared to previous syllabi, knowledge in and about the specific language was emphasized through explicit goals oriented toward language competence, whereas goals concerning culture were reduced to "reflect over traditions, cultural phenomena and social questions in areas where the mother tongue is spoken based on comparisons with Swedish conditions" (SNAE, 2011, p. 83). However, students' identities were no longer expressed in terms of a *double cultural identity* but as their *cultural identity* and the goal of bilingual replaced by multilingual.

4.4 Revitalization: The special status of the national minority languages

As noted in previous sections, the MTT subject was directed toward both students with an immigrant background and toward students from minority groups, and no separation was made with regard to either content or goals. In 1999, the Swedish government decided to accept the European Charter for Regional or Minority Languages, which was followed by a national policy framework recognizing five national minority languages in Sweden: Yiddish, Romani Chib, Saami, Finnish, and Meänkieli. In 2009, the Swedish Language Act was established, stipulating that "all residents of Sweden are to be given the opportunity to learn, develop and use Swedish" and, in addition, "persons belonging to a national minority are to be given the opportunity to learn, develop and use the minority language" (SFS, 2009, p. 600). People using languages other than the national minorities or Swedish Sign Language were to be given the opportunity to develop and use the language, although learning was not mentioned. Thus, the Language Act gave a stronger legal framework for the national minority languages vis-à-vis other languages with regard to learning and education. This marked a shift from a general policy of MTT toward a separated policy for the national minority languages. With regard to regulations, since 2015 there has been no requirement for students belonging to one of the national minority groups to have basic skills or to use the language on a daily basis at home to be eligible for MTT. Whereas the goal for MTT had previously been to maintain and develop the language, the goal of MTT with regard to the national minority languages was now also to be understood as revitalization (SNAE, 2015). Hence, students who had no previous knowledge in the specific language also became eligible to study the national minority language as MTT. In other words, the aim for MTT for students of a national minority became not only to maintain and develop one language, but also to have the possibility to revitalize the language that could have been lost over generations because of its long-term weak status in society (see Lainio, 2015) (see also Hammine, this volume).

In 2015, a new syllabus was introduced for MTT, dividing the subject into two parts: one syllabus for MTT for all languages besides the national minority languages, and one part with syllabi for MTT for each of the five different national minority languages (in total six different syllabi). In the syllabus for MTT for all other languages, a strong focus on language skills remained; the main aim became for students to develop knowledge in and about the mother tongue (SNAE, 2018). A comparative perspective toward culture prevailed, as students were expected to develop their knowledge about cultures and societies where the language was spoken and to develop a comparative approach to culture and language (SNAE, 2018). Whereas MTT for languages other than the national minorities has many similarities with other language-focused subjects (such as English and modern languages in the curriculum), the syllabi for MTT for the national minorities were oriented toward culture, history and traditions perceived as heritage, and the language was perceived as a strong tie to a specific minority group. For example, in the first paragraph of the syllabi in the MTT for Yiddish as a national minority language, it was stated: "Jews are a national minority with several hundred years of ancestry in Sweden. Their language – Yiddish – is an official minority language" (SNAE, 2018). Similar statements are made with regard to Meänkieli, Finnish, Romani Chib, and Saami. The comparative perspective is not present in these syllabi but rather to develop the students' ability to "reflect about social, historical and cultural phenomena in environments where the language is used and to reflect about the heritage, development and contemporary status of the language" (SNAE, 2018). Further, the ability to use the MTT as a tool for language development and learning was not mentioned in the MTT for the national minority languages, which it was in the syllabus for MTT for other languages.

To sum up, MTT for languages other than the national minority languages could be characterized as a language-focused subject, motivated by the importance of the mother tongue for language development and learning as well as its importance for identity and the ability to operate in a pluralistic society. MTT for the national minority languages became strongly tied to the minority group in essentialist terms, not problematizing the complex relations between language, culture and heritage. The importance of languages as cultural carriers that express common experiences, values, and knowledge, according to the syllabi, united the national minorities in Sweden with people using the same language in other parts of the world. The aim of revitalization was also manifested by a separation with regard to core content and knowledge requirements, whether the language was a first language or a second language of the student in the syllabi for the MTT for the national minority languages. The differences between the core-content with regard to first or second language learners were further developed in the commentary material (SNAE, 2016). A state-mandated inquiry in 2017 suggested that a new subject called National Minority Language be imposed (SOU, 2017, p. 91). Below, we will present our interview data with a focus on teachers' talk concerning the aims of MTT and we will discuss our research findings in the light of the theoretical frameworks presented above.

4.5 Ambiguous aim: Voices of the school teachers

During the interviews, the six primary school teachers were, among other things, asked about their views regarding the aims of MTT. The aims concerning MTT and values attached to it that they expressed were (1) to help students keep the language, (2) to develop the language, (3) support for their development of Swedish, (4) to enable the comparison between the mother tongue (MT) and Swedish, (5) for cultural values and identity development, (6) for contact with relatives, and (7) as an asset for the country.

That teachers expressed support for the value of MTT to help students keep their language may be expected as this follows official norms and policies. Two of the teachers specifically mentioned that they expected students to learn to read and write in the mother tongue and Teacher 3[4] elaborated what she meant by developing the MT[5]:

That you read nuances and in the language and that you sort of (.) no but well express oneself the way you want [. . .] how you may express yourself deeper [. . .] express yourself the way you want [. . .] everything from work to studies [. . .] in more detail and expressive yes better, is it you why, well better it is (.) as a human being as well.

4   Teachers are numbered 1–6.
5   (.) stands for pause with the dots marking seconds, and [. . .] stands for excluded speech.

Also, the fact that teachers express the importance of MT for students' development could be expected with regard to the discourse of national policy documents analyzed in previous sections. A strong discourse of the importance of MT is also expressed by teachers' concerns that a lack of skills in MT may impede students' learning in general and the development of Swedish specifically. Teacher 4 claims that

> *Students who lack a base in their language do not make the same progress in Swedish either [. . .] we've said to those who do not have enough Swedish language that (.) but you may write in Arabic and then you may work with that during study guidance that you go through and then (.) but then there are some students who are not able to write in Arabic either [...] then it is difficult to help them develop when they neither know Swedish but [. . .] had they had Arabic then you could have yes but discuss*

The citation partly reflects a discourse of semi-lingualism, which was strong in the Swedish context during the 1970s (see Hansegård, 1968) and argued that children who are not given the opportunity to develop their MT may risk becoming what they termed "semi-lingual". However, the citation also expresses a discourse of MT as a resource for learning, when students are said to be encouraged to use their strongest language for content learning. Teacher 2, who is herself a second language speaker of Swedish, expressed the value of comparing the mother tongue with Swedish as an aide for the development of language proficiencies in Swedish.

> *the main aim as I see it is that they all the time you should be able to compare [. . .] there should be more cooperation with Mother Tongue Teachers so that you could find these oh yes [in] your language you do like this but in Swedish we have to remember*

[. . .] you should climb over these obstacles much faster if we had someone that knew their language and would be there to explain [. . .] I work with Mohammed sometimes (MTT) and sometimes he says: Yes but in Syria there we do like this and then I understand [. . .] I know that there are different systems.

The value of MTT concerning culture and students' identity development was mentioned by four of the teachers in terms of traditions and that ways to address people may differ. One teacher specifically mentioned the value of MTT to preserve students' identity and "not to forget their origin." Hence, the value expressed for MTT was that students may develop a sense of value for their cultures and traditions. Teacher 1 mentioned the importance the mother tongue may have for students for their contact with relatives, and also the value of language knowledge for the country as a whole.

It is good for the whole of Sweden that there are many languages we will benefit from that when we will communicate with other countries then.

This teacher was also the only one that mentioned a negative aspect in direct relation to MTT and that was the workload for students learning two writing systems since they strive with two alphabets.

Even though teachers expressed strong support for MTT, they did not express high expectations for the subject and its teachers. The only concrete expectations on MTT teachers were that they should teach. Teacher 4 confessed, "I have no expectations because it feels like it's sort of an island outside, so I barely think of MTT I know it's there they do their thing (.) but it feels like a separate part of the school."

In summary, we can note that the teachers reproduce the official discourse regarding values with MTT. In their reflections, the teachers highlight three main aims of MTT: (i) language maintenance of MT (see 1 and 2 above), (ii) support for learning Swedish (see 3 and 4 above), and (iii) cultural values and identities, including contact with family and country of origin (see 5, 6, and 7 above).

5. Discussion

In this chapter, we have shown the variation and shifts over time with regard to the curricula and syllabi for MTT in Sweden, addressing questions of maintaining, developing, and revitalizing languages. Analysis of the empirical data showed how language hierarchies and ideologies are negotiated on different policy layers, from national curricula to school level, as it was shown in the interviews with the teachers. The teachers voiced different aims for MTT such as mentioned above: (1) language maintenance of MT, (2) support for learning Swedish, and (3) cultural values and identities including contact with family and country of origin. These aims are also expressed in the national policy documents regarding MTT although with a shifting focus over time from emphasizing MTT as a part of culture and cultural identity (during the 1970s and 1980s) to a stronger language focus (from 2000 until 2018), where culture and heritage are once more accentuated but then concerning national minority languages. In terms of language ideology, the analysis shows that, despite shifts in policy and the concepts used to describe the goals for the students' language use (active bilingual, bilingual, multilingual), the idea of separate bilingualism has not been challenged (compare Creese & Blackledge, 2010; García & Li, 2015).

Although we find it positive that students are encouraged to study MTT and become bi/multilingual, it is apparent that linguistic repertoires are labeled as two different languages or codes. Comparing the two languages is expressed as a goal in the syllabi, and also by the interviewed teachers, which indicates first a perception of two different languages (and cultures) that can be compared to each other and, secondly, that comparing them is important for the learning and development of the student. Even though such practices may support students' development of metalinguistic awareness, teachers should be made aware of their own perceptions of the linguistic repertoires of their students. Categorizations such as "their language" that is contrasted with Swedish are problematic, since they exclude MTT students from an ownership of Swedish and contribute to a discourse of otherness. Furthermore, the language ideology of separate bilingualism is reproduced by the division of languages in time and space during the school day, as students' use of the MT is positioned to the MTT classes and otherwise outside of school. Such discourse may counter translanguaging practices among teachers and students and especially as part of instruction.

Finally, the analysis has shown that MTT as a subject was developed during a time of labor migration in Sweden. Since then, the pattern of globalization and migration has changed, resulting in changes in official language policies. Thus, questions of maintaining, developing, and revitalizing home language are tied to the status of certain languages on a national level but the subject may, on a local school level, still face similar challenges.

References

Bagga-Gupta, S. (2012). Privileging identity positions and multimodal communication in textual practices. Intersectionality and the (re)negotiation of boundaries. In A. Pitkänen-Huhta & L. Holm (Eds.), *Literacy Practices in Transition. Perspectives from the Nordic Countries* (pp. 77–100). Cleveland: Multilingual Matters.

Blommaert, J. & Rampton, B. (2011). Language and Superdiversity. *Diversities, 13*(2), 1–21. Retrieved [20190209] from http://newdiversities.mmg.mpg.de/?page_id=2056

Bonacina, F. (2010). *A Conversation Analytic Approach to Practiced Language Policies: The example of an induction classroom for newly-arrived immigrant children in France.* Unpublished PhD Thesis. Edinburgh:

The University of Edinburgh.

Borevi, K. (2002). *Välfärdsstaten i det mångkulturella samhället*. Diss. Uppsala: Univ., 2002

Cabau, B. (2014). Minority language education policy and planning in Sweden. *Current Issues in Language Planning, 15*(4), 409–425.

Creese, A. & Blackledge, A. (2010). Translanguaging in the bilingual classroom: A pedagogy for learning and teaching? *The Modern Language Journal, 94*(1), 103–115.

Education Ordinance [Skolförordningen] (2018). *Skolförordning 2011: 185*. https://www.riksdagen.se/sv/dokument-lagar/dokument/svensk-forfattningssamling/skolforordning-2011185_sfs-2011-185

Ganuza, N. & Hedman, C. (2015). Struggles for legitimacy in mother tongue instruction in Sweden. *Language and Education, 29*(2), 125–139.

Ganuza, N. & Hedman, C. (2018). Modersmålsundervisning, läsförståelse och betyg: Modersmålsundervisningens roll för elevers skolresultat [Mother tongue instruction, reading comprehension and grades – the role of mother tongue instruction for school achievements]. *Nordand. Nordisk tidskrift for andrespråksforskning, 13*(1), 4–22. DOI: 10.18261/issn.2535-3381-2018-01-01.

García, O., & Li Wei. (2015). Translanguaging, bilingualism and bilingual education. In W. Wright, S. Boun, & O. García (Eds.), *Handbook of bilingual education* (pp. 223–240). Malden, MA: John Wiley.

Hansegård, N. E. (1968). *Tvåspråkighet eller halvspråkighet?*. Stockholm: Aldus/Bonnier.

Hélot, C. (2012). Linguistic diversity and education. In M. Martin-Jones, A. Blackledge, & A. Creese (Eds.), The *Routledge handbook of multilingualism* (pp. 214–231). Milton Park, Abingdon, Oxon: Routledge.

Hornberger, N. H. & Johnson, D. C. (2007). Slicing the onion ethnographically: layers and spaces in multilingual language education policy and practice. *TESOL Quarterly, 41*(3), 509–532.

Huss, L. (2003). Assimilaatiosta pluralismiin ja uuteen integraatiopolitiikkaan: Ruotsin kouluhistoriaa kielivähemmistöjen näkökulmasta. In R. Kangassalo & I. Mellenius (Eds.), *Låt mig ha kvar mitt språk. Antakaa minun pitää kieleni. Den tredje SUKKA-rapporten. Kolmas SUKKA-raportti. Skrifter från moderna språk 11* (pp. 33–49). Institutionen för moderna språk. Umeå: Umeå universitet.

Hyltenstam, K. (1986). Politik, forskning och praktik. In C. Wadensjö (Ed.), *Invandrarspråken - ratad resurs?* (pp. 6–24). Källa/25. Utgiven av Forskningsrådsnämnden. Stockholm.

Hyltenstam, K. & Milani, T. (2012). Flerspråkighetens sociopolitiska och sociokulturella ramar. In M. Axelsson, K. Hyltenstam, & I. Lindberg (Eds.), *Flerspråkighet: en forskningsöversikt* (pp. 17–152.) Stockholm: Vetenskapsrådet.

Hyltenstam, K. & Tuomela, V. (1996). Hemspråksundervisningen. In K. Hyltenstam (Ed.), *Tvåspråkighet med förhinder? Invandrar- och minoritetsundervisning i Sverige* (pp. 9–109.) Lund: Studentlitteratur.

Johnson, D. C. (2009). Ethnography of language policy. *Language Policy, 8*(2), 139–159.

Jørgensen, J. N. (2008). Polylingual languaging around and among children and adolescents. *International Journal of Multilingualism, 5*(3), 161–176.

Kroskrity, P. V. (2010). Language ideologies: Evolving perspectives. In J. Jaspers, J. Verschueren & J.-O. Östman (Eds.), *Society and language use (Handbook of pragmatics highlights (HoPH)* (pp. 192–211). Amsterdam: John Benjamins.

Lainio, J. (2012). Modersmålets erkända och negligerade roller. In M. Olofsson (Ed.), *Symposium 2012: Lärarrollen i svenska som andraspråk* (pp. 66–96). Stockholm: Stockholms universitets förlag.

Lainio, J. (2015). The art of societal ambivalence: A retrospective view on Swedish language policies for Finnish in Sweden. In M. Halonen, P. Ihalainen, & T. Saarinen (Eds.), *Language policies in Finland and Sweden: Interdisciplinary and multi-sited comparisons* (pp. 66–96). Bristol: Multilingual Matters.

McCarty, T. L. (2011). *Ethnography and Language Policy.* New York: Routledge.

Menken, K. & García, O. (2010). *Negotiating Language Policies in Schools. Educators as Policymakers.* London/New York: Routledge.

ME/Ministry of Education (1980). *1980års läroplan för grundskolan..*

Inledning, mål och riktlinjer. Stockholm: Ministry of Education.

ML (1974). *Invandrarutredningen 3. Invandrarna och minoriteterna. Huvudbetänkande av invandrarutredningen. [The Royal Commission on Immigration 3. The Immigrants and the Minorities. Report from the Royal Commission on Immigration]* SOU 1974:69. Stockholm: Ministry of Labor.

NBE/National Board of Education (1978). *Läroplan för grundskolan. Allmän del. Tillägg och ändringar från 1 juli 1978.* Stockholm: National Board of Education [Skolöverstyrelsen].

NBE (1985). *Elever med språk och kulturbakgrund från andra länder.* Kommentarsmaterial. SÖ publikationer. Läroplaner 1985:2. Stockholm: National Board of Education [Skolöverstyrelsen].

NBE (1988). *Hemspråksklasser och sammansatta klasser. Kommentarmaterial Lgr 80.* Red: Kerstin Thorsén. Stockholm: National Board of Education [Skolöverstyrelsen].

NBI/National Board of Immigration (1977). *Hemspråksreformen: en sammanfattning.* Stockholm: National Board of Immigration [Statens invandrarverk].

Nauclér, K. (1997). Den uppgivna läroplanen: Tvåspråkighet i förskolan. In *Svenska som andraspråk och andra språk.* Festskrift till Gunnar Tingbjörn. Utgiven av Anders-Börje Andersson, Ingegerd Enström, Roger Källström & Kerstin Nauclér. *Institutionen för svenska språket* (pp. 283–294). Göteborgs universitet. Göteborg.

Norberg Brorsson, B. & Lainio, J. (2015). Litteratur och språk. Flerspråkiga elever och deras tillgång till utbildning och språk i skolan: Implikationer för lärarutbildningen. Uppföljningsrapport till EUCIM-TE-projektet. *Litteratur och språk.* Nr 10. Mälardalens högskola.

Paulsrud, B. & Rosén, J. (2019). Translanguaging and language ideologies in education: Northern and Southern perspectives. In S. Brunn & R. Kehrein (Eds.), *Handbook of the Changing World Language Map* (pp. 1–15). New York: Springer.

Prop. 1975:26. *Regeringens proposition om riktlinjer för invandrar- och minoritetspolitiken m.m.* Regeringens proposition 1975: 26.

Prop. 1978/79:180. *Regeringens proposition om läroplan för grundskola m.m. Regeringens proposition* 1978/79: 180.

Prop. 1997/98:16. *Sverige, framtiden och mångfalden – fråninvandrarpolitik till integrationspolitik.* Regeringens proposition 1997/98: 16.

Reath Warren, A. (2017). *Developing Multilingual Literacies in Sweden and Australia: Opportunities and Challenges in Mother Tongue Instruction and Multilingual Study Guidance in Sweden and Community Language Education in Australia.* Diss. (sammanfattning) Stockholm: Stockholms Universitet, 2017.

Ricento, T. & Hornberger, N. H. (1996). Unpeeling the onion: Language planning and policy and the ELT Professional. *TESOL Quarterly, 30*(3), 401–427.

Rosén, J. (2017). Spaces for translanguaging in Swedish education policy. In B. Paulsrud, J. Rosén, B. Straszer, & Å. Wedin (Eds.), *New Perspectives on Translanguaging and Education* (pp. 38–55). Bristol: Multilingual Matters.

Rosén, J. & Bagga-Gupta, S. (2015). Prata svenska, vi är i Sverige! [Talk Swedish, we are in Sweden!]: A study of practiced language policy in adult language learning. *Linguistics and Education, 31*, 59–73.

Runblom, H. (1995). Swedish multiculturalism in a comparative European perspective. In S. Gustavsson, & H. Runblom (Eds.), *Language, Minority, Migration.* Yearbook 1994/1995 from the Centre for Multiethnic Research. Uppsala Multiethnic Papers 34 (pp. 199–218). Uppsala: Uppsala University.

Salö, L., Ganuza, N., Hedman C., & Karrebaeck, M. (2018). Mother tongue instruction in Sweden and Denmark. Language policy cross-field effects, and linguistic exchange rates. *Language Policy, 17*, 591–610.

SFS 2009:600. *Language Act.* [Språklagen (2009:600).] Swedish Code of Statutes no: 2009:600. Stockholm: Ministry of Culture.

SNAE (1994). *Läroplan för det obligatoriska skolväsendet, förskoleklassen och fritidshemmet.* Stockholm: Skolverket.

SNAE (2000). *Grundskolan. Kommentarer till kursplaner och betygskriterier.* Stockholm: Swedish National Agency for Education.

SNAE (2002). *Flera språk – fler möjligheter: Utveckling av modersmålsstöd och modersmålsundervisningen 2002.* Rapport till regeringen 15 maj 2002. Dnr 01-01:2751. Stockholm: Swedish National Agency for Education.

SNAE (2011). *Curriculum for the Compulsory School, Preschool Class and* the *Recreation Centre 2011*. Stockholm: Swedish National Agency for Education.

SNAE (2015). *Nationella minoriteter i förskola, förskoleklass och skola.* Stockholm: Swedish National Agency for Education.

SNAE (2016). *Kommentarmaterial till kursplanen i modersmål utom nationella minoritetsspråk (reviderad 2016).* Stockholm: Swedish National Agency for Education.

SNAE (2018). *Läroplan för grundskolan, förskoleklassen och fritidshemmet (reviderad 2018).* Stockholm: Swedish National Agency for Education.

SOU (2017). *Nationella minoritetsspråk i skolan – förbättrade förutsättningar till undervisning och revitalisering. Betänkande av Utredningen förbättrade möjligheter för elever att utveckla sitt nationella minoritetsspråk.* Statens offentliga utredningar 2017: 91. Stockholm: The Government Office [Regeringskansliet].

Spetz, J. (2014). *Debatterad och marginaliserad: Perspektiv på modersmålsundervisningen. [Debated and marginalised: Perspectives on mother tongue tuition]* Rapporter från Språkrådet 6. Stockholm: The Swedish Language Council [Språkrådet].

Straszer, B. (2010). *Ungrare, ungerska och ungersk kultur i Sverige och Finland.* Digitala skrifter från Hugo Valentin-centrum 1. Uppsala universitet. Uppsala.

CHAPTER 9

Embracing multilingualism in school through multilingual educational staff: Insights into the interplay of policies and practices

Simone Plöger and Galina Putjata

1. Introduction

Educational systems in most countries are characterized by monolingual norms (Fürstenau, 2015). In light of migration and transnational mobility all over the world, researchers from educational as well as linguistic disciplines request a "multilingual turn" (Gogolin, 2005; Cummins, 2010). Educational staff[1] play a key role in this process, acting as agents between language policies and practices. This paper will present key findings from an ongoing research project on a particular school form – an integrative model that aims to integrate newly arrived pupils and their language practices[2] in the mainstream classes from the very beginning (Dewitz & Massumi, 2017) and includes multilingual staff in the process. This case is particularly interesting, as multilingual educational staff are extremely rare and

---

1   The term embraces teachers as well as pedagogues, mentors, and social workers in school.
2   The term "heritage language" is subject to controversial discussion in German pedagogical discourse as it bears an idea of a (foreign) heritage with no actual relevance for the child's life. Hence, the present paper adopts the term "family languages" or "language practices."

migration-related multilingualism is usually not considered as part of pedagogical expertise, as we will show in the literature review (2). What does a "multilingual turn" in school look like if multilingual staff is employed in the mainstream system? In order to answer this question, a qualitative study was conducted based on Bourdieu's concepts of language as capital and linguistic market. This theoretical framework as background to our research will be presented (3.1) followed by the specific context of the multilingual school team (3.2) as well as the methods *interview* and *participatory observation,* which we applied for data collection (3.3). These qualitative data allow a deep insight into the perception of multilingualism of policy makers, the teaching staff and of multilingual actors themselves. Completed by insights from participatory observation, our findings (4) present a multi-dimensional perspective of the case, which we will discuss focusing on the role of multilingual staff for a multilingual turn (5). We will finally draw a conclusion for policy makers as well as educational practitioners (6).

2. Brief literature review

Multilingualism is a social reality. In Germany, the exact number of children and young people growing up multilingually is not known and not statistically recorded. Indirect indications can be found in statistics on the so-called migrant background with approximately 30–50% (Beauftragte für Migration, Flüchtlinge und Integration, 2016, p. 40). These figures neither reflect the language constellations (languages of parents, siblings, common family languages) nor the actual language practices of the children. However, for pedagogical practice, these figures have a significant consequence: teachers work in increasingly heterogeneous groups with respect to the children's language biographies. In addition, "German", as any other language embraces a series of sociolects, regiolects, and different linguistic registers that children bring with them as a learning resource.

Transnational mobility increases this linguistic heterogeneity even further. Socio-economically or politically motivated, as "refugee migration," or supported by internationalization funds such as Erasmus, this voluntary and involuntary mobility continues to shape social multilingualism in Germany.

2.1 "Multilingual turn": Multilingualism in educational contexts

At the same time, this multilingual reality is opposed by the monolingual approach at school in many countries, including Germany (Cummins, 2010; Gogolin, 2005). This discrepancy puts all those at a disadvantage who deviate from the dominant linguistic norm and has an effect on the educational success of children that grow up multilingual. It has also consequences for their linguistic development: multilingualism, how it emerges and how it develops, depends largely on how society deals with languages. The monolingual orientation of educational institutions shapes individual linguistic development and can lead to language rejection (Blommaert, 2010; Irvine & Gal, 2000).

As a reaction to this development, researchers across disciplines and countries have called for a so-called "multilingual turn" – the perception of multilingualism as a social reality and hence as a linguistic norm. In the field of multilingualism education, this call draws on psycholinguistic and socio-political arguments concerning cognitive and linguistic transfer, the importance of all linguistic resources in learning and development processes, the socio-political need to overcome the deficit perspective on linguistic minorities as well as the use of migration-related resources in a democratic society (Allemann-Ghionda & Pfeiffer, 2010; Cummins, 2010; Poarch & Bialystok, 2017). Over the past ten years, data from empirical teaching and school research have supported these psycholinguistic and socio-political arguments. Empirical studies confirm that when migration-related multilingualism is constructively included in the classroom, it has positive effects on multilingual students as well as their peers. This has been corroborated by findings on multilingual literacy activities (Melo-Pfeifer & Helmchen, 2018), studies on methods of multilingual didactics in foreign language teaching (Candelier *et al.,* 2012), but also on the productive use of family languages in mathematics and subject teaching (Prediger, 2011). Finally, studies on classroom interaction complement these findings (Bührig & Duarte, 2013).

Despite the normative-theoretical discourses, scientific arguments, the proven effectiveness of methods at the teaching level and school development concepts at the structural level depicted above, however, teachers in most countries, including Germany, continue to orient themselves toward a monolingual norm (Huxel, 2018, for Germany; Pulinx & van Avermaet, 2015, for Belgium; Young, 2017, for France). The question in multilingualism education remains: How can a multilingual turn be achieved?

2.2 Multilingual teachers as change agents
In recent years, a key role in the transformation process of the educational landscape has been (politically) assigned to immigrant teachers as "role models" for a successful educational career, as bridge-builders between parents, teachers, and students, and as experts on multilingualism and intercultural communication (Bräu et al., 2013). This perspective has led different actors around the world to call for a more diversified teacher population (BReg., 2015; Ingersoll & May, 2016) arguing that "[t]eachers with immigrant background are an example for a successful upward mobility through education. Because of their specific bicultural and bilingual competences as well as their function as a role-model, they can play a significant role for the cultural opening of the school" (MSW NRW, 2012).

Even though the immigrant background of those teachers appears as a potential from this perspective, the political call reveals a series of underlying deficit-oriented assumptions. First, it implies that immigrant students need a role model in order to be motivated, which leaves the responsibility for academic achievement to the students themselves and diminishes the role of the school system and the institutional discrimination processes (Allemann-Ghionda & Pfeiffer, 2010). It further implies that a bridge has to be built between teachers and students (most of them born in the country of education), as they still belong to a "different culture." And finally, it is based on the assumption that immigrant teachers are per se competent in dealing with linguistic and cultural diversity even without a specialized training in linguistics or language teaching.

Broadly criticized as "othering" in sociological discourse (Döll & Knappik, 2015), the legitimation of these assumptions still lacks empirical basis. Interview studies on the self-perception of pre-service teachers illustrate that immigrant background as such is not the reason for choosing the teacher's profession (Georgi et al., 2011). The interviewees appear reluctant to assume the role of language and cultural mediators, and open themselves to this role only after having experienced injustice in treatment of children with immigrant backgrounds (Karakaşoğlu et al., 2013). In most cases, however, this role is ascribed to them by school principals and colleagues: immigrant teachers are asked for translation or help in specific language support situations, often even though they have hardly any experience, knowledge, or opportunity to reflect on this task. Recent studies show that teachers go so far as to distance themselves from this task and rather request to be accepted as professionals (Lengyel & Rosen, 2015).

While these perspectives on immigrant students and teachers have been broadly investigated, there are hardly any studies that address their potential for initiating in the educational system transformation processes toward a multilingual approach. As a reaction to this lacuna, we have conducted a qualitative study that investigates this potential from a multidimensional perspective using interviews with multilingual educational staff as well as participatory observation.

3. Research background

The study draws on Bourdieu's (1990) theory of language as capital and linguistic market. This theoretical framework will be presented in the following section.

3.1 Theoretical framework: School as linguistic market and multilingual staff as change agents

The model of the linguistic market and the economy of linguistic exchange enables us to analyze social power relations, in which language practices are regarded as strategies of self-positioning in social space (cf. Bourdieu, 1990). According to Bourdieu, each individual holds different forms of capital: cultural capital, social capital, and economic capital. The position of the individual within the social space is hence determined by the capital it holds, i.e. by competencies and educational qualifications, by social contacts and by material possessions.

Language represents a particular form of cultural capital, because languages and linguistic varieties have different market values within a society that correspond to hierarchical power relations. A certain way of speaking always subliminally refers to the origin of the individual, his or her educational career, and his or her position in social space. Thus, speakers of dialects or minority languages are unconsciously socially classified and are often ascribed a low level of professional competence. The socially legitimate majority language, on the other hand, functions as cultural capital that can be transformed into economic capital (cf. Bourdieu & Wacquant, 1996, p. 107).

These hierarchical differences between languages are not natural, however, but socio-politically constructed (Bourdieu & Wacquant, 1996, p. 108). The school plays a central role here as a place of socialization where students experience the significance of a language: while knowledge of the legitimate language (e.g. German) is rewarded, deviations from the linguistic norm are sanctioned. Finally, the students' equipment with cultural capital is documented in testimonials. The average grade but also certificates for certain language skills are regarded as decisive criteria for being allocated to a particular type of school, for obtaining access to higher education or to vocational training. Consequently, linguistic capital determines the educational and professional career. What is considered relevant knowledge, for example, whether Latin and Ancient Greek are of higher value than Italian or Russian, is influenced by the groups with the largest volume of capital – policy makers. Hence, schools as institutions and teachers as their actors produce and reproduce the existing linguistic power relations (cf. Bourdieu, 1990, p. 20).

Following this conceptual framework, immigrant teachers would play an important role in transforming the linguistic market of school. Being persons of authority and representing a societal group with power themselves, they would be able to question the existing language hierarchy in their feedback on immigrant languages and represent the legitimacy of migrant languages in everyday interactions (see also, Amosa Burgess & Fiti, this volume). However, research on new immigrant teachers is extremely scarce, as teachers from other countries are rarely integrated into the national school system. Hence, their actual potential for transforming the monolingual mindset at school remains unclear. In order to investigate this question, one specific educational context has been selected. In the next chapter, we thus turn to this specific context where multilingual staff were purposely integrated in a mainstream school.

3.2 Contextual framework

The study takes place in Hamburg, which is a city-state in Northern Germany. Normally, newly arrived pupils in Hamburg attend a preparatory class called IVK[3] for one year, which focuses on the systematic acquisition of German as a second language. After this

3   Internationale Vorbereitungsklasse = international preparatory class.

year, they pass on to the mainstream system. In contrast, the school our research is based on educates newly arrived pupils in an *integrative* way (Dewitz & Massumi, 2017, p. 32). Already after a few weeks, the pupils are assigned to mainstream classes and get language support in a preparatory class once a day. By doing so, the school represents a special case in the educational landscape of Hamburg.

When the school started a preparatory class in October 2015, they employed a multilingual cultural mediator, Mrs. Akbar[4]. In August 2018, they employed a multilingual educational consultant for Romani children, Mrs. Albu. Following the presented theoretical background on language as capital and multilingual actors' role as change agents on the linguistic market of school, the following questions arise:

- Which reasons and expectations are linked to the employment on behalf of the decision makers?
- How do multilingual educators themselves perceive their role with regard to multilingualism in the mainstream school system?
- If so, how do they use their multilingual repertoire while working with newly arrived pupils?

3.3 Methodology
3.3.1 Data collection
This paper focuses on data from an ongoing dissertation research project[5]. In order to answer the presented questions on the perspective

---

4   All names are pseudonyms.
5   The project is called "Language education during the transition from preparatory to mainstream class: An ethnographic study on experiences of newly arrived pupils." The field research of two years consists of participatory observations, informal conversations and qualitative interviews with students, teachers and educational staff. These data will be presented elsewhere, as it is beyond the scope of the present paper (Plöger, forthcoming).

of policy makers and multilingual staff, we will draw on interviews and participant observation of their pedagogical practice. In order to access the perception of multilingualism on different levels, interviews were conducted with policy makers as well as school employers and the multilingual actors themselves. Hence, the paper is based on the following data: four guideline-based interviews with the teacher of the preparatory class (Andrea Berger), the cultural mediator of the school (Leyla Akbar), the educational consultant of the school (Marina Albu), and the director of the department of refugee education (Lucas Romano), as well as an informal conversation with the head teacher of the school (Ludwin Hildebrandt). The interviews and informal conversation provide the main data of our analysis, but they are complemented by excerpts of protocols from the participatory observation. This allows us to enrich the experts' perspective by using very specific examples of multilingual practices in classroom interactions.

3.3.2 Data analysis

Subsequent to the data collection, interviews were transcribed and field notes were developed to protocols that contain "thick description" (Geertz, 1983). The data analysis aims at reconstructing (1) the (self-)perception of the multilingual staff's role in school, and (2) the multilingual practices in (classroom) interactions.

In order to reconstruct perceptions and self-perceptions, the conducted interviews and informal conversations were analyzed according to coding methods of the Grounded Theory (Charmaz, 2014): First, we coded the transcripts initially in order to determine "analytical themes" (Breidenstein et al., 2015, p. 17; translation S.P.). This allowed us to identify those themes that were relevant both to our research questions and to the participants themselves. If they repeated themes and aspects during the interviews, we interpreted them as being significant. Mrs. Akbar, the cultural mediator of the school, for example, repeated several times how she gained the trust of the newly arrived pupils by using some words in their family language. We coded all those sequences with the code "Language as access to the children". In presenting the data, we would only refer to one of those quotes.

Second, we re-coded those relevant sequences axially in order to identify connections between the codes, as well as overlapping, and contradictory themes in the interviews. This made it possible to develop the categories that are central to our research question with reference to our theoretical background.

As all observation protocols of this research project have been coded initially, we were able to identify sequences relevant to our research question there, too. Those sequences were coded in the same way as described above in order to find examples of multilingual practices that would fit or contradict the findings of the interviews.

3.3.3 Data representation

To represent the data, we will directly quote the most concise examples. Due to the ethnographic methodology, we are further able to extend our analysis beyond the quoted examples and to relate them to the larger context. Additional information from interviews and observation protocols were thus paraphrased if not directly quoted. Direct interview quotations and excerpts from observation protocols will be indented and italicized if longer than two lines.

Interviews were conducted and observation protocols were written in German by the PhD researcher herself. When translating them into English, we tried to remain as close as possible to the sense. Therefore, language mistakes were not adjusted.

4. Findings and analysis

As shown in the contextual framework, the school employed two multilingual pedagogues in the last three years. Our analysis provides evidence that this employment is based on the consensual valuation of multilingualism as being aspirational between policy makers, the school itself, and its actors. The following analysis shows how multilingualism is valued by different actors and how those perceptions reflect in everyday interaction. Hence, the analysis is divided into two major categories: the role of multilingual staff (4.1) and multilingualism (4.2). Each category is subdivided into several themes in order to point out specific aspects.

4.1 The role of multilingual staff
This category contains the aspects employment (4.1.1), function (4.1.2) and self-perception of multilingual staff (4.1.3).

4.1.1 Employment
Lucas Romano, director of the department of refugee education, explains that schools in Hamburg get financial resources from the municipality by way of public grants if they have preparatory classes. These grants enable schools to employ cultural mediators, for instance. People who are interested in becoming cultural mediators can attend a training at the State Institute for Teacher Training and School Development (LI). This allows the department to implement quality assurance and provide "a real curriculum: What do I have to know about school in Hamburg?" (Interview, 10.10.2018). This demonstrates the expectation that cultural mediators have to be well informed about the school system.

The official flyer about cultural mediators calls them "Bridge-builders in the education system" and explains that they can help with communication difficulties "due to their linguistic and cultural knowledge and a specific interest in the education system" (LI; translation S.P.). This underlines the expectation pointed out by Mr. Romano and highlights that cultural mediators have a certain "linguistic and cultural knowledge" that might be interpreted as being multilingual and/or cultural (cf. 2.2 on critical discussion).

Leyla Akbar, cultural mediator of the school, was employed in autumn 2015 when the school set up a preparatory class as a reaction to the high numbers of immigrants. Prior to that, Mrs. Akbar already worked for the school on an honorary basis helping with translations and parental conversations. Hence, the school's staff and principal knew Mrs. Akbar and her work, which led to the employment. The school's conference (consisting of teachers, parents, and pupils) decided collectively about the employment. Before starting work, Mrs. Akbar completed a course for cultural mediation. As her "years of experience" (Interview, 12.12.2018) were accepted, Mrs. Akbar did not have to do the whole training, however. She works part time (75%) in school and part time (25%) in migrant organizations on an honorary basis.

The school's head teacher, Ludwin Hildebrandt, emphasizes that the whole teaching staff supports the decision about the employment of Mrs. Akbar. With regard to financial resources, he explains that they arranged the post by economizing elsewhere. Apparently, the public grants mentioned by Mr. Romano were not sufficient.

Since August 2018, Marina Albu has worked as an educational consultant at the school, taking special care of Romani children. After a training at the LI to supplement her training as a cultural mediator, she had the option to choose a school she wanted to work for, according to her statement. Mrs. Albu works half-time at the school. In addition, she continues her previous work as an interpreter. In the following, we will clarify the function of those roles at the school.

4.1.2 Function

Mr. Romano describes the functions of cultural mediators as being "active, somewhere in the triangle of parents-pupils-school" (Interview, 10.10.2018) (see also Abas, this volume). The brief comment that cultural mediators could, for instance, support teachers in the classroom by "promoting *their* language group" shows that he expects a cultural mediator to be a multilingual person (cf.

2.2 for "othering"). This is in line with the official information document of the LI. Nonetheless, neither Mr. Romano nor the LI state it explicitly, which can be analyzed as being totally obvious to them. A multilingual repertoire as well as the active use of it seems to be an unspoken condition for working as a cultural mediator.

This can also be seen in the actual work of Mrs. Akbar. Participatory observation for almost a year provides evidence about her functions: she works as an interpreter; she represents the first point of contact for newly arrived pupils and their parents and accompanies them from then on; she visits pupils at home; she gives extra classes for pupils who need special support in learning German; she organizes excursions, debates, and co-ops; she runs a swimming class for newly arrived pupils, and much more. The diversity of her duties stands in line with the vague description provided by Mr. Romano. Whereas Mr. Romano describes the work rather as an auxiliary work – "It may be joining lessons [. . .]. It may be organizing parents' evenings. It may be translating a flyer" (Interview 10.10.2018) – Mrs. Akbar points out the importance of her work for the pupils as well as for herself.

Mrs. Albu, the educational consultant for Romani children, describes her function as follows:

> *Me as an educational consultant, I should be available as teacher, which means teaching language and history; I should be available as social worker, which means building bridges between family, pupils and schools, colleagues; I should be available as interpreter for discussions with parents.* (Interview 15.11.2018)

When asked whether she is actually teaching, she says no and outlines that her position has been newly created and that the school is still in the process of determining her actual functions. At the moment, she primarily works as a social worker and gives individual tuition to a Romanian-speaking girl who arrived a few months ago.

We will now focus on *how* both women perceive their position and their role in school.

4.1.3 Self-perception of the multilingual staff

Mrs. Akbar is enormously proud of being "elected" by the school's conference: "And I was *elected*, I was elected by the parents, the pupils and colleagues *and* the school administration" (Interview 12.12.2018). She emphasizes the word "elected" and says it two times. Furthermore, she names the groups that elected her and points out that she also has been elected by the school administration which underlines her pride.

Furthermore, Mrs. Akbar perceives the employment not as her right but as an opportunity for herself. She emphasizes that she worked for 20 years on an honorary basis before getting the position as cultural mediator. Through the employment she finally got a secure legal status, after fleeing from Afghanistan and living in Germany for 23 years. She says that she is "thankful" for the position and traces it to specific actors of the school, inter alia, the school administrator. She repeats the word "thankful" several times and describes her job as "standing on solid ground." She says, "But now I'm happy, so I gladly come to work here, *very* gladly." This makes clear, that she perceives her job very positively.

Mrs. Akbar says ironically that she is a cultural mediator as she knows a lot about "all kinds of cultures." Her focus on culture extends throughout the interviews. She often stresses her own culture as well as her knowledge about "*lots* of cultures," for instance through journeys and visits. She values this knowledge as a certain form of capital saying, "For my work as a cultural mediator, it is very very important that you have some knowledge about these cultures. If you have that, you manage to solve 60 or 70% of all problems on your own." So she indirectly says that most of the "problems" are culture-based. She perceives her role as one who shows newly arrived pupils and families how to "adapt" to the German system and culture:

"They have their circle and culture. Of course, I don't think it's bad but they should adapt a little more."

In her statements, the role of her multilingualism often coincides with her cultural knowledge (cf. language as capital in 3.1). We will take a closer look at this when presenting the findings of the category *multilingualism* (4.2).

Mrs. Albu emphasizes the fact that she, herself, has chosen the school (and not the other way around). In contrast to Mrs. Akbar, she sees her employment as her right and not as an opportunity to be thankful for. She also points out her prior working places (European Commission, Parliament, and Court of Justice). She strongly emphasizes her qualification.

As well as Mrs. Akbar, Mrs. Albu combines language and culture with regard to her functions in school. As educational consultant, she is explicitly employed for Romani children, but she says:

> *It also is a question of self-determination. Most will say that they aren't Romani, they say that they are Romanian and then I say that's okay, or Serbian and I say that's okay, too, I know your language, too and I help you, too, even if you're not Romani.* (Interview 15.11.2018)

Mrs. Albu does not limit her function to Romani children, which is her official target group, but extends her help to all pupils whose language she speaks. The relationship between language and culture is demonstrated when she answers the question of whether she thinks that a lot works through the use of different languages:

> *Yes of course, of course! I once had a pupil who was perceived as being very problematic here in school. And when he came to me and I talked to him in Romani, he couldn't stop laughing because he had never seen that a teacher spoke his language. And he really*

was good-natured during the discussion, being always polite and kind and he promised to join. And it has a certain impact when somebody of your culture, of your community comes and knows your rules from home and then you can't cheat anymore. (Interview 15.11.2018)

In this quote, we see two issues: First, her experience of a child's reaction toward her use of his family language, which we will discuss when talking about the pupils' multilingualism. Second, her connection between language and culture. Just like Mrs. Akbar, Mrs. Albu perceives language and culture as interlinked and almost identical. The interesting thing about the quote is the last subset: "Then you can't cheat anymore." This underlines the "problematic" view of the pupils' behavior that Mrs. Akbar points out as well. Obviously, the work and function of both has to do with "problematic" children whose problems arises because of cultural aspects. As Mrs. Akbar and Mrs. Albu know "their" culture, the children can't take the cultural difference as an excuse. Both see their role in guiding them to "the German culture."

There seems to be an overall consensus that Mrs. Akbar and Mrs. Albu as multilingual – and multicultural – staff are "bridge-builders." The information document of the LI as well as Mrs. Albu use this term, which is also often cited in publications (see 2.2; Bräu et al., 2013). All agree that both women have specific linguistic and cultural competencies that they can use in their everyday interaction with pupils. Strikingly, both describe that they work especially with "problematic" children. As "bridge-builders" they can solve problems that arise because of cultural differences.

4.2 Multilingualism
In this chapter, we will focus on multilingualism in school. First, we will describe the multilingualism of Mrs. Akbar and Mrs. Albu

(4.2.1). Second, we will show how they and the teacher Mrs. Berger deal with the pupils' multilingualism. This also includes the role of the German language in school. Therefore, we will give exemplary insights into the interactions, using protocol excerpts from participatory observation (4.2.2).

4.2.1 The own multilingualism

In answer to the question of which languages she speaks, Mrs. Akbar says,

> I understand a little Turkish, Arabic, Russian, Polish, Indian, Iraqi, so now Kurdish and I also speak my mother tongue. That is Dari and Farsi, it's similar. So I also know Farsi perfectly and I know Pashto perfectly. (Interview 12.12.2018)

She is a person who likes to explore languages through traveling and interacting with speakers. She does not rank her knowledge of different languages – except for the languages spoken in Afghanistan which she speaks "perfectly." But she names those languages she "understand[s] a little" before those she knows "perfectly." Mrs. Akbar is willing to explore languages she does not know and to use even little knowledge in any language in her interaction with pupils, which we will point out in detail in the next subtheme. Her good experiences guide her actions. Mrs. Akbar originally comes from Afghanistan. Her own migrant background plays an important role for her work with newly arrived pupils. She points out that she often reflects on her own situation coming to an unknown country without speaking the majority language.

Mrs. Albu was raised bilingual, speaking Romanian and Romani. She describes these two languages and English as her "working languages" with reference to her job as a professional interpreter. She says that she learned French at school and names Russian, saying,

"Unfortunately, I don't know Russian, I can only read." She learned German as her seventh language when she came to Germany 13 years ago. Mrs. Albu ranks her language knowledge and judges, for instance, that she does not know Russian even though she can read the language.

She actively uses her multilingual repertoire in school, as we can see in her statement cited above (cf. 4.1.3): she helps pupils using a language they speak. However, she does not see her multilingualism as being related to her employment. She says that it was rather important to have *any* educational consultant. This is contradicted by the perception of the parents, however:

> *When I introduced myself to the parents on the first day of school [. . .], my work itself wasn't important, wasn't interesting, but my multilingualism. They were surprised and it caused positive feedback. [. . .] If something positive can be achieved through it [the multilingualism], that's okay to me.* (Interview 15.11.2018)

She perceives her function as an educational consultant to be reduced to her multilingualism by the parents. However, this fact does not upset her. In contrary, she is glad to achieve positive outcomes through her linguistic capital (cf. 3.1).

In the following section, we will present how Mrs. Akbar and Mrs. Albu use their multilingualism with regard to the multilingualism of the pupils. Furthermore, we will outline how Mrs. Berger as teacher of the preparatory class deals with the pupils' multilingualism and which role the German language plays in interactions.

4.2.2 The pupils' multilingualism

When Mrs. Akbar is asked how she uses her multilingual repertoire in the interaction with pupils, she describes what it does with the children when she uses or tries to use their family languages. In doing so, she focuses on the children's well-being[6]. For her, language can be a key to well-being. Besides this socio-emotional aspect of multilingualism, she also points out a functional aspect. She explains that she integrates multilingualism into classroom interaction through dictionaries and mobile phone translations. This is particularly interesting, as she does not focus on her own multilingualism and its integration in classroom interaction, but on multilingualism in general.

As mentioned above, Mrs. Akbar says that she often puts herself in the pupil's position by referring to her own migration background. This is how she "directly find[s] a way," meaning an access to the pupils. She even points out that the job would "not be easy to accomplish" if "one is not affected oneself." She tells three anecdotes showing how she gains the pupils' trust using some words in their family languages when they first came to school. We would like to present one as an example:

> *Haias didn't want here, he cried so loudly and I said, in Russian I said to him "Come on, don't cry, everything will be fine". And he came to me, took me like this and kissed and said: "Mum, she knows Russian"* [Mrs. Akbar laughs]. *I said "But don't fool yourself please, little". He said "That's enough!" The next day he came at 7.30h. By chance, I was here, I looked, and he sat outside. He knocked on the door and said "Open the door" in Russian. I opened the door and then directly* [Mrs. Akbar laughs and shows a hug with her arms]. (Interview 12.12.2018)

Even if Mrs. Akbar does not speak Russian and only knows a few words, she uses the language in order to calm down Haias. From this

6   The pupils' well-being plays a central role in the interactions. However, we are not able to draw detailed attention to it at this point. For further information on this, please refer to Van Der Wildt et al. (2017).

moment on, she becomes an important reference person for the boy. She describes her use of the pupil's family languages as follows: "And by doing so, I can also win their confidence and then also give them this security."

Mrs. Albu also uses the family languages of the pupils she advises. She has had similar experiences regarding the pupils' reactions as Mrs. Akbar. As cited above (cf. 4.1.3), a Romani-speaking boy could not stop laughing when Mrs. Albu used "his" language. According to Mrs. Albu, he showed a friendly and cooperative behavior in the later discussion.

Mrs. Albu accompanies Felicia, a Romanian-speaking girl who had only been in Germany few months when they started an individual tuition two times a week in September. Mrs. Albu teaches her not only the German language but also shows her how to learn autonomously by explaining and training her in the use of a dictionary, for instance: "This makes her independent, obviously. And she is happy, it's a feeling of success 'Ah, I have the solution with me. I only have to know how to deal with it.'" (Interview 15.11.2018). Mrs. Albu thus helps her to help herself.

Mrs. Albu speaks German and Romanian with Felicia. She agrees that it is a great opportunity for Felicia to speak Romanian with her and to ask questions. The researcher has observed Felicia not only since September, but also before the summer break: she seemed to be a shy girl that did not talk much. In the interaction with Mrs. Albu the researcher got a totally different impression about Felicia, which we would like to point out with an exemplary excerpt from a protocol shortly after the start of school in September:

I hear Felicia telling Mrs. Albu something in Romanian, with a broad smile. First I don't understand what she is talking about but then I hear the word "cacao" and Mrs. Albu asks "la mensa"? [which is similar to the German word "Mensa" for "canteen"].

This is why I suppose that Felicia might tell that she drank hot chocolate in the canteen. She then turns back to the worksheet, still smiling. (Observation protocol, 03.09.2018)

In the interaction with Mrs. Albu, Felicia seems much more open and laughs a lot. This excerpt stands for many similar observations. After some time, the researcher could also observe this behavior in the preparatory as well as in her mainstream class, without being accompanied by Mrs. Albu. The many examples suggest that the work with Mrs. Albu gives Felicia self-confidence and a sense of well-being.

When newly arrived pupils come to an unknown country and go to school for the first time, "an open and constructive way of handling multilingualism" can help in facilitating their start (Fürstenau, 2017, p. 52; translation S.P.). Mrs. Akbar and Mrs. Albu give them security by using or by trying to use their family language – independent of their degree of mastery. They not only give them security but also appreciation. The pupils take from the experience that their family languages are recognized in school.

When the interview with Mrs. Berger, teacher of the preparatory class, comes to the aspect of multilingualism, the first thing she points out is the fact that she also teaches English to the newly arrived pupils. As the pupils are taught in an integrative way, Mrs. Berger is not obligated to teach them subjects other than German. However, it is important to her. This may be due to the fact that she is an English teacher originally. Indirectly, this shows a certain hierarchization of languages, with German and English as being important languages to know – i.e., important capital.

Mrs. Berger also points out that one should "absolutely" take up the pupils' multilingualism in class and directly connects it to "multiculturalism": "I think it's really important that they never forget their roots" (Interview 28.08.2018). As for Mrs. Akbar and Mrs. Albu, language for Mrs. Berger is directly linked to the culture and cultural heritage that she would like to maintain. She explains that this was the reason why she dedicated herself to the Arabic class. Nonetheless, Mrs. Berger draws a distinction between situations where the use of multilingualism is obvious (e.g. when pupils need help and translations) and others, where it is not allowed (e.g. when pupils discuss). She, as the teacher, takes control over the use of languages other than German. However, she does not make the legitimate and illegitimate use of languages plain to the pupils. Thus, many situations could be observed in which pupils were either reprimanded for using their family language or even asked to use it:

When they start talking in Arabic, [Mrs. Berger] gets angry and says, that the game does not work like this and if anybody said one more word in Arabic, he or she would not be allowed to participate anymore. (Observation protocol, 20.08.2018)

[Mrs. Berger] then asks for the word "water well" in different languages (Arabic, Persian, Kurdish) and repeats the words the children tell her. (Observation protocol, 28.08.2018)

Mrs. Akbar also shows an ambivalent behavior toward the use of family languages. She sometimes initiates its use and sometimes prohibits it:

When Naim is ready with reading the exercise about syllables, Mrs. Akbar says: "We also have it [syllables] in our languages, e.g. in Arabic." She says an Arabic word and emphasizes each syllable. (Observation protocol, 24.09.2018)

Batin and Hafza speak in Arabic which is curbed by Mrs. Akbar: "Pscht, not in Arabic, please!" (Observation protocol, 03.09.2018)

Both women emphasize in the interviews that multilingualism is an important resource and appreciate the pupils' linguistic diversity. But they assume control over the use of languages. This demonstrates that language prohibitions are situative and personalized. This finding is in line with recent research emphasizing the tension between the task of the school to convey German language skills and to acknowledge the pupils' multilingualism at the same time (Huxel, 2018). And it shows that language prohibitions are imposed by monolingual German-speakers as well as by multilingual staff.

The prohibition of multilingualism is often directly referred to the German language. In all interviews, the acquisition of German is the focus of the education of newly arrived pupils. Knowledge of the majority language is considered the key to education.

Mrs. Berger says, "Everyone has to speak German" is the "headline of the class" (Interview 28.08.2018). As German is the common language of all pupils in the preparatory class, pupils are expected to speak German. She formulates language rules. Our observation shows that these rules remain vague in the preparatory class. There is no explicit rule, but Mrs. Berger consistently admonishes pupils who use their family language:

> *Listen girls, I would like to please you to speak German at school. In the tube and [at home] and everywhere in the world, you can speak Arabic."* (Observation protocol, 26.09.2018)

Mrs. Berger makes a difference between being inside and outside of school. In their free time, the pupils can talk whatever language they would like to; in school, they are expected to speak German.

Language prohibitions and rules are not only initiated by the educational staff but also by the pupils who, apparently, take over their behavior as shown in the following exemplary excerpts:

Mrs. Akbar is not yet present. "Fettah says something to the girls in Arabic. Naim [an Arabic-speaking boy] says quietly, "Not Arabic!" but the others don't seem to hear him or don't care about his objection. (Observation protocol, 03.09.2018)

Some pupils start talking in Arabic when Mrs. Akbar leaves the classroom in order to get her book. She directly comes back and says: "Firstly, not in Arabic, but in German and secondly, quiet!" When she leaves, the pupils continue talking in Arabic. Fettah says loudly: "In German, please!" (Observation protocol, 24.09.2018)

Naim and Fettah, both Arabic-speaking themselves, admonish their classmates for speaking in Arabic. Apparently, they internalized the language prohibitions.

This analysis is in line with the finding that teachers and educational staff in most countries, including Germany, continue to orient themselves toward a monolingual norm (see 2.1). This not only applies to monolingual German-speaking actors but also to multilingual actors in school. Moreover, even multilingual pupils seem to adapt and internalize these orientations. This raises the question as to whether the employment of multilingual staff really can achieve a multilingual turn. We will discuss this question with reference to the theoretical background in the next chapter, including implications and recommendations for policy makers as well as practitioners.

5. Discussion

With the aim of supporting newly arrived pupils as well as pupils with migrant backgrounds, multilingual staff were employed in school. Our findings show that this employment is the result of an extremely positive perception of multilingualism on all levels of agency: on behalf of policy makers, and on the level of decision makers at school as well as its staff. The qualitative data from interviews as well as participatory observation allow deep insights into how multilingual practices are valued by different actors and how these perceptions are reflected in everyday interaction. These findings could be reconstructed for the role of multilingual staff during their employment (4.1.1), with regard to their function at school (4.1.2) as well as the perceived high valorization on behalf of multilingual educational practitioners themselves (4.1.3). Hence, these findings reveal that multilingualism, on the one hand, is perceived as something natural and positive.

On the other hand, a closer look at multilingualism in everyday interaction (4.2) reveals discrepancies between policies and practices in school, which result in ambivalences on the actor's behalf. Sometimes, the use of multilingual resources is naturally integrated into class, whereas in other situations, it is reprimanded. This ambiguity shows that educational staff – irrespective of whether they are multi- or monolingual – are still uncertain about how to handle multilingualism in a system oriented toward monolingual norms. Interpreted in terms of Bourdieu's theory of language as capital and school as linguistic marketplace, these findings reveal that the goal of valuing and acknowledging the linguistic capital of the pupils is challenged by the norms and linguistic, as well as social, hierarchies of the school environment. At this point, the ethnographic method used for our study, particularly the participant observation, reveals its importance as it enabled us to document such ambiguities.

Hence, multilingual staff can play a key role for a multilingual turn, but they cannot achieve it if they are not supported by the whole system. The case we analyzed shows how first steps can be done: Mrs. Akbar and Mrs. Albu work in a school where they are supported by the teaching staff and the school's administration. This is still not the rule in German schools but an important and indispensable component for intercultural school development (Fürstenau, 2017). Both Mrs. Akbar and Mrs. Albu took special training at the LI before being employed as cultural mediator and educational consultant. In their work, they focus much more on culture than on language, which raises the question of whether the training emphasizes culture as well. For both, Mrs. Akbar and Mrs. Albu, it is absolutely obvious that they use their multilingual repertoire every day in order to help pupils. Nonetheless, they restrict the pupils' use of family languages to promote the acquisition of the majority language, German.

These results open a further question on the need to professionalize the existing multilingual practices. Hence, training programs must not only consist of elements with reference to culture and "bridge-building," but should especially emphasize the constructive handling and inclusion of multilingualism in everyday interaction and teaching practices. These findings are in line with results on language diversity management of multilingual teachers in other national contexts (Putjata, 2018). This allows us to draw the conclusion that, in future, training programs, as well as studies, must not only contain cultural aspects but should also focus on linguistic ones, in particular, as emphasizing cultural aspects often implies deficit-oriented and problem-oriented assumptions. Policy makers should further engage in promoting (heritage) language classes by introducing them as regular subjects.

However, despite these factors that could be improved, the school is on a good path to achieving a multilingual turn: all actors on all levels – the policy makers, school principals as well teaching staff – consider the reality as being multilingual.

6. Conclusion

The presented qualitative study from a selected secondary school in Hamburg allows deep insights into the possibilities and limitations of a "multilingual turn" in educational systems and the role of multilingual educational staff in this process. Our findings reveal that multilingual staff can play a decisive role in a multilingual school's development.

However, they also show that their presence as such is not sufficient. More complex changes on different levels of agencies are necessary starting from individual persons as policy and decision makers at school as well as processes of school development as a whole structural process. These changes should also include a specific training on linguistic diversity management in the classroom as well as the use of multilingual staff's own linguistic repertoires, which would encourage the acceptance of multilingualism as a capital, not only for multilingual educational practitioners or multilingual students themselves, but for the school and the modern society in times of globalization and transnational mobilities.

References

Allemann-Ghionda, C. & Pfeiffer, S. (2010). *Bildungserfolg, Migration und Zweisprachigkeit: Perspektiven für Forschung und Entwicklung*. Berlin: Frank & Timme.

Beauftragte für Migration, Flüchtlinge und Integration (2016). *11. Bericht der Beauftragten der Bundesregierung für Migration, Flüchtlinge und Integration - Teilhabe, Chancengleichheit und Rechtsentwicklung in der Einwanderungsgesellschaft Deutschland*. Retrieved from https://www.bundesregierung.de/Content/Infomaterial/BPA/IB/11-Lagebericht.

Blommaert, J. (2010). *The Sociolinguistics of Globalization*. Cambridge: Cambridge University Press.

Bourdieu, P. (1990). *Was heißt sprechen? Die Ökonomie des sprachlichen Tausches*. Wien: Braumüller.

Bourdieu, P. & Wacquant, L. (1996). *Reflexive Anthropologie*. Frankfurt a. M.: Suhrkamp.

Bräu, K., Georgi, V. B., Karakasoglu, Y., & Rotter, C. (2013). *Lehrerinnen und Lehrer mit Migrationshintergrund: Zur Relevanz eines Merkmals in Theorie, Empirie und Praxis*. Münster: Waxmann.

BReg. (2015). Rede von Bundeskanzlerin Angela Merkel beim Deutschen Fürsorgetag am 17. Juni 2015. Retrieved from http://www.bundesregierung. de/Content/DE/Rede/2015/06/2015-06-18-merkel-fuersorgetag.html.

Breidenstein, G., Hirschauer, S., Kalthoff, H., & Nieswand, B. (2015). *Ethnografie. Die Praxis der Feldforschung.* Konstanz: UVK.

Bührig, K. & Duarte, J. (2013). Zur Rolle lebensweltlicher Mehrsprachigkeit für das Lernen im Fachunterricht – ein Beispiel aus einer Videostudie der Sekundarstufe II. *Gruppendynamik und Organisationsberatung, 44*(3), 245–275.

Candelier, M., Camilleri-Grima, A., Castellotti, V., de Pietro, J-F., Lörincz, I., Meissner, F-J., Schröder-Sura, A., Noguerol, A., & Molinié, M. (2012). *A Framework of Reference for Pluralistic Approaches to Languages and Cultures. Competences and Resources.* Strasbourg: Council of Europe. Retrieved from http://carap.ecml.at/CARAP.

Charmaz, K. (2014). *Constructing grounded theory.* 2nd edition. Los Angeles: SAGE.

Cummins, J. (2010). *Language, power, and pedagogy: Bilingual children in the crossfire. Bilingual education and bilingualism.* Clevedon England, Buffalo N.Y.: Multilingual Matters.

Dewitz, N. von & Massumi, M. (2017). Schule im Kontext aktueller Migration. Rechtliche Rahmenbedingungen, schulorganisatorische Modelle und Anforderungen an Lehrkräfte. In: N. McElvany et al. (Eds.), *Ankommen in der Schule. Chancen und Herausforderungen bei der Integration von Kindern und Jugendlichen mit Fluchterfahrung.* Münster: Waxmann, 27–40.

Döll, M. & Knappik, M. (2015). Institutional mechanisms of inclusion and exclusion in Austrian pre-service teacher training. *Tertium Comparationis. Journal Für International Und Interkulturell Vergleichende Erziehungswissenschaft, 21 (2),* 185–204.

Fürstenau, S. (2015). Transmigration und transnationale Familien. Neue Perspektiven der Migrationsforschung als Herausforderung für die Schule. In R. Leiprecht & A. Steinbach (Eds.), *Schule in der Migrationsgesellschaft. Ein Handbuch: Grundlagen – Diversität – Fachdidaktiken.* Debus, 143–156.

Fürstenau, S. (2017). Unterrichtsentwicklung in Zeiten der Neuzuwanderung. In N. McElvany, A. Jungermann, W. Bos, & H. G. Holtappels (Eds.), *Ankommen in der Schule. Chancen und Herausforderungen bei der Integration von Kindern und Jugendlichen mit*

Fluchterfahrung. Münster: Waxmann, 41–56.

Georgi, V. B., Ackermann, L., & Karakas, N. (2011). *Vielfalt im Lehrerzimmer. Selbstverständnis und schulische Integration von Lehrenden mit Migrationshintergrund in Deutschland.* Münster: Waxmann.

Geertz, C. (1983). Dichte Beschreibung. Beiträge zum Verstehen kultureller Systeme. Frankfurt am Main: Suhrkamp.

Gogolin, I. (2005). *Migration und sprachliche Bildung. Interkulturelle Bildungsforschung: Bd. 15.* Münster: Waxmann. Retrieved from http://www.socialnet.de/rezensionen/isbn.php?isbn=978-3-8309-1541-6.

Huxel, K. (2018). Berufskultur und Lehrersein. Kulturtheoretische Zugänge in der Lehrerforschung. *Zeitschrift Für Interpretative Schul- Und Unterrichtsforschung, 7*(1–2018), 109–121.

Ingersoll, R. & May, H. (2016). *Minority Teacher Recruitment, Employment and Retention: 1987 to 2013.* Stanford: CA.

Irvine, J. T. & Gal, S. (2000). Language ideology and linguistic differentiation. In P. V. Kroskrity (Ed.), *School of American Research advanced seminar series. Regimes of language: Ideologies, polities, and identities.* Santa Fe: School of American Research Press, 35–84.

Karakaşoğlu, Y., Wojciechowicz, A. A., Bandorski, S., & Kul, A. (2013). *Zur Bedeutung des Migrationshintergrundes im Lehramtsstudium. Quantitative und qualitative empirische Grundlagenstudie und Reflexion von Praxismaßnahmen an der Universität Bremen.*

Lengyel, D. & Rosen, L. (2015). Minority teachers in different educational contexts: Introduction. *Tertium Comparationis. Journal Für International Und Interkulturell Vergleichende Erziehungswissenschaft. 21*(2), 153–160.

Melo-Pfeifer, S. & Helmchen, C. (2018). *Plurilingual literacy practices at school and in teacher education.* Berlin: Peter Lang.

MSW NRW (2012). Mehr Lehrkräfte mit Zuwanderungsgeschichte. Handlungskonzept. *Ministerium Für Schule Und Weiterbildung Des Landes Nordrhein-Westfalen.*

Plöger, S. (forthcoming). Chancen und Grenzen einer integrativen Beschulung für die Sprachbildung neu zugewanderter Schüler_innen. Ein ethnographischer Einblick in einer Hamburger Stadtteilschule. *InfoDaF, Themenheft "Vorbereitungsklassen".*

Poarch, G. & Bialystok, E. (2017). Assessing the implications of migrant multilingualism for language education. *Zeitschrift Für Erziehungswissenschaft, 20*(2), 175–191.

Prediger, S. (2011). *Mathematiklernen unter Bedingungen der Mehrsprachigkeit: Stand und Perspektiven der Forschung und Entwicklung in Deutschland.* Münster: Waxmann.

Pulinx, R. & van Avermaet, P. (2015). Integration in Flanders (Belgium) – Citizenship as achievement: How intertwined are 'citizenship' and 'integration' in Flemish language policies? *Journal of Language and Politics, 14*(3), 335–358.

Putjata, G. (2018). Immigrant teachers' integration and transformation of the linguistic market in Israel. *Language and Education, 21*(2), 1–17.

Van Der Wildt, A., Van Avermaet, P., & Van Houtte, M. (2017). Multilingual school population: ensuring school belonging by tolerating multilingualism. *International Journal of Bilingual Education and Bilingualism, 20*(7), 868–882.

Young, A. S. (2017). "Non, moi je lui dis pas en turc, ou en portugais, ou en, j'sais pas moi en arabe": Exploring teacher ideologies in multilingual/ cultural preschool contexts in France. *Bellaterra Journal of Teaching & Learning Language & Literature, 10*(2), 11–24.

CHAPTER 10

New to the classroom: Experiences of attitudes to translanguaging

Vesna Busic and Kirk P. H. Sullivan

1. Introduction

After a recent public lecture in a café, an experienced teacher came up to us and asked if we really meant that students should use their home languages in school as this might help them solve questions more effectively as they could use all their cognitive resources. This teacher continued that school is the only place that some students use Swedish, and we have to make sure they use it all the time or their Swedish will not improve. This experienced teacher was not convinced by the arguments presented in the lecture, but rather appeared to promote a view of language similar to the ones from early last century when Welsh could not be spoken in school, when Indigenous languages could not be spoken in school, and when any language other than the majority national language could not be spoken in school, even when the other language was the student's strongest linguistic resource for thinking and communicating.

This way of thinking about a language in school is surprising and hints at a strong current of language ideology and attitudes that support monolingualism and Swedish as the dominant national language. This way of thinking jars with current language in education policies in Sweden that, among other things, support mother tongue development through mother tongue education and Indigenous and national minority language education, as evidenced in much Swedish research on translanguaging (See, for example, Paulsrud, Rosén, Straszer, & Wedin, 2018a). In Umeå, for example, 33 mother tongue languages, including Indigenous and national minority languages, are currently taught to school pupils from school year 0 to school year 13.

Ekberg (2017) overviewed Swedish education policies, specifically in relation to the political and social ideas that have created the current conflicting discourses in law and policy. There is a political discourse in Sweden about protecting the status of Swedish from English. This discourse is perhaps stronger than the discourse in the Netherlands about protecting the status of Dutch, and perhaps weaker than some of the discourse in Denmark in relation to protecting Danish. However, it has resulted in the status of Swedish being confirmed in law. This has been coupled, Ekberg (2017) argued, with a "monolingualizing component embedded in the different language policy measures to promote the integration of newly arrived pupils" (p.93), that these newly arrived pupils should learn Swedish as quickly as possible and move to regular instruction in school together with Swedish speakers. This, as Ekberg (2017) pointed out, creates not only a linguistic hierarchy with Swedish at the top, but also a conflict with educational policies promoting multilingualism, Indigenous and minority language rights, and investment in mother tongue teaching.

The teacher's way of thinking about school students' linguistic resources expressed after the public lecture in a café repeated itself in discussion with two final-year teacher trainee students who were running an intervention study in a primary school class for their final degree independent project paper – all teacher trainee students in Sweden are required to write an independent project paper as part of their degree program. These two teacher trainee students were introducing signage in a classroom to support communication and studying what happened when it was introduced. It gradually became clearer in our discussion that in this classroom the school students were not allowed to use any language other than Swedish, and the introduction of signage was to facilitate communication when Swedish was not understood by all. As teacher trainers, we were surprised at the classroom environment the final-year teacher trainee students had encountered.

Together, our two illustrative examples paint of picture of school that does not align with the ideas or practices of translanguaging; something that forms one of the core elements of teacher training at our university. How translanguaging is understood and taught at Swedish universities is presented by Paulsrud, Rosén, Straszer, and Wedin (2018b) in their introduction to their anthology *Transspråkande i svenska utbildningssammanhang [Translanguaging in the Swedish educational context]* (Paulsrud et al., 2018a). They summarized translanguaging based on Mazak's (2017) definition. Here we give a translation of Paulsrud's (2018b) summary including an additional aspect they add in their discussion based on García (2009).

1. Translanguaging is a language ideology based in multilingualism as norm.
2. Translanguaging is a theory about bi/multilingualism that builds on multilingual experiences and claims that bilingual or multilingual speakers do not separate their language into separate systems but rather they are integrated, linguistic repertoires that they use to navigate in their multilingual everyday life and existence.
3. Translanguaging is an educational approach in which teachers and students are allowed to use all their linguistic and semiotic resources in teaching and learning.
4. Translanguaging is a form of practice in which people use their linguistic and semiotic resources in an integrated manner that is more than, but includes, code-switching.

5. Translanguaging is transformative, in relation to our understanding both of language and language use, and of the lives that multilingual speakers create through their language use.
6. Translanguaging confirms social justice as it goes hand-in-hand with equality, and multilingual students' right to education and social inclusion.

We recognize that there is a continuum between full translanguaging in the classroom and forbidding other languages from being spoken in the classroom, but we did not expect that today's teacher trainee education, including its positive view on translanguaging and using all the school students' linguistic resources, would not be reflected school contexts.

Naturally, this awakened our curiosity about how teacher trainee students experience translanguaging in the classroom during their teaching practice. After teaching practice, we always hold a debriefing conversation with the teacher trainee students to give us more general feedback about how well we had prepared them for their teaching practice. Not least as we recognize that during teaching practice, teacher trainee students frequently experience a dissonance between current research and pedagogical ideas, and the advice given by the school-based mentors who are currently teaching in schools. Over a number of years teacher trainee students have informally reported encountering teaching practice mentors who discourage all languages other the national main language to be used in the classroom. This action is the opposite of what these teacher trainee students have been taught in university and the research articles they have studied as part of their teacher training degrees.

This chapter considers the experiences and observations of teacher trainee students who are new to the classroom. These teacher trainee students enter classrooms without the baggage of "experience," school tradition, and similar elements that delimit what is permitted in the classroom (see also Chen, this volume). They arrive with theoretical knowledge and untested teaching skills that are based in national policy and the university curriculum they are following. This allows them to experience and observe the tension between policy and practice in ways that experienced teachers may fail to do.

Given our recent surprise about the forbiddance of the use of languages other than Swedish in school in the 21st century, in combination with the informal reports from teacher trainees returning from their teaching practice, we decided to invite Swedish as an Additional Language teacher trainees to participate in a formal focus group discussion after they had returned from teaching practice, to systematically discuss translanguaging, experience of teaching practice and potential dissonance between university teaching and learning, and school practice. It is this focus group discussion that forms the basis of this chapter.

Much of the literature reports on successful intervention studies and action research studies conducted together with teachers with positive views toward translanguaging. Further teachers who allow their teaching to be observed by researchers tend to be those whose views align with the research objective. These studies may not reflect the situation among the less research-interested teachers or in schools that are not influenced by university staff. We felt that accessing teacher trainee student experiences of teaching practice would provide a potentially more authentic snapshot of contemporary school than the ones given by much of the contemporary Swedish translanguaging research that has been published in the archived literature. For example, the research published in Paulsrud (2018a), the research looking at the perceptions of the linguistic potential of translanguaging (e.g., Torpsten, 2018), and interventions projects such as Svensson (2016), which demonstrated that translanguaging is possible in classrooms with many languages even if the teachers do not speak these languages, but only when the teachers are flexible in their educational practice and comfortable in involving mother tongue teachers in their teaching. Most of this research confirms what Williams (1994, 1996) argued. Translanguaging in the classroom leads to broader and deeper knowledge, along with the skills to access this knowledge, yet whether translanguaging is accepted figures infrequently in the archived literature.

1.1. Context of the study

The context of the study is Sweden, a country with indigenous languages, the Sámi languages, which are traditionally spoken in Sápmi, a region that today is divided across four countries (Finland, Norway, Russia, and Sweden) and four other official minority languages (Finnish, Romani, Yiddish, and Meänkieli). Moreover, Sweden has recently accepted many asylum seekers: 54,259 persons in 2013 (The Swedish Migration Agency, 2014) and 162,877 persons in 2015 (The Swedish Migration Agency, 2016). School students who speak languages other than Swedish at home are entitled to mother language teaching if there are at least five children in a municipality with that language who request such teaching. Currently in Umeå, a city of around 100,000 inhabitants, mother tongue teaching is offered in 33 languages. Sweden is therefore a country in which many school classes will have students who speak more than one language, and where for some students a language other than Swedish is the stronger language. This is the case when the student is studying Swedish as an Additional Language.

Teacher training in Sweden has changed many times over the years, and although there are national learning outcomes and some structural requirements set by the Swedish government, how these are achieved is left to each university to decide (see also Plöger & Putjata, this volume). There are national quality evaluations, so variation is in many respects delimited by this process of quality control.

The specific context for this study is a Swedish university town north of Stockholm with the full range of teaching training programs, and schools in and in the near vicinity of the town. All the schools have experience in welcoming teacher trainee students for their teaching practice and have experienced school-based mentors who work with the teacher trainee students during their teaching practice. Teacher trainee students are assigned a school-based mentor for their teaching practice. These mentors are experienced members of staff who have ideally also followed a brief mentor training program provided by the university. The mentors support and guide the teacher trainee students on a daily basis during their teaching practice. During teaching practice the teacher trainee students are observed by a university lecturer at least once. The observed teaching is then discussed with the teacher trainee student, and the teacher trainee student submits a written report that is examined. The context of this study is hence authentic.

2. Methodology

The aim of the present study is to gain an understanding of how those new to the classroom experience and observe the tension between their academic teaching training and their experiences when new to the classroom, specifically their experiences of attitudes to translanguaging. First, to provide an understanding of the directives teachers of Swedish as an Additional Language need to follow, including how they should assess their students, we undertook a preliminary discursive analysis of language in education directives, and for this analysis we selected the two curriculum documents for Swedish as an Additional Language (Skolverket, 2011, 2018) and the directives for the Introduction programs (Skolverket, 2019) that the teacher trainee students had taught during their teaching practice. Second, we designed a qualitative focus-group study based on semi-structured interview questions that consisted of four phrases: first, a discussion of experiences during teaching practice; second, a more researcher-directed phase focusing on aspects that were difficult to unify with their university-based learning; third, their understanding of translanguaging; and fourth, a discussion about their perceptions of their teaching practice mentors' understandings of translanguaging.

The research questions we pose are:

1. How is multilingualism represented in Swedish as an Additional Language curricula?
2. How do teacher trainee students define translanguaging and multilingualism in educational settings?
3. What are teacher trainee students' general experiences of teaching practice?
4. What things that teacher trainee students are taught at university do they have difficulty unifying with their teacher trainee student experience?
5. What are teacher trainee students' experiences of their mentors' attitudes toward translanguaging?

2.1 Participants

The criteria for participation in the study was that Swedish as an Additional Language was one of the disciplines the teacher trainee students were training to teach and that they had completed their second teaching practice. We decided to restrict participation to this group of teacher trainee students as it is in these classes that multilingualism is always present, and as Swedish as an Additional Language teachers, they have staffroom status on issues relating to linguistic best classroom practice for school students with other language backgrounds, as they are the specialists. Further, these teacher-trainee mentors are generally the teachers in a school who have studied most about multilingualism and education. We also decided to only include teacher trainee students after their second period of four weeks of teaching practice. From experience, we felt that the teacher trainee students might be too overwhelmed with the entire experience during their first teaching practice to have time to fully reflect and be able to contribute analytically to the focus group discussion. Three teacher trainee students who fitted our criteria agreed to participate. All were native speakers of Swedish and were advanced learners of English. One of the teacher trainee students also spoke Spanish. None of them spoke any of the languages spoken by the school pupils in the classes they taught during their teaching practice.

To give a greater understanding of our participants, we will now briefly overview the current structure of the teacher training at our university, which includes Swedish as an Additional Language as one of the teaching subjects, and the program that gives certification to teach at Upper Secondary (Gymnasiet) and the final three years of compulsory school, Lower Secondary (Högstadiet). Not only were those who participated in our focus group discussion following this program, but most teacher trainee students including Swedish as an Additional Language as one of their subjects follow this program as it gives them a greater choice of teaching positions after graduation.

The program requires that the teacher trainees have one other subject chosen from Art, English, French, Sport and Health Studies, Mathematics, Music, Swedish, Spanish, and German. Depending upon the combination of subjects, the degree is 10 semesters (5 years and 300 ECTS) or 11 semesters (5.5 years and 330 ECTS) long. This includes 210 or 240 ECTS in the two teaching subjects, depending on the national requirements for the chosen combination; 60 ECTS in what is called the educational core that considers the common aspects of teaching, policy, law, educational leadership, conflict, ethics, democracy, and assessment; and 30 ECTS of teaching practice in school. Swedish as an Additional Language provides 180 ECTS of the subject requirements and this means that the other subject has to provide 210 ECTS credits.

The teaching practice component of 30 ECTS is the total of both subjects and divided across two periods. Teacher trainee students in Swedish as an Additional Language have two periods of four weeks in two different schools, which is a total of eight weeks' teaching practice in the subject. Thus, even after their second teaching practice these teacher trainees can still be considered new to the classroom.

The three semesters of study, or 90 ECTS credits, at Umeå University is grounded in the principle that multilingualism is a resource in the classroom as "even if the class is being conducted in the dominant majority language only, students are constantly making sense of the new language through what they already know in their own language" (García & Seltzer, 2016, p. 21) and may want to translanguage with other members of the class and/or the teacher to make full use of the learning opportunity. Throughout the three semesters we continually return to the core topics of (1) multilingualism as a resource, (2) the problem with the label of "Swedish as an Additional Language," as it sends the message to the school students that the peers who have Swedish as their first language have better language skills, and (3) myths about school students studying Swedish as an Additional Language. Here we challenge the idea that these students only speak the other language at home and Swedish only at school and develop these into an understanding of dynamic use of languages without sharp boundaries among multilinguals. This allows the teaching of translanguaging in educational settings, such as the Swedish as an Additional Language classroom. Hence, our teacher trainee students are encouraged and supported in the use of translanguaging.

2.2 Data collection

The three teacher trainee students who agreed to participate in the study took part in a single focus group led by the first author. All the participants gave both written and oral informed consent following ethical guidelines (Swedish Research Council, 2017) with their written consent stored securely at Umeå University. All participants were informed that what they said and discussed would not affect their grades (which had already been set), and that they could leave the focus group discussion if they wanted without providing any reason for doing so. To increase anonymity, we do not report the participants' ages nor genders. We refer to the participants with gender-neutral names and their school placement (ie. the type of school in which they did their teaching practice): Kim-TTI, the teacher trainee student who undertook their teaching practice in a "Language Introduction" class; Storm-TTC, the teacher trainee student who undertook their teacher practice in a compulsory school class; and Alex-TTUS, the teacher trainee student who undertook their teaching practice in an upper-secondary school class.

The focus group discussions were conducted in an informal setting, which included a sofa and armchairs. The conversation was recorded using a mobile phone placed on the coffee table. The conversation was held solely in Swedish; the three teacher trainees were native Swedish speakers and none of them translanguaged into another language during the interviews. This included English, which might have been expected given that some literature in the area of translanguaging the teacher trainee students read in English. Three example questions (translated into English) that the first author used to stimulate participant discussion were (1) How would you describe your teaching practice in Swedish as an Additional Language? (2) I wonder what you think of when you hear the term "translanguaging"? and (3) Turning back to your classroom experiences, how would you describe translanguaging in the class and school that you were working in?

The protocol was used to assure that the main topics were covered, otherwise we allowed the discussion to develop naturally and at times topics became interwoven. The first author (Vesna Busic) led the focus-group discussion, and the conversation lasted around 50 minutes. Vesna is an experienced lecturer in Swedish as an Additional

Language and moved to Sweden as an adult from the Balkans. As Vesna teaches teacher trainee students specializing in Swedish as an Additional Language, she is an insider practitioner-researcher studying her teacher trainee students' experiences, perceptions, and attitudes. Thus, Vesna's position as an insider needs to be considered when interpreting the results presented and discussed in this chapter, even if Vesna is an outsider of the specific school contexts where the teacher trainees have their teaching practice. The interviewed teacher trainees do not appear to have been nervous or concerned to be interviewed by Vesna, one of their lecturers.

The second author (Kirk P. H. Sullivan) is a professor of linguistics and director of the Umeå University's postgraduate school within the field of the educational sciences, and supervises many students at BA, MA, and doctoral level, but does not teach or examine students of Swedish as an Additional Language. Kirk also moved to Sweden as an adult.

2.3 Data analysis

The focus group discussion was recorded and transcribed verbatim by the first author (Vesna Busic). Identifying information was removed and pseudonyms given to schools and teachers mentioned in the discussion. Both authors read the transcriptions and selected passages of the transcriptions, which they recursively grouped into themes aligned with the research questions. The outsider perspective of the second author is balanced by, and balances, the insider perspective of the first author. After we had decided on the quotes from the group discussions to illustrate our findings, the second author (Kirk P. H. Sullivan) translated these into English.

3. Findings

After first presenting our discursive analysis of language in education directives, we turn to the answers to our other four research questions, which provide a picture of how those new to teaching experience the dissonance between their university training and their teaching practice, specifically in relation to aspects of translanguaging and multilingualism. In this section, we foreground the teacher trainees' perspectives, experiences, and observations through English translations of their voices. In the presentation of our findings, we consider each research question in turn, even if the first research question was the one we asked last in the focus group. We did not want to influence the spontaneous reflections by immediately focusing the discussion around translanguaging as we hoped this would enter the conversation naturally, and it did. We also merge discussion into the presentation of our findings.

3.1 Discursive analysis of language in education directives

Teachers in Swedish as an Additional Language teach one of three national curricula in the subject: Introduction, Compulsory School, and Upper Secondary School. Here we focus on these curricula's references to multilingualism – there are no explicit references to translanguaging. That is, we do not present a full curriculum analysis of these curricula but rather focus on key concepts of direct relevance to this study, delimited to the groups taught by the teacher trainees participating in our study. We aim to provide the reader with an understanding of the context of our study. Further, the Introduction program for upper secondary school is an umbrella term for five similar, yet distinctive, programs and here we focus on the language program (Språkprogrammet) that is represented in our focus group discussion.

As mentioned above, the Introduction program represented among our teacher trainees is for upper-secondary-aged students. Thus, even if Swedish competence level progresses can be viewed as Introduction, Compulsory School, and then Upper Secondary School, this order does not follow school student age in this study. The Language

Introduction program's objective is to give the upper-secondary-aged students the Swedish skills to enter ordinary Upper Secondary School classes or another form of training to enter the job market. There are neither national goals nor a set structure for any of the introduction programs. School students following an introduction program have at least 23 hours per week and what this contains is based on the school student's needs and the individual plan the school has written based on an assessment of the student's background, school experience, language and disciplinary knowledge, and any work experience. This plan can include that a school student studies only Swedish as an Additional Language. The relevance of multilingualism in the education of these school students is potentially visible in the assessment of the school student's language knowledge. However, there are no directives that this needs to be more than assessment of Swedish; assessment prefers Swedish as it is the national language. The Swedish National Agency for Education refers to material available for compulsory school that can be used. In relation to language, this compulsory school material assesses general literacy skills such as familiarity with an alphabet, writing, and the reading of fiction, rather than purely knowledge of Swedish. In fact, it is possible to use a translator during the assessment.

Turning to Swedish as an Additional Language in compulsory school, the objective is to develop the school student's knowledge in and about Swedish with a focus on communicating in Swedish based on their competence level, yet without demanding a focus on correct form "too early." A first analysis of the syllabus does not suggest any value to multilingualism in education or the use of translanguaging in the compulsory school Swedish as an Additional Language classroom (see also, Rosén, Straszer, & Wedin, this volume). There are also some phrases that hint at possibilities, for example, "to develop their [...] own identity and understanding of the world," where the pupil's multilingual self is central. Yet, in context it is clear that this idea relates to Swedish:

In meetings with different text types, drama and other aesthetic forms the school students are given the possibility to develop their Swedish language, own identity and understanding of the world.

Even if the syllabus requires the use of fictional literature from different periods and world literatures, this will be in translation.

Another example is the paragraph that ends, "In this way, the school pupils are given the possibility to take responsibility for their own language use in various contexts and media," yet the paragraph begins,

> Through teaching the school students are given the possibility to develop their knowledge of the Swedish language, its norms, structure, pronunciation, lexicon including how language use varies based on social context and media.

Hence, the aims of the compulsory school syllabus for Swedish as an Additional Language only implicitly suggest that multilingualism has a place in education, but this is heavily moderated by a focus on Swedish only. However, the learning outcomes for end of compulsory school open for teachers to use translanguaging in education and assessment (see Schissel, De Kornn, & López-Gopar [2018] for a discussion of the challenges of assessment using translanguaging). The teaching and learning *opportunities* are provided via the learning outcomes:

- Linguistic strategies to understand and be understood in school disciplines when one's Swedish is not sufficient.
- Sentence structure in Swedish in comparison with the school student's own mother tongue.
- Differences in language due to context, with whom and with what goal one is communicating.

- Language's importance for influencing others and for one's own identity development.

Thus, even if an initial reading of the syllabus suggests few possibilities for multilingualism in this educational setting and for translanguaging to have support in the guiding document for the school subject, there are clear opportunities that would support a teacher working in these ways.

The syllabus for Swedish as an Additional Language for the Upper Secondary School is more open (and closed) to multilingualism in education and translanguaging as a resource and the subject is described as follows:

> The subject [Swedish as an Additional Language] contributes to strengthening the school student's multilingualism and belief in their own language ability, at the same time they gain an increased respect for the language of others and their ways of expressing themselves.

And among the objectives for Upper Secondary School we find:

- The school students will also be given the possibility to reflect on their own multilingualism.
- The content will be aligned so that the school students' previous experiences and knowledge are made the most of.
- Multilingualism is a resource for the individual and society, and through comparative linguistic knowledge and language experiences with others the school students are given the possibility to develop a better understanding of the functions of language in communication, thought, and learning.

In this syllabus, we see a development from the compulsory school syllabus in that the syllabus recognizes that the school students may have knowledge of languages other than their mother tongue: "Ability to compare the Swedish language with their own mother tongue *and other languages* [our emphasis] in which the school student has competence." This comparison has moved from Language A in comparison to Swedish, to language S in comparison to Swedish. However, the learning outcomes for the most advanced module do not refer at all to other languages or multilingualism. Here the learning outcome has been transformed into "Reflection on language learning, with a focus on developing strategies for continued learning." Oddly, as the school student progresses through the modules of Swedish as an Additional Language in the upper secondary school, the importance of their multilingualism and opportunities for use in the classroom through, for example, translanguaging decreases. Naturally, restricting the use of translanguaging for assessment does not exclude the use of translanguaging for learning, and our reading of this syllabus is that there is much support for translanguaging and the recognition of the multilingual competencies among the school students in the Swedish as an Additional Language classroom.

3.2 Defining translanguaging and multilingualism in educational settings

In order to interpret the other research questions it is necessary to understand what the teacher trainee student believes is being discussed in the focus group discussion, and for the findings we present here to have validity. Thus, even though we did not create a discussion about understandings of translanguaging until toward the end of the focus group discussion we present our findings in this area first. It became apparent even before Vesna explicitly asked about understandings of translanguaging that they held the view that García's (2009) two strategic principles, namely social justice and social practice, should be interwoven into the teaching. They felt that when it comes to social justice, it is important to show through their teaching that all languages have equal value and that they should be used as a source of knowledge and a starting point for learning.

These three teacher trainee students are convinced that the most important thing is to show respect and interest for the school students' languages and cultures in order to create a positive working environment that benefits everyone. The teacher trainee students think that the school students' multilingualism should be seen as a resource and that it is something that can be relatively easily acknowledged in the teaching and strengthened via collaboration with mother tongue teachers and other multilingual adults, for example, parents and other teachers who can act as resources in the multilingual classroom. They all expressed a dislike of the monolingual norm. For example, Kim-TTI said, "No talk in different languages, they never got to talk about their languages." Another teacher trainee student, Storm-TTC, expressed surprise that they encountered classes that are "a normal Swedish class," rather than classes that offer all pupils the opportunity to acquire new knowledge through multilingual books / multilingual material, and prepare and present their school information in the languages they have in their repertoire in order to not have to lower the cognitive level of teaching – something that can happen if everything is to be done in Swedish only and no translanguaging is allowed in the classroom. Storm-TTC's thoughts were echoed by the other two teacher trainee students, and, in discussion, they expressed a desire for monolingual and multilingual teachers to collaborate across the subject boundaries in order to erase the sharp boundaries between different school subjects as well as between Swedish and Swedish as a second language, thereby promoting translanguaging as a resource for education and learning.

The teacher trainee students' thoughts in the discussion, and their interest in running a project where their school students would create their own identity texts (Cummins & Early, 2011) once they are working in school after completing their teacher training, need to also be considered in the light of the final Swedish as an Additional Language assessment that they undertook immediately prior to their second teaching practice. Their final assessment was creating a short presentation on their understanding of translanguaging and how they intended to apply translanguaging in their teaching practice. The audience for these presentations included not only the course teachers and students, but also their peers with other subject combinations. Hence, the teacher trainee students participating in the focus group interview had recently worked with translanguaging as part of an assessment. The assessment included questions from their peers that triggered both thoughts, questions, and discussion as to how to work with translanguaging among the Swedish as an Additional Language teacher trainee students and those with other subject combinations who wondered how they could work with translanguaging. In sum, these teacher trainee students have an excellent and nuanced understanding of translanguaging.

3.2 Surprises during teaching practice

In this section, we have decided to focus on surprises that the teacher trainee students discussed that are not directly or explicitly related to multilingualism in education or translanguaging. The surprises we have decided to present here provide a backdrop to the following section, which considers the dissonance between the teacher trainee students' university learning and their experiences during their teaching practice. Interestingly the surprises that the teacher trainee students raised in discussion, which we present in this section, are a precursor to the dissonance they experienced while on teaching practice and in their mentors' views on multilingualism in the classroom and translanguaging.

Alex-TTUS, whose teaching practice was in a large upper-secondary school, found a lot of time was spent doing administrative work with the school students' schedules. The Swedish as an Additional Language school students came from many different classes and timetabling clashes became part of the working day. The mentor reported that they would have preferred that the Swedish as an Additional Language class was timetabled first, but this was not the preference of the other teaching staff. Alex-TTUS interpreted this as a question of status. Swedish as an Additional Language is not viewed as a real subject and the students are seen as the weak ones who cannot communicate clearly and correctly in Swedish. The monolingual norm of the school was very clear to this teacher trainee student.

Kim-TTI agreed with Alex-TTUS about status and describes how Swedish as an Addition Language classes were low priority. Kim-TTI did her teaching practice in a medium-sized upper secondary school and describes the classrooms this course was assigned as follows:

They are in a side building to the school, small rooms with poor lighting without any projector, separated from the other students. So it very rarely happens that they [language introduction students] meet the students (predominantly Swedish-speaking) who read national programs in the main building.

Further, both Kim-TTI and Alex-TTUS noted that, even if the Swedish as Additional Language teachers were not happy with their low-status classrooms and had "talked about the poor study environment with the head" (Kim-TTI), they did little to improve the situation. Kim-TTI reported that "the only thing that was on the walls were some signs about how to behave *in Swedish* [Kim-TTI's emphasis]." Storm-TTUS observed that in their classroom "there were posters and signs in German because my mentor also teaches German, but nothing else." Here we see first that language classes are placed in the periphery and that the Swedish as an Additional

Language students are ignored in the classroom. The underlying attitude that is given to the school students is that they are not as important as the other students; indeed, in one of the schools these students did not even have the same lunch break time as the majority students. In Storm-TTUS's classroom, the teacher used this classroom for teaching in German without considering the identities and languages of the students studying Swedish as an Additional Language but rather focused on the school students learning German as a foreign language.

Another aspect that all the teacher trainee students brought up in the discussion is the monolingual physical school environment. None of the teacher trainee students reported seeing any information in a language other than Swedish in places such as the school cafeteria. Alex-TTUS not only commented on the "German" classroom, "there were no books other than in Swedish, German and dictionaries," but also noted that in the school library "there were very very few books in any languages other than Swedish and English." Alex-TTUS also noted that there were no fiction books in the school apart from books in Swedish and English (and German in the "German" classroom). They never saw any information in any other language except Swedish in the other school premises, such as the school cafeteria.

These surprises during teaching practice align with Jaspers (2015) and Stroud (2004). The physical marginalization in these schools is a way of legitimating linguistic hierarchies in schools and classrooms in the way "language ideologies and discourses of integration provide a means of legitimating racial and class hierarchies" (Jaspers & Madsen, 2018). Thus, even in schools with many multilingual students there is "an [. . .] affection for monolingualism" (Jaspers, 2015, p. 110).

3.3 Dissonance during teaching practice

In our teacher training for students of Swedish as an Additional Language, we work from the assumption that multilingualism in the classroom is an important tool to enhance the learning of the multilingual school student, who may be multilingual in many ways. These school students may be speakers of Sweden's official minority languages, they may be speakers of internationally major languages such as English, German, and Spanish, or speakers of smaller languages who have moved to Sweden and applied for asylum. We avoid the term "minority language speakers" not least as this suggests a power relationship. Further, following García (2009), we discuss translanguaging as the individual's use of their languages in education and do not delimit translanguaging to multilingual teaching. We work from the assumption that the contexts our students will encounter are culturally and linguistically diverse and rarely, if ever, bilingual contexts where the teacher is bilingual in the languages of the classroom.

Hence, the meeting of a monolingual norm in which the school students spoke Swedish in class, or as Storm-TTC reflected, "They talk their own languages in the breaks, conversation in Swedish in class is difficult for many," and Alex-TTUS said, "They talk only Swedish in the classroom, already a norm." This was not what we have prepared the teachers to encounter. Their mentors motivated the monolingual norm by saying "that the school students learn Swedish better in this way and that they should not 'mix' the languages because it creates confusion in the classroom" (Storm-TTUS). All three teacher trainee students noticed that at school the school students' tasks were simplified so that they would be easy to understand. They reflected, as Storm-TTC expressed it, "There is gap between what we read and reality." They problematized that in their teacher training they were encouraged to consider how translanguaging could be applied to challenge the school students intellectually, but in their teaching practice they encountered something else. They heard, as Storm-TTC reported that he heard during his teaching practice, that "translanguaging is nothing for compulsory school." An explanation for the monolingual norm in the class is that the teachers' side wanted control over what was said between the students in order to avoid "unpleasant conflicts" (KIM-TTI) between the students.

Storm-TTC linked his experiences of teaching when observed by a mentor with his desire to know what to do when he graduates:

> *What should I do? The school students are interrupted, as the teachers don't understand, they talk in their languages but preferably only during breaks, and they are examined in Swedish. The teacher says that we must know what they are talking about. We mustn't lose control. They say to the students "Is it something that can't wait?" and the school student ends the conversation. The teachers say they are pro translanguaging in theory but not in practice and not in the classroom, everything should be in Swedish, that is what is examined.*

All three teacher trainee students noticed that the school students used many types of dictionaries and Google Translate, but neither in a focused way nor in one that was supported by classroom teaching. They noticed no focus on which languages were in the classrooms or how the school students could be organized into project groups based on these languages. In fact, the school students' previous language and subject knowledge was not noticed at all, according to the focus group discussion, with the teaching being driven by a focus on external national testing.

Oddly, teaching assistants in these classrooms who spoke some of the school students' languages were more used as interpreters by the teachers, for example, to convey changes to the schedule and the occasional word, but as Storm-TTC expressed it, "The teaching assistant was asked about the translation of the occasional word but that was it . . . they were more a 'peer' support person than a teaching assistant."

When asked to add anything important to the discussion about their teaching during their teaching practice when thinking about language in the classroom, these teacher trainees' thoughts can be summarized as follows:

Kim-TTI said that some of the Swedish as an Additional Language pupils in her class said it was better to speak Swedish at school all the time and that they could speak their languages at home and in their spare time. These school students did not realize that they had use of their languages at school, even if the school was a Swedish school.

Storm-TTC said that a librarian at the school tried to set up a project involving both school students with Swedish as their first language and those studying Swedish as an Additional Language, by organizing a reading project in which they would choose a book, and read and discuss the book. The librarian hoped to create an open environment where the students would discuss and use all their linguistic resources to express themselves. However, the school students formed groups based on their first language, no teachers became involved because the book project was not part of compulsory school and the project failed. Storm-TTC seemed frustrated that an attempt to set up a learning environment that permitted translanguaging was unsuccessful.

Alex-TTUS's biggest impression of her teaching practice was how their mentor felt that the goal of the Swedish as an Additional Language teaching was to move to Swedish-only as soon as possible. The mentor focused on the form (eg. grammatical) elements of the Swedish language mentioned in the syllabus and paid less attention to those that focused on multilingualism. The mentor allowed the use of other languages individually or in small groups in the first year of Upper Secondary School, but never in full class or in examination tasks. This mentor aimed for Swedish-only in the final year of Upper Secondary School. Alex-TTUS, however, did not reflect on the gradual removal of comparison with other languages and multilingualism from the learning outcomes at Upper Secondary School. These are not major elements of this mentor's first year of upper-secondary classes, but the reduction toward the final year aligns with the national learning outcomes for Swedish as an Additional Language. We interpret Alex-TTUS's impression as surprise at not only the move to Swedish-only, but also the lack of understanding about the value in allowing school students to use all their linguistic resources, including through translanguaging, to learn. Language ability as described by García (2009) – a dynamic and complex system where individual languages are intertwined into each other, which should be the basis when, for example, teaching Swedish as a second language – was not something that was experienced in the school during teaching practice.

The monolingual language view that all three teacher trainee students encountered on teaching practice jarred with what they had read and were taught in our university courses, which is characterized by a democratic view that all languages spoken by school students are seen as parts of the same language ability – one common underlying proficiency which is described by Cummins (2007) as an iceberg with protruding peaks that represent individual languages. This dissonance between the university, where multilingualism runs as a common thread throughout the university courses for prospective teachers in Swedish as an Additional Language, and practice was experienced by the teacher trainee students at large.

In discussion the teacher trainee students also considered how their mentors' attitudes to their school students' multilingualism were reflected in how they talked about the students and how this was framed by the monolingual affection (Jaspers, 2015). All three teacher trainee students discussed how their mentors talked about their school students in terms of shortcomings, rather than in terms of success. Storm-TTC expressed this as follows: "The students never get to become experts at anything, for the most part they receive written teacher responses to their tasks where it was 'wrong' and how they could train Swedish to correct the errors."

In sum, it is clear that the teacher trainee students experience a dissonance or even a head-on collision between university and school practice. The schools have many years of experience, yet in spite of research and changes over many years in teacher training they maintain a preference for a monolingual context for education.

3.3 Understandings of translanguaging

In our discussion of dissonance, we reported on Alex-TTUS's impression that his mentor lacked an understanding of the benefits of translanguaging. During the focus group interview, Alex-TTUS referred to a conversation during their teacher training practice about translanguaging, and that the mentor expressed scepticism about working with translanguaging in the classroom: "The students do not get enough Swedish at home nor in their spare time and school has to fill the gap and this leaves no space for any other language." This mentor, Alex-TTUS felt, taught to the text with a focus on grammar exercises and reading comprehension exercises without any meaningful context. Similar feelings relating to the pressure to produce monolingual language in the school students are reported in Schissel et al. (2018), "Teachers fear they [the school students] will not succeed on the standardized, monolingual tests that are crucial to academic achievement" (p. 8), and thus avoidance of interference from other languages is necessary. Indeed, Schissel et al. (2018) report that "teachers expressed how translanguaging has traditionally been viewed as a problem or a barrier to overcome" (p. 8).

Kim-TTI and Storm-TTC did not have the same negative experience as Alex-TTUS. They pointed out that their supervisors were more positive about translanguaging (at least when they talked about it), but that they did not see this positive attitude reflected in classroom teaching. Both of these mentors thought that multilingualisam was a resource and could be used in education, but they would need more education and time, more resources, and better support from the other staff to introduce translanguaging in their teaching. Jaspers (2015) suggested that often multilingualism is seen as located in the individual but that nations, including the classroom, are territorially monolingual. Teachers can thus be positive about translanguaging in the individual but not in "territories," such as the classroom, that are monolingual. The acceptance of translanguaging and multilingualism is spatialized to the individual rather than the national state.

4. Discussion and conclusion

The situations our teacher trainee students report on after their teaching practice is neither accepting of multilingualism in education nor accepting of translanguaging. This situation deviates from much research that promotes translanguaging, reporting on successful translanguaging in the school classroom. Our findings align more with the work of Jaspers (2015), which considered translanguaging in a Dutch language school in Belgium where most pupils were not native Dutch speakers. Thus, even though this chapter discusses only the experiences of three teacher trainee students it resonates with other studies.

We posed four research questions of our focus group data, and we found that (1) the teacher trainee students had a good understanding of the theoretical and educational aspects of translanguaging and multilingualism in educational settings, (2) the multilinguals are pushed to the spatial periphery, (3) the teacher trainee students were frustrated that what they had learned about the educational advantages of multilingualism and translanguaging was not found in their teaching practice placements, which suffocated anything that represented multilingualism outside of the individual, and (4) even if the mentor was positive toward translanguaging and multilingualism it was not going to happen in their monolingual territory of the Swedish as an Additional Language classroom.

We notice throughout that the teacher trainee students are frustrated with the situations they have encountered. However, we wonder whether they will turn into agitators when they graduate and work in schools alongside teachers with many years of experience in getting school students to pass their exams, or simply slide into the same patterns as their mentors. The question thus becomes: What are the education implications of this study and how can we create a situation that encourages new teachers to apply what they have learned about multilingualism in education and translanguaging in their classrooms?

First, we need to continue publishing and spreading examples of best translanguaging practice. Second, recognizing that teachers are limited in what they do by the national curriculum and subject syllabi, we need to agitate for multilingual perspectives to percolate all subjects and levels. Here we need to be vigilant and make sure the importance does not decrease as it currently has in the Swedish as an Additional Language syllabus for Upper Secondary School. Third, teacher education has a large role to play. It is currently playing a big role, but in our university this is limited to courses for future Swedish and Swedish as an Additional Language teaching.

We argue that for multilingualism and translanguaging to not be seen as peripheral approaches, they need to be included in teacher training regardless of discipline and age group. Finally, we would argue that most importantly, an open dialogue with experienced school teachers (in Swedish as a second language and other subjects) needs to be opened. This dialogue needs to respect their concerns and experience, listen and respond to their questions by designing collaborative projects where researchers and teachers can together create translanguaging spaces in the school, and overcome teachers' concerns that school students do not get "enough" Swedish if a translanguaging pedagogy is applied.

Returning to the illustrative examples with which we opened this chapter, it is clear that opening such a dialogue is difficult, and the contradictory messages of the law, in relation to multilingualism versus a linguistic hierarchy with Swedish at its apex (see Ekberg, 2017), suggest that the clash between Swedish at the apex and multilingualism and translanguaging as positive penetrates all of Swedish society. School is thus a microcosm of a greater challenge.

Many experienced teachers start from a deficit perspective and see students with other first languages as a problem to be pushed to the periphery. These students, they believe, achieve lower results in international studies such as PISA and TIMMS. Further, these attitudes feed into and come from stereotypes, the need for teacher control in the classroom, and a belief that the other should become Swedish. These positions are reflected in current political flows toward the political right internationally and, in Sweden, the demands for language tests for citizenship and the idea that language is indexical of identity. This means that without strong Swedish skills one cannot be Swedish. Thus, the creation of an open dialogue is difficult. One possibility is that teachers who are positive toward translanguaging could become involved in social action and be seen in the political arena to counterbalance the move to the political right and linguistic monolingual states. This would challenge views in a similar way to public lectures by academics. However, organizing a structured dialogue that does not become a traditional competence development project is challenging. Another possibility is facilitated school-based discussions on issues relating to non-native Swedish speakers and how to improve their school results in a Swedish language–dominant assessment system. In these discussions translanguaging can be discussed in such a way that it is not promoted as a solution or as non-starter. An open discussion alongside other open discussions may provide a route to its broader acceptance.

In sum, this chapter has indirectly considered three schools and their translanguaging practices. The experience of three teacher trainee students was one of dissonance between university teaching that is positive toward the advantages of translanguaging and school practice that favors monolingualism. We have suggested a number of actions that we hope will reduce the frustration of our future teachers and keep them interested in working with translanguaging approaches to teaching once they graduate and start work.

References

Cummins, J. (2007) Rethinking monolingual instructional strategies in multilingual classrooms. *Canadian Journal of Applied Linguistics, 10*(1), 221–240.

Cummins, J., & Early, M. (2011). *Identity Texts: the Collaborative Creation of Power in Multilingual Schools.* Stoke on Trent, UK: Trentham Books.

Ekberg L. (2017). Finnish, Meänkieli, Yiddish, Romany and Sami in Sweden. In C. A. Seals & S. Shah (Eds.) *Heritage Language Policies around the World.* (pp. 84–96). Abingdon, UK: Routledge.

García, O. (2009). *Bilingual education in the 21st century: a global perspective.* Hoboken, NJ: Wiley.

García, O., & Seltzer, K. (2016). The Translanguaging current in language education. In B. Kindenberg (Ed.), *Flerspråkighet som resurs. Symposium 2015 [Multilingualism as a resource. Symposium 2015]* (pp. 19–30). Stockholm, Sweden: Liber AB.

Jaspers, J. (2015). Modelling linguistic diversity at school: The excluding impact of inclusive multilingualism, *Language Policy, 14,* 109–129.

Jaspers, J., & Madsen, L. M. (2018). Fixity and Fluidity in sociolinguistic theory and practice. In J. Jaspers & L. M. Madsen (Eds.) *Critical Perspectives on Linguistic Fixity and Fluidity: Languagised Lives* (pp. 1–26). Abingdon, UK: Routledge.

Mazak, C. (2017). Introduction: Theorizing translanguaging practices in higher education. In C. Mazak & S. Kevin (Eds.) *Translanguaging in higher education: beyond monolingual ideologies.* (pp. 1–10). Bristol, UK: Multilingual Matters.

Paulsrud, B., Rosén, J., Straszer, B., & Wedin, Å. (Eds.) (2018a). *Transspråkande i svenska utbildningssammanhang [Translanguaging in a Swedish educational context].* Lund, Sweden: Studentlitteratur.

Paulsrud, B., Rosén, J., Straszer, B., & Wedin, Å. (2018b). Introduktion [Introduction]. In B. Paulsrud, J. Rosén, B. Straszer, & Å. Wedin (2018a). *Transspråkande i svenska utbildningssammanhang [Translanguaging in a Swedish educational context]* (pp. 11–26). Lund, Sweden: Studentlitteratur.

Schissel, J., De Kornn, H., & López-Gopar, M. (2018). Grappling with translanguaging for teaching and assessment in culturally and linguistically diverse contexts: teacher perspectives from Oaxaca, Mexico. *International journal of bilingual education and bilingualism* (online first). *doi: 10.1080/13670050.2018.1463965*

Skolverket (2011). Läroplan, examensmål och gymnasiegemensamma ämnen för gymnasieskola 2011. Stockholm, Sweden: Skolverket. https://www.skolverket.se/publikationer?id=2705

Skolverket (2018). *Läroplan för grundskolan, förskoleklassen och fritidshemmet, reviderad 2018. [Curriculum for elementary school, preschool class and the after-school center, revised 2018]* Stockholm, Sweden: Skolverket. https://www.skolverket.se/publikationer?id=3975

Skolverket (2019). *Introduktionsprogram [Introduction programmes]* Stockholm, https://www.skolverket.se/undervisning/gymnasieskolan/laroplan-program-och-amnen-i-gymnasieskolan/gymnasieprogrammen/introduktionsprogram

Stroud, C. (2004). Rinkeby Swedish and semilingualism in language ideological debates: A Bourdieuean perspective. *Journal of sociolinguistics, 8*(2), 196–214.

Svensson, G (2016). Translanguaging för utveckling av elevers ämneskunskaper, språk och identitet. In B. Kindenberg (Ed.), *Flerspråkighet som resurs. Symposium 2015 [Multilingualism as a resource. Symposium 2015]* (pp. 31–43). Stockholm, Sweden: Liber AB.

The Swedish Migration Agency (2014) *Inkomna ansökningar om asyl, 2013* [Applications for asylum received, 2013]. See https://www.migrationsverket.se/download/18.7c00d8e6143101d166ddae/1485556207418/Inkomna+ans%C3%B6kningar+om+asyl+2013+-

+Applications+for+asylum+received+2013.pdf (accessed 4 February 2019).

The Swedish Migration Agency (2016) *Inkomna ansökningar om asyl, 2015* [Applications for asylum received, 2015]. See https://www.migrationsverket.se/download/18.7c00d8e6143101d166d1aab/1485556214938/Inkomna+ans%C3%B6kningar+om+asyl+2015+-+Applications+for+asylum+received+2015.pdf (accessed 4 February 2019).

Swedish Research Council. (2017). *God forskningssed [Good research practice]*. Swedish Research Council: Stockholm, Sweden.

Torpsten, A.-C. (2018). Translanguaging in a Swedish Multilingual Classroom. *Multicultural perspectives 20*(2), 104–110.

Williams, C. (1994) *Arfarniad o ddulliau dysgu ac addysgu yng nghyddestun addysg uwchradd ddwyieithog [Evaluation of learning and teaching methods in the context of Bilingual education]*. Unpublished Doctoral Dissertation. Bangor: University of Wales.

Williams, C. (1996). Secondary education: Teaching in the bilingual situation. In C. Williams, G. Lewis, & C. Baker. *The language policy: Taking stock: Interpreting and appraising Gwynedd's policy in education* (pp. 39–78). Langefni, UK: CAI.

CHAPTER 11

Remixing pedagogies and fluidity of spaces in a community-based schoolscape

Suriati Abas

1. Introduction

In recent decades, language teaching has evolved from a monolingual to a multilingual perspective in most parts of the predominantly English-speaking world. The influx of migrants from different areas, which brings together speakers of languages other than the dominant language of the host country, caused the one-state monolingual language ideologies to be re-examined. In the United States (US), the number of speakers of minority languages such as Arabic, Chinese, Korean, Pashto, and Russian, to name just a few (with the exception of French, German, and Spanish), has more than doubled, increasing from 23 million to 46.9 million, between 1980 and 2000. In 2011, 21% of the 291.5 million people aged five and over spoke a language other than English at home (US Census, 2011). These languages, also referred to as "less commonly taught languages" (LCTLs) in the US or, widely known as "community languages" in Australia and the UK, grew more (or less) important over time, due to economic interests and changing immigration trends. Although efforts have been made since a decade ago to incorporate other languages as part of the US bilingual education system, 45.3% of the 528 programs are in Spanish (Directory of Foreign Language Immersion Programs in US Schools, 2011). With students coming from multilingually diverse backgrounds, there is a need to recast the atrophied discourse over minority languages.

Minority languages should be valued beyond the expediency of meeting current diplomatic, defense, and economic needs of the country. They play a vital role in preparing students for the globalized workforce. Hence, to evince how young children can be introduced to minority languages in a convivial environment, I proposed an expanded view of schoolscape. Initially acknowledged as materials within a school-based environment (Brown, 2005, 2012), I redefined this notion and termed it as "community-based schoolscape," incorporating remixed pedagogies and community involvement in fluid, ever-shifting spaces. To demonstrate the characteristics of a community-based schoolscape, I present an autoethnographic account reflecting on my own experiences as a language learner and coordinator, juxtaposing them with the experiences of those whom I observed (for a similar approach, see also Hammine, this volume). I employed Scollon and Scollon's (2003) geosemiotics theory to vividly describe the intricate intersections that occurred during critical learning moments of the "others." The purpose is to contribute to an understanding of how multilingual education, specifically the teaching and learning of minority languages, can be facilitated in non-traditional settings where the learning spaces are unfixed, and/or not fully equipped with facilities that are commonly found in classrooms (e.g. computer, whiteboard, table, chairs).

The normative questions underpinning my writing are: How can language learning happen outside traditional classroom settings? In what ways can spaces be utilized for teaching minority languages to children in the community? What particular pedagogical approaches can be applied for the benefit of the children and the community? The chapter concludes by (a) reiterating key characteristics of a community-based schoolscape, and (b) reflecting on the larger meanings behind the architecture of fluid spaces and resource limitations, leaving advocates from among researchers, practitioners, language activists, and the community to continue promulgating minority languages in the most creative ways.

1.1 Schoolscapes and redefinition

As aforementioned in the introduction, Brown (2012) conceptualized schoolscapes as "the school-based environment where place and text, both written (graphic) and oral, constitute, reproduce and transform language ideologies" (p. 282). Motivated by existing studies on linguistic landscape (LL), widely cited as "[t]he language of public road signs, advertising billboards, street names, place names, commercial shop signs, and public signs on government buildings combine to form the linguistic landscape of a given territory, region, or urban agglomeration" (Landry & Bourhis, 1997, p. 25), the notion of schoolscapes was proposed in Brown's study of signages at Estonian schools to examine LL in educational spaces. Literature on schoolscapes has focused on the utility of LL for raising language awareness (e.g. Dagenais, Moore, Sabatier, Lamarre, & Armand, 2009; Sayer, 2010), promoting cultural and linguistic diversity (e.g. Hancock, 2012), and language acquisition (Malinowski, 2015; Rowland, 2013). Advancing these investigations, I chose to look at schoolscape from a semiotic perspective, widening my examination of signs from a "heteropological" (Malinowski, 2015) or all-encompassing, non-traditional school context. Following Jaworksi and Thurlow's (2010) view of semiotic landscape, rather than LL, I considered "the interplay between language, visual discourse and the spatial practices and dimensions of culture" (p. 1). Aside from examining written signs, I focused on additional discursive modalities that took the form of "visual images, non-verbal communication, architecture, and the built environment" (p. 2). I included remixed pedagogies and community involvement in fluid, ever-shifting spaces to my definition of community-based schoolscape drawing from a project known as PLAYnLEARN.

2. The context

Located within the vicinity of a midwestern city in the US, PLAYnLEARN is home to linguistically and ethnically diverse populations. The city's multilingualism is reflected in its public schools, which bring together immigrant children from various parts of the world with other multilingual and monolingual children born in the city. Thus, providing free minority language classes presents opportunities for parents to expose their child/children to either a new language or a language that is spoken at home. The flexibility of the project is evident through its enrollment procedure: parents may send their child, aged pre-K through 6, at any time of the semester although they are highly encouraged to join from the first lesson. The classes are held once a week, for 50 minutes over ten to eleven weeks, in a semester. A key feature that stands out in PLAYnLEARN is the concept of utilizing a combination of scholarly capital and intellectual capacity from the university and the community, for the benefit of the children in the community, itself. Similar to the UK complementary school model, classes in PLAYnLEARN differ greatly in organizational structure and processes, size, pedagogy, and curriculum (Wei, 2006; Issa & Williams, 2009) when compared to traditional language classes that are supported by instructor expertise and material resources. Instructors of the language classes are volunteers, from among the undergraduate and graduate students who are either learners of the minority language and/or heritage speakers of the language. On some semesters, parents from among the community volunteer to teach. The spaces for learning are often unfixed; the lessons are either developed using minimal resources such as colored construction papers and marker pens, creatively drawn from readily available materials, or the physical built environment. Enrollment for the ten-week classes frequently fluctuates in response to erratic weather conditions, school events and/or weekend family arrangements. However, regular updates on children's learning occur on social media via Facebook, at the end of each lesson.

Unlike typical language classrooms, which maintain the rigidity of language separation, the lessons in PLAYnLEARN are conducted in two languages, with English being used as the medium of instruction while the minority or target language is introduced through learner-centered activities such as role-playing, singing songs and/ or visuals (see also, Seals, Pine, Ash, Olsen-Reeder, & Wallace, this volume). This fluid movement between English and the minority language is what García (2009) describes as translanguaging. The term "translanguaging," although widely used in the study of multilingualism, has taken on varying perspectives. In the Welsh context, it is defined as a pedagogical strategy that alternated input and output in two different languages (Baker, 2011) with the objective of increasing proficiency in both languages. For García and Wei (2014), translanguaging refers to new language practices that occur spontaneously. From this view, the boundaries between languages are frequently shifting, fluid and therefore, it is drawn from the learners' linguistic repertoires as a whole, rather than two separate languages. According to Kleyn (2016), translanguaging is a viable approach for both learning majority and minoritized languages" (p. 217).

As an insider, I had vested interest in articulating my personal experiences of being a part of this project to document my trajectory; the engagements provide opportunities for me to reflect on the fecundity of language education in the US. I decided to employ autoethnography to explicate key characteristics of a community-based schoolscape through four language classes – Arabic, Japanese, Persian, and Russian – offered by PLAYnLEARN.

3. Methodology
Autoethnography can be understood as a form of self-study (auto) with the aim of inquiring into everyday experiences to which the

author is a full member. In autoethnography, the personal stories of the author and their larger meanings were revealed (Creswell, 2013). My intention in applying autoethnography is primarily to merge my personal narratives with reflections on theoretical elements in order to clarify, make available, and put together a wider understanding of the issue in focus – pedagogical constructs that facilitated minority language learning and how spaces in places contributed to its sustainability. As Goodall (2000) says, one of the merits of employing autoethnography is that it provides a means for "personally and academically reflecting on lived experiences" (p. 137). While prescribed methodological procedure such as a case study methodology may be equally helpful for investigating a phenomena within its real-life context (Yin, 2009), I pursued autoethnography to engage in "a rewriting of the self and the social" (Reed-Danahay, 1997, p. 4) in order to make my work accessible to a broad range of audiences: researchers, practitioners, language activists and community members. This self-study framing enables me to "invoke" readers (practitioners who are working within the limitations of space and material resources, in particular) to be involved in my experience (Bochner & Ellis, 1996; Pavlenko, 2007). Although contemporary autoethnographers have provided compelling evidences for crediting autoethnography in educational contexts (e.g. Hughes, 2008; Pennington, 2007; Romo, 2005) and attributed high "ecological validity" (Brock-Utne, 1996) afforded by this method, the shortcomings of autoethnography lies in its epistemological status (Walford, 2004); the social realities constructed in the exemplar lessons given in the next section were, to a certain extent, limited by my interests and what I chose to disclose. To establish methodological rigor, I exercised reflexivity, a process of being "[f]ocused on the self and ongoing intersubjectivities" (Mann, 2016, p. 28). Through a reflexive journal (cf. Lincoln & Guba, 1985), I consistently recorded my methodological decisions, the events that happened, my personal reflections, the "a-ha" moments in PLAYnLEARN and provided excerpts of them in this chapter. All these were made possible given my omniscient role and positionality.

3.1 Positionality

Following Ellis's (2009) autoethnographic approach, I positioned myself as both the author and the focus of the story. However, in pursuing a self-examination of my experiences, the attention to self involves a variety of others – "others of similarity" (those with similar experiences to self), "others of difference" (those with different experiences to self), and "others of opposition" (those with experiences irreconcilable to self) (Chang, 2008). While I bring my experiences of acquiring a foreign language and learning in a bilingual education system to mind, I chose to narrate another experience of mine, in relation to different others, in terms of the ways I was raised to learn languages to those that I observed. This experience draws from my position as a language and program coordinator of PLAYnLEARN. My role placed me as an omniscient participant; I was overseeing six language classes – two Arabic, and one Chinese, Japanese, Persian, and Russian; and supervising 18 volunteer instructors who were undergraduate and graduate students in a midwestern university in the US. I conducted pedagogical training sessions, provided weekly feedback to lesson plans and did post-lesson observation debriefings to the volunteers. For this chapter, I randomly chose to illustrate selected lessons from my personal diary entries that vividly portray how the lack of space and resources can fuel creative, transformative learning of minority languages.

During lesson observations, I typed quick notes on my cell phone to document best practices (if any), areas for improvement and my reactions to specific situations. These notes were not deliberately part of the data collection, but rather, meant for debriefing the volunteers at the end of the lesson. It is also a way of talking to myself: what I noticed and learned from the lesson. The other aspect of my position involved social media outreach. I photographed every single lesson at various community sites. With the consent of parents and volunteers, these photographs were uploaded onto a Facebook page for publicity, documenting the project and updating parents on their children's learning experiences. These photographs concurrently served as reflective notes.

Throughout my two years of serving in this position, I often had to think on the feet whenever the spaces that were assigned for PLAYnLEARN had to give way to more contingent activities such as public or school events. Hence, the question of how spaces can be utilized to maximize language learning grew germane to me. This concern also arose as I was managing volunteers instead of salaried instructors; volunteers who are investing time out of their volition to teach children in the community, concomitantly struggling to fulfil their responsibilities as full-time university students and having to develop lesson plans and materials for the program. Despite the space and resource limitations, the community-based schoolscape thrives. In the next section, I provide a brief explanation of the theoretical framework that guided my personal narratives – geosemiotics, a portmanteau of geography (spaces) and semiotics, to mean "the social meanings of the material placement of signs (semiosis, to use Peirce's term) particularly in reference to the material world of the users of signs" (Scollon & Scollon, 2003, p. 4).

3.2 Viewing community-based schoolscape geosemiotically
With classes being taught in open fields, hallways, and any other freely available, public spaces at the community partner sites, the ways that learning took place was not only shaped by classroom instructions, but also space, place, and the visuality of materials. These ecological contributions to PLAYnLEARN can be vividly described using Scollon and Scollon's (2003) geosemiotics where the

physical, material, and symbolic aspects of places are foregrounded and viewed as resources for meaning-making. Hence, answering to the question of "What is happening here?" involves looking at the lessons holistically in terms of the activities, physical space, and their interactions. It may also be possible to link "What is happening here?" to many "theres" due to spatial connections that bind one thing with the other (Massey, 2000). For example, in one of the Russian classes, the children did a Matrosyka paper craft (See https://www.dltk-kids.com/world/russia/m-matryoshka.htm) and this activity was used to introduce them to Russian folk art and more vocabulary. Hence, the paper crafting activity is incidentally immersing the children into Russia and the artefacts symbolic to the country.

In all, viewing the community-based schoolscape geosemiotically means directing attention to three elements: Firstly, the ways in which interaction occurs in a particular space, which in this case are through the pedagogies and the respective community partner sites (interaction order). Secondly, the visual materials used for teaching and the context where it takes place (visual semiotics). Thirdly, the physical environment, in terms of the positioning, aesthetics, and materials, which contributes to how the space is "read" (place semiotics). These three elements are brought together through the concept of the "semiotic aggregate," a complex space in which "multiple semiotic systems [are] in a dialogical interaction with each other" (Scollon & Scollon, 2003, p. 12). For example, in a classroom setting, there are multiple potential and actual interactions among students, instructors, the texts, and signs that coalesce for meaning-making. Likewise, in the community-based schoolscape of PLAYnLEARN, the semiotic aggregate is intricate and the systems within it are constantly working with one another, to negotiate meanings. The pedagogical approach inherently plays a role in the interaction order that ensued at particular learning spaces.

3.3 Main pedagogical approach: Communicative Language Teaching (CLT)

Focal to PLAYnLEARN is the pedagogy of Communicative Language Teaching (CLT), an established teaching method. CLT, as according to Larsen-Freeman (2000), is a broad approach to teaching that promotes communication, with clearly defined classroom practices. It is often viewed as a set of general principles. The five tenets generally acknowledged for CLT are

- an emphasis on learning to communicate through interaction in the target language
- the introduction of authentic texts into the learning situation
- the provision of opportunities for learners to focus on not only language, but also on the learning process, itself
- an enhancement of learners' own personal experiences as important contributing elements to classroom learning
- an attempt to link classroom language learning with language activities outside the classroom. (Nunan, 1991, p. 279)

Applying a communicative approach to language teaching involves role-play, games, singing songs, map reading, and other activities that build in interaction and communication (For more CLT-related activities, see Richards, 2006). In a CLT classroom, the activities often incorporate pair or group work, draw on authentic experiences that develop students' understanding about the target language and its country and/or culture, and require learners to negotiate and cooperate with one another. These are the types of activities that were emphasized in PLAYnLEARN. While I advocated CLT as the approach that has been adopted for this program since I took over the position, my current ability to read and write in Spanish also made me believe in the potential of CLT; I acquired Spanish through authentic exposure during my sojourn to Spain, Argentina, Chile, and Peru. My on-going research work in Buenos Aires, Argentina, inherently led me to acquire more Spanish. Upon reflection, my language learning experiences guided me in my professional work as a language and program coordinator of PLAYnLEARN.

I trained all volunteer instructors and their assistants in the foundations of CLT during the orientation and mid-semester training sessions. They were given first-hand experience in how CLT can be applied to teaching languages, with the opportunity to do a demo team teaching and be shown exemplar videos for more ideas. One of the merits of using CLT is that it emphasizes fluency rather than grammatical accuracy. In this way, learners of the target language would feel more confident when interacting with other people (Brown, 2001) since errors in communication are tolerated. The focus on communicative competence additionally enables learners to utilize the target language for real-life communication (Richards, 2006). For young children, the communication can be as simple as using the target language for greetings, introducing themselves and expressing gratitude to one another. In CLT, learner-centeredness is highly valued; the instructor assumes a role as a facilitator for the most part of the language learning process, providing leads only for instructional tasks while gradually passing on the role to the learners.

3.4 Remixing pedagogical approaches

Although CLT is highly emphasized, the community-based schoolscape constructed by PLAYnLEARN is one that involves combinations of two pedagogical approaches. With instructions given in English language, also the language spoken by the majority in the US, and the target/minority language introduced through learner-centered activities, there is clearly a remixing of pedagogical approaches. Translanguaging, in this case, occurs due to two main reasons: (a) the children who attended PLAYnLEARN are either heritage speakers of the language but may not have acquired enough to follow instructions in the target language, or (b) the children are non-speakers of the target/minority language. These remixed pedagogical approaches are part of the interaction order that exists in geosemiotics. The physical language learning activities transcended onto the digital space, through a Facebook page. I uploaded photographs capturing the children, volunteers and people in the community in action as they were learning a language. In some instances, I added snippets of video recordings to document the language learning process, thus establishing permanence of record for future references. In the section below, I illustrate my experiences of navigating around the fluidity of spaces to ensure that language learning is made possible. I provide a photographic commentary of a community-based schoolscape from the lens of Scollon and Scollon's geosemiotics at four different sites: (a) an open-spaced area inside a public museum, (b) a room at a university with limited technological facilities, (c) a corner of a school library, and (d) an open area outside a daycare center.

4. Enactment of geosemiotics in a community-based schoolscape
(Excerpts from personal diary entry, USA, Fall 2016 – Spring 2018)

4.1 Exemplar Lesson #1
Class: Elementary Arabic
Venue: Hallway of a public museum
Grade level: Pre-K to 3
Total number of children: 10
Theme: Revisiting numbers, colors, fruits, and household items

4.1.1 Brief description of the space
On a Saturday, at 1:15pm, I was informed that PLAYnLEARN was assigned a lecture theater that could contain fifty people; the room that was used by the team of two volunteer instructors and two assistants had to give way to a one-day public event. Although

the lecture theater was equipped with a computer and a projector, it was more suited for adults rather than children. To ensure that there were ample space for movements, I directed the team to use the hallway, directly outside the lecture theater where there were rarely any visitors. The volunteers mounted their teaching materials onto a carpeted floor. They created a hopscotch together and transformed the hallway into a temporary, mini playground. I assisted them with positioning the wooden chairs that we could find from the lecture theater, in semicircles as if extending invitations to an audience. Hence, the set-up for that day was as shown in Figure 1.

Figure 1. Left: A child recalling the name of a fruit in Arabic. Right: A hopscotch created using colored construction papers, tape and artificial fruits. Photographer: author.

4.1.2 *What is happening here?*

The lesson began with simple greetings of مرحبا [Merhaba; Hello], among the instructors, their assistants, children, and parents, as they made their way to the empty wooden seats. While all parents made themselves comfortable at the other end, one of them sat with her three-year-old daughter to support her in learning elementary Arabic. Mr. Ahmed (pseudonym), the Arabic instructor, kneeled down on the carpeted floor to maintain eye contact with the young children, who were seated in a semicircular seating arrangement. The interaction order that occurred between him and the children was one that was personal and up-close; his straight body posture made the children feel comfortable for he was almost the same height as them. Using a red, attractive-looking bag, which he called "My magic bag," Mr. Ahmed invited volunteers from among the children to pick a fruit in the bag, without looking into it. The conversational encounter proceeded with the entire instructions delivered in the dominant language, English language. However, when a fruit was picked and shown to all, the child had to name the Arabic word for it. For each correct word, Mr. Ahmed said, ممتاز [mumtaz; excellent]. The entire class repeated the Arabic word for the fruit together, before the next child got to feel and name another fruit. After a quick recall activity, the review of lesson based on the themes of numbers, colors, and fruits continued with a simple hopscotch activity.

The impermanence of the hopscotch was seen through the A4-sized colored construction papers taped onto the carpeted floor by the hallway of the public museum. On the papers, the numbers were handwritten in black ink to create visibility. Beside each of the colored papers, an artificial fruit was placed. Each child took turns to throw a token. The team of three counted in Arabic up to the position where the token had landed. The player named the Arabic word for the color and the fruit that was laid beside the token.

After three rounds of hopscotch, Mr. Ahmed and his assistants moved the review activity to another area of the museum that had household items. Together with his assistants and the parents, joined by the children, all of them made a line, jogging on the spot and sounding out like a train starting its engine, "Choo . . . choo . . . choo . . . تسعة ، عشرة خمسة ، ستة ، سبعة ، ثمانية ،، واحد ، اثنان

ثلاثة ، أربعة [wahid, ithnin, thalatha, arba'a, khamsa, sitta, sab'a, thamaniya, tis'a, 'ashra; one, two, three, four, five, six, seven, eight, nine, ten] . . . choo, choo, choo . . ." The children continued making the engine sound, counting one through ten in Arabic till they reached the dining area exhibit. I thought this was a very creative way of getting the children to move. The children played another game, which required them to recall at least one word in Arabic from the household items. In this game, parents and slightly older children assisted the younger ones while Mr. Ahmad and his assistants made attempts at sounding out the first syllable as a clue, where necessary.

At the dining area exhibit, Mr. Ahmed used the artefacts – table, chair, window and door – without having to move any of them, to revisit the Arabic words. The small square area of this space made it easy for him to engage in conversational encounters with the children and their parents. Thus, enabling communication to occur at a personal distance, in a non-threatening way. Establishing a closed yet safe and comfortable distance is important when managing young children.

The lesson culminated with the children saying, مع السلامة [Ma'a salama; Goodbye], waving at Mr. Ahmad and his assistants. To help parents review the words with their children, the team of volunteers created a simple handout that drew on the notion of translanguaging. They provided both the English words, the Arabic abjad and its transliteration, in three separate columns parallel to one another. While the handout appeared presentable, if CLT had been applied, the English words could have been substituted with visuals as a form of meaning-making. Having learned in classrooms privileging text-based materials, the thought of including visuals may not have crossed the minds of the volunteers.

4.2 Exemplar Lesson #2

Class: Elementary Russian

Venue: A spacious room in a university with limited facilities

(no computer and audio)
Grade level: Pre-K to 3
Total number of children: 10
Theme: A review of words related to food and practice saying "I want . . ."

4.2.1 Brief description of the space

Every Saturday, at 11:00 am, the children who attended elementary Russian came to a class equipped with only tables and chairs. The volunteer instructors and their assistants came at least half an hour earlier to move the tables outside of the room and create space for the planned activities. I assisted them with rearranging the chairs to one side of the classroom. These chairs were meant for parents who would like to sit in and watch over their young child. As a team, we usually decide on the spatial arrangements on the day itself. A typical set up for the weekly lesson is shown in Figure 2.

Figure 2. Two of the children interacting with visual materials for an activity that requires them to name the Russian word. Photographer: author. Used with permission.

4.2.2 What is happening here?

The lesson began with a simple greeting of привет [privet], to mean "Hello" in Russian language, among the instructors, their assistants, children, and parents, as they made their way to the room. While some parents sat on the chairs, most of those with pre-K or younger children sat on the carpeted floor with their child, Ms. Lisa (pseudonym), the volunteer instructor, and her assistants. Following a semi-circular arrangement, the conversational encounters took place within a personal distance that enabled the children to know one another and learn together in a cosy, open space. Since there were three newcomers in this session, Ms. Lisa began by placing the palms of her hands together onto her chest, saying, меня зовут Lisa [Menya zovut Lisa; My name is Lisa]. Then she pointed at Anna, who has been attending the classes regularly, Как тебя зовут? [Kak tebya zovut?; What is your name?] This particular gesture was what I did during the orientation training session. Using Malay language, I said, "Nama saya Su" [My name is Su] and the introduction of names in Malay circulated from one volunteer to another. I saw Anna asking the same question to the person next to her and it went on till it was Tim's, Bill's, and Sam's turn. Lisa and the other children assisted each of them by saying out the words меня зовут [Menya zovut] slowly for them to repeat after. For each child's attempt, Ms. Lisa responded with a thumbs up sign, concurrently saying Отлично! [Otlichno!; Good!], while some of the children mimicked her gestures and words. To ensure that the newcomers would not be left out, Ms. Lisa asked for volunteers from among the children who had been attending the class regularly, to be a buddy to Tim, Bill, or Sam. Each of the buddies took turns to introduce at least two Russian words that they could recall from the visuals on the whiteboard (see Figure 2). Being able to get a young child to articulate two words is a huge success. As an adult, I struggle to recall new vocabulary that does not have cognates with English or a language that I frequently use in my daily communication.

In the first activity, "Waiter! Waiter!", the children moved from the carpeted floor facing the whiteboard to a rectangular table with seats and assumed roles as customers. One child took the role of a waiter. Through this activity, the conversational encounter initiated by the instructor shifted to service encounter, in a simple game that involved role-playing as a waiter and customers in a restaurant; the waiter came to the dining table and asked, "What would you want?" in English. Each customer expressed their desires by saying я хочу ... [ya khochu ...; I want ...] and one of the foods, fruit, or drinks displayed on the whiteboard in Russian, if he/she recalled the word. I noticed that translanguaging in the role-play was unintentionally introduced to motivate children who are new to Russian language. With English words accepted for food, fruit, or drinks, the activity opened up opportunities for other children to articulate the Russian word by whispering into their friend's ears if they knew it. Thus, providing assistance to those who needed more time to be familiar with simple Russian words that were taught in the previous sessions through CLT. The assigned waiter, assisted by Ms. Lisa's volunteer assistants and their parents, took the orders (i.e. visual images placed on a paper plate) from the kitchen area (another table placed in the same room), and walked back to serve the customers. For each correct order, the waiter was awarded a point. The game continued till each child had their turn. The person who accumulated the most points was the winner.

The next part of the activity incidentally introduced the children to major Russian cities: Moscow, St. Petersburg, Sochi, Volgograd, Tula (see images at the topmost part of Figure 3) through a game known as Соль Train. Using prominent cities in Russia as visual materials for the game, the team of volunteers created "spaces" that featured Scollon and Scollon's concept of indexicality when the language activity was linked to well-known places in Russia. In this game, the children worked in pairs to pick a picture that matched with what Ms. Lisa or her assistants said in Russian language. They had to identify the picture and the said word to reach one of the cities. The team that managed to move up to a city and shout out the name of the city first, was the winner. The lesson culminated with Ms. Lisa asking the children and their parents what they would like to learn for the following week. I encouraged the volunteers to informally ask the children and/or parents for suggested topics/themes. By tailoring the lessons to the children's interest, parents would be motivated to return with their child for more language learning opportunities.

A simple handout was distributed to all parents as take-home words that they may want to revise with their children, at leisure. On all the handouts created by this team of volunteers, a visual image of St Basil Cathedral was incorporated, signifying that the list of words was specific for a Russian lesson. This visual, positioned at the top part of the handout, indexed a distinctive architecture recognized by many as a symbol of Russia. Hence, implying that the handout is specifically created for children who are learning Russian language. The instructors engaged in translanguaging to ensure that the words, typed in the target/minority language, Russian, were accurately interpreted. However, visuals were added on top of the English word, transliteration and Russian Cyrillic words to help the children visualize the new vocabulary. While on one hand I discouraged the volunteers from including translations, to align with the notions of CLT, this handout sets me to think of the limitations of CLT – how might words such as tasty and non-tasty be accurately represented using visuals?

4.3 Exemplar Lesson #3

Class: Elementary Japanese
Venue: A corner of a library in ABC elementary school
Grade level: 3 and 4
Total number of children: 15
Theme: Weather

4.3.1 Brief description of the space

On Tuesdays at 4:30 pm, the children in ABC elementary school who were signed up for a daycare program attended elementary Japanese. Although a corner of the library was allocated for PLAYnLEARN, there was no teaching equipment (i.e. whiteboard, computer, projector). I instructed the volunteers to use the topmost edges of the bookshelves as a display board for the students to see the visual materials. At other times, I got them to utilize the windows by the school library. One of them brought a personal laptop, so the team used it to retrieve a song from YouTube for the day's lesson (click on どんなてんき？by SuperSimple to listen). The set up in this particular place is often as shown in Figure 3.

Figure 3. Visuals used as teaching materials and displayed by the book shelves of a library. Photographer: author.

4.3.2 What is happening here?

The lesson began with a simple greeting of こにちは [Konichiwa], to mean "Hello" in Japanese language, among the instructors, their assistants, children, and the daycare assistants. Mr. Jamal (pseudonym), the instructor, then informed the children that they would be learning words related to weather. The conversational encounters in this space took place with the instructor standing in front of a book shelf that functioned as a display board, with the children seated on a carpeted floor. Although they had to look up as they listened to him, the personal distance contributed to their attentiveness. Using self-created materials depicting images of different types of weather conditions, Mr. Jamal introduced the children to one word at a time, sounding it out slowly and clearly, for them to say out loud together. He said, "晴れ [ha-re], repeat after me, 晴れ, 晴れ" and 良い [yoi, meaning "good"]. To ensure that the children understood the word and the visual attached to it, he asked them, "So what is ha-re?" They responded, "Sunny!" and he commented, "良い" [yoi; good]. Although the children were learning new Japanese words, based on CLT approach, there should not be any room for translations. Mr. Jamal could have asked the children to respond to him visually or through bodily movements. On hindsight, I feel that it was only natural for him to draw on a dominant linguistic repertoire understood by the children, to support them in learning a minority language such as Japanese.

The lesson went on with Mr. Jamal and his assistants singing the Japanese song, どんなてんき? [Don'na tenki?; How's the weather?] from a YouTube resource. Their voices and actions created a platform event for the children to watch. In the next two rounds, the children sang to the tune, with actions, taking charge of the platform event for Mr. Jamal, his assistants, and the daycare assistants to watch as they learned the new vocabulary. Through the song sung in Japanese accompanied by vivid visuals with English subtitles, the children picked up the target/minority language. For the second part of the activity, the children moved from the carpeted floor and sat on a circular table. The conversational encounters took place among *withs,* or groups of trios, assigned by the daycare assistants. Ms.

Lily, another volunteer instructor, reinforced the weather-related words that have been taught using a Tenki board game (see http://japaneseteachingideas.weebly.com/weather.html). The team of volunteers had taken this template from a publicly available and copyright-free Japanese teaching website. Printed on A4-sized white paper, this Japanese game aims to provide sufficient practice for asking, "How's the weather today?" For this game, I realized that translanguaging was visible on the board itself. The directions were printed in English. Each visual had English words below it while the target vocabulary that was introduced to the children (i.e. weather-related words) was printed in Japanese characters with transliterations. To ensure equitable participation, the daycare assistants moved around. They sat and played with the children, assuming the role of facilitator, while learning Japanese language with the volunteers as the lesson continued. The Tenki board game was given to each child as a take home vocabulary for reference. They left the room, saying, さよなら [Sayōnara; Goodbye] to everyone.

4.4 Exemplar Lesson #4

Class: Elementary Persian
Venue: An open space outside a daycare center
Grade level: One pre-K (native speaker of Persian) and the others are grade 3 to 4
Total number of children: 10
Theme: Body parts - head, shoulders, knees and toes

4.4.1 Brief description of the space

On Wednesdays at 4:45 pm, the children who signed up for a daycare program attended Elementary Persian as one of the activities. The volunteer instructor works with one volunteer assistant but is supported by two other daycare assistants from the daycare center. The space that was available to them on the day that the children were supposed to be learning body parts was taken up for photo-taking sessions. Left with very little space in the daycare center, I sought the permission of the personnel to conduct the lesson at an open space outside of the daycare center. The weather was perfect for a movement activity. The setup is as shown in Figure 4.

Figure 4. **The children and community partners singing with actions, outside a daycare center. Photographer: author.**

4.4.2 What is happening here?

The lesson began with a simple greeting of سلام [Salam], to mean "Hello", in Persian language, otherwise known as Farsi, among the instructor, her assistant, the children, and the daycare assistants. Ms. Ann (pseudonym) informed the children that they would be learning words related to body parts. She then assigned Yasmin (pseudonym), a four-year-old native speaker of Farsi, to be her co-teacher in a simple game of "Simon Says." Yasmin, well-versed in Farsi, attended this class upon request from her parents. They liked the little girl to be engaged in activities that build her foundational understanding of their heritage language and home language, Farsi. The conversational encounters for this lesson occurred in a circular formation, with everyone standing at a personal distance, close to one another. Ms Ann and Yasmin took turns to introduce the children to different parts of the body, asking them to repeat the Farsi words, showing each body part as they articulated it aloud. To reinforce learning, Ms Ann had them sing the song "Head, shoulders, knees, and toes" in Farsi with actions, outside of the daycare center (see Figure 4). She drew on the perceptual spaces that were present in the same social-physical space and time to engage the children in the target language. These included looking at Yasmin's actions as she pointed at specific body parts (visual space) to learn the vocabulary in Farsi, while listening to and singing the song (auditory space) in an open space on a clear, sunny day (thermal space). The song was initially sung word-by-word to allow the children to pronounce the Farsi words accurately and synchronize them with their bodily actions. It was later on sung slightly faster to add joy and to check that the Farsi words came to their mind naturally.

With the permission of the daycare personnel, Ms. Ann and the children were given colored chalk to draw onto the cemented floor, for an impromptu hands-on activity, "Draw a monster." The cemented floor was transformed into a visual space where the children demonstrated their learning through a simple, creative, imaginative drawing. Ms. Ann, Yasmin, and the community assistants gave instructions on the number of eyes, noses, ears, hands in Farsi, to draw, gradually giving the older children an opportunity to take the lead with the activity using Farsi numbers and body parts. To close, the children took a look at the monster that were drawn by their friends. They bade one another, خدا حافظ [Khoda hafez; Goodbye] once their parents were there to pick them up.

On the whole, geoseomiotics of a community-based schoolscape in each of the abovementioned lessons can be summarized as in Table 1.

Table 1. Geosemiotics of a community-based schoolscape

Language classes	Venue	Interaction order [The ways in which interaction occurs]	Visual semiotics [The visual materials and the context]	Place semiotics [The positioning, aesthetics and materials contributing to how the space is "read"]
Arabic	A public museum	Closed, personal distance Conversational encounter – "What's in my magic bag?" Files and processions – Mimicking a train Perceptual spaces – visual, auditory, thermal and haptic	Hopscotch created from colored construction paper with handwritten numbers and artificial fruits; Selected objects in the dining area exhibit: window, door, table, and chair Handout printed in English, Arabic abjad and transliterations	Visual materials and artefacts on the carpeted floor functioning as a temporary "playground" for children; Physical artefacts permanently installed in the museum used as teaching resources
Russian	A room in a university	Closed, personal distance Conversational encounter – Self-introduction for newcomers Service encounter – "Waiter! Waiter!" game Conversational encounter – "Соль Train" game Perceptual spaces – visual, auditory, thermal and haptic	Visuals depicting food, fruits and drinks Handout with visuals in English, Russian Cyrillic and transliterations	Visual materials taped onto a wide-spaced wall Visual materials displayed onto a wide-spaced table, to simulate a kitchen area

Language classes	Venue	Interaction order [The ways in which interaction occurs]	Visual semiotics [The visual materials and the context]	Place semiotics [The positioning, aesthetics and materials contributing to how the space is "read"]
Japanese	A corner of a library in ABC elementary school	Closed, personal distance Conversational encounter – Introducing new vocabulary using visuals Platform event – Singing with actions Perceptual spaces – visual, auditory, thermal	Visuals of different types of weather with Japanese transliterations Japanese board game printed with visuals accompanied by the English word below, and Japanese transliterations as handouts	Visual materials taped onto bookshelves functioning as a display board
Persian	An open space outside a daycare center	Closed, personal distance Conversational encounter – Instructor and a native-speaker child as a co-instructor introducing body parts – "Simon says" game Platform event – Singing with actions Conversational encounter – "Draw a monster" Perceptual spaces – visual, auditory, thermal and haptic	Physical parts of the body	The circular formation of the children in a safe, open space outside of the daycare center

5. Larger meanings and implications

The results of this autoethnographic study as summarized on Table 1, suggest a nexus of theory–practice–person, all of which influence one another. As a language and program coordinator, my personal experiences of acquiring Spanish through real-life interactions led me to attach a high value to CLT. While initially I picked up the language for survival purposes, my vocabulary widened as I started embarking on field-based research in Argentina where Spanish is predominantly used (see Abas & Damico, 2018; Abas, in press). As I reflected on how the children in PLAYnLEARN may benefit, I conjectured that the language activities could be a great headstart. Similar to how I had become acquainted with Spanish, I foresee these as teasers for developing the community's interest (both children and parents) in pursuing minority languages, in future. Although my exposure to language learning prior to the US took on the path of a language separation policy, I must admit that there are merits and demerits in any type of language learning models. However, to privilege my past over current views on language education in the US or vice versa, would not justify the sustainability of minority languages or language programs that tailor to children of heritage or minority language speakers. To this end, I believe effective language learning requires a holistic approach. PLAYnLEARN opens up opportunities for embracing a new emergent paradigm in accordance with recent trends of globalization and digital communication. By virtue of its fluidity, a community-based schoolscape thrives because of the strong support from the volunteers, parents, community partners and children. Based on my experiences of being a part of the lessons that I had described earlier, the semiotic aggregates that constantly come into play can be graphically represented as follows:

Figure 5. Semiotic aggregates of a community-based schoolscape. Adapted from Scollon and Scollon (2003, p. 3); the arrows were included to indicate physical-digital transference of experiences.

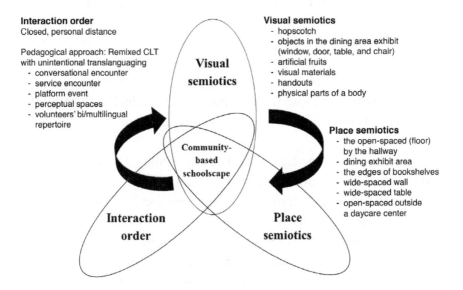

As can be seen in Figure 5, there are "multiple semiotic systems in a dialogical interaction with each other" (Scollon & Scollon, 2003, p.12) in a community-based schoolscape such as PLAYnLEARN. This included my own background to language learning as it impacted my beliefs and hence, the ways I trained the volunteers. In reality, the configurations of interactions are far more complex and might not be captured neatly as above since all of the semiotic systems converged with one another despite the limitations. Through Scollon and Scollon's geosemiotics, I evinced that language learning can happen outside of the classroom or in non-traditional settings for as long as the semiotic systems – interaction order, visual semiotics and place semiotics – converged to support the learning of minority languages.

Given limited resources and the fluidity of spaces, it is still possible to engage in the process of meaning-making. In Exemplar lesson #1, the volunteers constructed two hopscotches that transformed the hallway into a mini playground and leveraged available resources from the dining area exhibit to review the Arabic words. In Exemplar #2, the whiteboard and tables were utilized as visual display and kitchen areas for the purpose of revisiting food items and incorporating a simple role-play activity. Exemplar lesson #3 however, had the computer-printed visuals on the topmost edge of the bookshelves and windows for the children to view. The volunteers in Exemplar lesson #4 totally did away with the limited space by occupying the open space outside the daycare center.

In terms of the pedagogical approach, while CLT is emphasized, translanguaging should be credited as a natural way in which bilinguals express themselves (Kleyn, 2016) or, to be specific, articulate their understanding of particular words. However, to train volunteers to use translanguaging as a valid pedagogical approach for this program may be challenging; some of them are learners of the minority languages themselves, and therefore, they may not be prepared to engage in the target/minority language with the children and the community with fluency. Embracing translanguaging as peripheral, in this case, is recommended rather than placing it as central to the pedagogy of teaching minority languages. Moving forward, at the basic level, elementary schools could potentially design the curricula based on the "language awareness" (LA) approach to transform minority languages into legitimate knowledge. LA activities are typically task-based, focused on comparing different languages and promoting metalinguistic reflection (Hélot, 2008). This approach envisages language learning drawing from learners' own linguistic repertoire and thus, it creates awareness on the diversity of languages and multilingualism (for examples of LA activities, see Wright and Bolitho, 1993).

Conclusively, I argue that minority languages can best be served when the entire community is involved in making voluntary contributions to promote and sustain them. As the saying goes, "It takes the whole village to raise a child."

Acknowledgements
Special thanks to dedicated volunteers, community partners, parents, and the children who have been a part of this wonderful project.

References
Abas, S. (in press). Repatriating desaparacidos across spaces. In D. G. Pyles, R. M. Rish, & J. Warner (Eds.), *Negotiating place and space in digital literacies: Research and Practise* (pp. 261–276). Denver, CO: Information Age Publishing.

Abas, S. & Damico, J. (2018). The language of activism. Representations of social justice in a university space in Argentina. In N. Avineri, L. R. Graham, E. Johnson, R. Riner, & J. Rosa (Eds.), *Language and social justice in practice* (pp. 157–165). New York, NY: Routledge. doi:10.4324/9781315115702

Baker, C. (2011). *Foundations of bilingual education and bilingualism.* Bristol, UK: Multilingual Matters.

Bochner, A. P. & Ellis, C. (1996). Talking over ethnography. In C. Ellis & A. P. Bochner (Eds.), *Composing Ethnography: Alternative Forms of Qualitative Writing* (pp. 13–45). Walnut Creek, CA: Alta Mira Press.

Brock-Utne, B. (1996). Reliability and validity in qualitative research within education in Africa. *International Review of Education, 42*(6), 605–621.

Brown, H.D. (2001). *Teaching by Principles: An Interactive Approach to Language Pedagogy.* New York: Longman.

Brown, K. D. (2005). Estonian Schoolscapes and the Marginalization of Regional Identity in Education, *European Education, 37*(3), 78-89, doi: 10.1080/10564934.2005.11042390

Brown, K. D. (2012). The linguistic landscape of educational spaces: Language, revitalization and schools in southeastern Estonia. In D.

Gorter, H.F. Marten, & L. Van Mensel (Eds.), *Minority languages in the linguistic landscape* (pp. 281–298). Basingstroke: Palgrave-Macmillan.

Center for Applied Linguistics. (2011). *Directory of foreign language immersion programs in U.S. schools.* Retrieved March 31, 2019, from http://webapp.cal.org/Immersion/

Chang, H. (2008). *Autoethnography as method.* Left Coast Press, Walnut Creek, CA.

Creswell, J. W. (2013). *Qualitative inquiry and research design: Choosing among five approaches.* Thousand Oaks, CA: Sage.

Dagenais, D., Moore, D., Sabatier, C., Lamarre, P., & Armand, F. (2009). Linguistic landscape and language awareness. In E. Shohamy & D. Gorter (Eds.), *Linguistic Landscape: Expanding the Scenery* (pp. 253–269). New York: Routledge/Taylor & Francis Group.

Ellis, C. (2009). *Revision: Autoethnographic reflections on life and work.* Writing Lives: Ethnographic Narratives series. New York: Routledge.

García, O. (2009). Education, multilingualism and translanguaging in the 21st century. In M. Ajit, P. Minati, P. Robert, & S. Tove (eds.) *Multilingual Education for Social Justice: Globalising the Local* (pp. 128–145). New Delhi, India: Orient Blackswan.

García, O., & Wei, L. (2014). *Translanguaging: Language, bilingualism and education.* London, England: Palgrave Macmillan.

Goodall, H. L. (2000). *Writing the new ethnography.* Lanham, MD: AltaMira Press.

Hélot, C. (2008). Awareness Raising and Multilingualism in Primary Education. In N. Hornberger (Ed.). *The Encyclopedia of Language and Education.* New York: Springer.

Hughes, S. A. (2008). Toward "good enough methods" for autoethnography: Trying to resist the matrix with another promising red pill. *Educational Studies, 43,* 125–143.

Issa, T., & Williams, C. (2009). *Realising potential: complementary schools in the UK.* Stoke on Trent: Trentham Books.

Landry, R. & Bourhis, R. Y. (1997). Linguistic landscape and ethnolinguistic vitality: An empirical study. *Journal of Language and Social Psychology, 16*(1), 23–49.

Larsen-Freeman, D. (Ed.). (2000). *Techniques and principles in language teaching* (2nd Ed.). Oxford: Oxford University Press.

Lincoln, Y. S. & Guba, E. G. (1985). *Naturalistic inquiry.* Newbury Park, CA: Sage.

Malinowski, D. (2015). Opening spaces of learning in the linguistic landscape. *Linguistic Landscape 1*(1–2), 95–113. doi: 10.1075/ll.1.1-2.06mal

Mann, S. (2016). *The research interview: Reflective practice and reflexivity in research processes.* London: Palgrave Macmillan.

Massey, D. (2000). The conceptualisation of place. In D. Massey & P. Jess (Eds.), *A place in the world? Places, cultures and globalisation* (pp. 45–85). New York: Oxford University Press.

Nunan, D. (1991). Communicative tasks and the language curriculum. *TESOL Quarterly, 25*(2), 279–295.

Pavlenko, A. (2007). Autobiographic narratives as data in applied linguistics. *Applied Linguistics, 28,* 63–188.

Pennington, J. L. (2007). Silence in the classroom/whispers in the halls: Autoethnography as pedagogy in White pre-service teacher education. *Race, Ethnicity and Education, 10,* 93–113.

Reed-Danahay, D. E. (2001). Autobiography, intimacy and ethnography. In P. Atkinson, A. Coffey, S. Delamont, J. Lofland, & L. Lofland (Eds.), *The handbook of ethnography* (pp. 407–425). London: Sage.

Richards, J. C. (2006). *Communicative Language Teaching Today.* New York: Cambridge University Press.

Romo, J. J. (2005). Border pedagogy from the inside out: An autoethnographic study. *Journal of Latinos and Education, 4,* 193–210.

Sayer, P. (2010). Using the linguistic landscape as a pedagogical resource. *English Language Teaching Journal, 64*(2), 143–154. doi:10.1093/elt/ccp051

Scollon, R. & Scollon, S. (2003). *Discourses in Place: Language in the Material World.* London: Routledge.

United States Census Bureau (2000). Language use in the United States: 2011. American community survey reports. Retrieved from https://www.census.gov/topics/population/language-use.html

Walford, G. (2004). Finding the limits: Autoethnography and being and Oxford University proctor. *Qualitative Research, 4,* 403–417.

Wei, L. (2006). Complementary Schools, Past, Present and Future. *Language and Education, 20*(1), 76–83, DOI: 10.1080/09500780608668711.

Wright, T. & Bolitho, R. (1993). Language awareness: a missing link in language teacher education? *ELT Journal, 47*(4), 292–304.

Yin, R. K. (2009). *Case Study Research Design and Methods* (4th ed.). Thousand Oaks, CA: Sage Publications.

CHAPTER 12

Multilingual education: Encouraging students to use their language backgrounds

Verbra Pfeiffer

When you think about language, it's really about skills – and those skills are fluid and transferable. —Tonya Gilchrist (2018)

1. Introduction

Research has found that students who have more than one language at their disposal believe that they should be able to master their academic language and forget their home or community language so that they can strengthen their academic performance and concept literacy. Such a perception may be found in countries like South Africa and Switzerland that have an array of multilingual students at their universities. This study looks at ways in which the academic writing of students is influenced by their code-switching and translanguaging skills. This is a qualitative, longitudinal study presenting data from South Africa and Switzerland, addressing the topic of what is good writing in the respective communities. The data of this study is a written account of ways in which the students gave nuance to their understanding of good writing from an academic perspective. Attempts were made by students to find ways in which they used their home language when writing for academic purposes. A comparison of the answers of the students from the two countries was made, where the differences and similarities in answers were identified. This research looks at discerning ways in which students' writing can be strengthened by leaning on their home language (L1) to assist them in their academic writing. The aim of the study was to make students aware of the fact that having more than one language at their disposal could enrich their academic writing. In conclusion, an attempt was made to demonstrate that multilinguals should be made aware that they can draw on different strategies and practice that can be activated for learning, depending on the languages they have available for reading or writing or discussions.

1.1 Point of departure

Student population at universities has become increasingly diverse, creating new challenges for students and university lecturers. It appears that university students worldwide are studying in a multilingual context where English occupies the dominant position (Mazak, 2017; Palfreyman & van der Walt, 2017; Kaufhold, 2018). Hyland (2018, p. 384) argues that, even if it were possible in the past to rely on the communicative readiness of school leavers for academic study, this linguistically, socially, and culturally diverse body of students now makes such assumptions extremely questionable. In addition, higher education institutions often support the use of English at postgraduate level so that they can internationalize their universities (Mortensen, 2014; Kaufhold, 2018). Lillis and Curry (2010, p. 1) have labeled English "the default language of Science and academic research and dissemination," noting that it is "considered by prestigious institutions to be the global language of Science."

In this chapter, I will look at the way in which learning to write in English, whether it is one's first, second or third language, continues to be a major educational venture throughout the world (more specifically South Africa and Switzerland). According to Freedman, Pringle, and Yalden (2014, p. 3), in the second-language (L2) context, the difficulties involved in learning combined with the difficulties in learning to write in one's own language at a level beyond that of minimal literacy are joined by all the further complexities inherent in trying to master a second language. Hence, it is no longer only a matter of trying to master a different medium and learning how to handle its special exigencies, "it is also a matter of learning how to express oneself appropriately in a different language and in a different culture" (Freedman et al., 2014, p. 3).

In our universities our classes have become linguistically diverse and our academic literacy lecturers themselves display a variety of "linguistic repertoires" (Carstens, 2016, p. 1). As a result, we tend to view writing as one manifestation of a multilingual repertoire (see also Hammine, this volume). Accordingly, due to the multilingual nature of South African classrooms as well as Swiss classrooms, it is required that students are able to describe what they regard as good writing to show that they are aware of the importance of developing this skill. For this purpose, I gathered students' opinions of what they thought good writing may be. As such, the study goes beyond common assumptions that language proficiency in English is the main ingredient in academic success. With this in mind, I will discuss the importance of those academic writing skills (planning, writing, revising).

Through the medium of English, students have come to realize the importance of being proficient in English. However, students should also realize that English is not the alpha and omega, and the learning of it should not necessarily mean the avoidance or loss of other languages (Klapwijk & van der Walt, 2015, p. 3). In light of this, this study will be addressing the role the students' home or community languages may play in their writing and moving away from the importance of being proficient in a language that is not their home language, in this case English.

Finally, in this chapter I will explore ways in which the use of translanguaging and code-switching affects writing skills in a bi/

multilingual context. Research demonstrates that code-switching is a sophisticated, rule-governed, and systematic communicative behavior used by linguistically competent bilinguals to achieve a variety of communicative goals (Gingràs, 1974; Pfaff, 1979; Timm, 1975, Gort, 2012). In this chapter, I will demonstrate the way in which the students use code-switching techniques to assist them in their academic writing.

Translanguaging has been viewed as the "planned and systematic use of two languages for teaching and learning inside the same lesson" (Lewis, Jones, & Baker, 2012, p.643) to facilitate understanding, L2 learning, and L1 development. In this chapter I will focus on the value of improving writing skills and the extent to which translanguaging occurs when students write in one language and think in another in South Africa as well as in Switzerland.

2. Literature framework

In a bi/multilingual educational context, where students are presented with lectures and study material in more than one language, students are allowed to exploit their bi/multilingual proficiency, that is, without focusing on one language only (van der Walt & Dornbrack, 2011). Thus, academic language proficiency requires high levels of writing fluency in English. In a multilingual country, the focus in this chapter is to determine what students regard as good writing.

Writing may be viewed as central to postgraduate study, irrespective of the discipline (Vivian & Fourie, 2016, p. 147). In a study conducted by Cameron, Nairn, & Higgins (2009, p. 269) it was found that "[w]riting is the foundation of an academic year." They argue that, often, students' writing is at the center of teaching and learning in higher education, "fulfilling a range of purposes according to the various contexts in which it occurs" (Coffin, Curry, Goodman, Hewings, Lillis, & Swann, 2003, p. 2). According to Coffin et al. (2003, p. 2) students' writing relates to assessment ("the major purpose for student writing"), learning ("which can help students grapple with disciplinary knowledge"), and entering particular disciplinary communities ("whose communication norms are the primary means by which academics transmit and evaluate ideas"). For students, academic writing can be quite a stressful process when they are writing in their L2/L3 because they are aware that writing relates to assessment, learning, and getting their points or arguments across. For this purpose, I examine ways that students view the importance of writing well.

Rohman (1965, pp. 107–8) defined "good writing" as that discovered combination of words that allows a person the integrity to dominate his subject with a pattern both fresh and original. He continues to say that "bad writing," then, is an echo of someone else's combination that we have merely taken over for the occasion of our writing . . . "Good writing" must be the discovery by a responsible person of his uniqueness within his subject. In this chapter, I will demonstrate students' understanding of good writing and the use of words to dominate their subject-specific content.

In addition, good writing may be viewed as good dialogue – always mixing, changing, incorporating, answering, anticipating – merging the writer and the reader in the construction of meaning (Middendorf, 1992; DeLyser, 2003, p. 172). Learning to write is not just a question of developing a set of mechanical "orthographic" skills; it also involves learning a new set of cognitive and social relations (Tribble, 1996; Pfeiffer, 2015). Writing alone is typically grounded in the cognitive processes such as planning, translating, and reviewing/revising, rather than on the levels of language involved in translating ideas into the written product (Abbott, Berninger, & Fayol, 2012).

Ruíz (1984, p. 27) makes a distinction between "language-as-problem," "language-as-right," and "language-as-resource" approaches in language planning. Recently, researchers have started to investigate multilinguals' academic writing by combining approaches to bilingualism, second language learning and academic writing.

312   EMBRACING MULTILINGUALISM

Results indicate that students can benefit from their knowledge and experience of academic writing across language codes (Gentil, 2005; Kobayashi & Rinnert, 2013). It appears that switching languages occurs naturally and is a strategy that multilingual students employ intuitively (Cumming, 2013; Canagarajah, 2011; Gentil, 2005; van der Walt, 2013; Kaufhold, 2018). Linked with multilingualism there are two main concepts that I will address, which are code-switching and translanguaging.

Johanssen (2013, p. 2) found that code-switching is a phenomenon that exists in bilingual societies where people have the opportunity to use two or more languages to communicate. She continues to say that being able to speak more than one language, bilinguals can code-switch and use their languages as resources to find better ways to convey meaning. Code-switching has also been defined as "the alternation of two languages within a single discourse, sentence, or constituent" (Jamshidi & Navehebraim, 2013, p. 186). Basically code-switching "involves the transfer of linguistic elements from one language into another: a sentence begins in one language, then makes use of words or grammatical features belonging to another" (Crystal, 2003, pp. 78–79). This implies that code-switching lends into several functions such as filling linguistic gaps, expressing ethnic identity and achieving particular discursive aims (Bullock & Toribio, 2009; Johanssen, 2013). In addition, Palmer, Mateus, Antonio Martinez, & Henderson (2014, p. 759) echoed that code-switching is shifting between two languages within or between utterances. This practice may be seen by teachers in dual language education. They argue that bilingual students use language in complex and dynamic ways. In light of this, code-switching may be viewed as strict language separation advocates (Cloud, Genesee, & Hamayan, 2000); however, it is generally acknowledged by a large body of research in the field of linguistics that supports the notion of code-switching as a normal, intelligent, and socially meaningful linguistic phenomenon (Blom

& Gumperz, 1972; Jaffe, 2007; MacSwan, 2000; Toribio, 2004; Woolard, 2004; Zentella, 1997). In the discussion section of this chapter, I will demonstrate the way in which the students used code-switching when writing. This may be seen when the student uses the two or more languages available to them to assist in writing as they attempt to convey meaning in academic writing.

Translanguaging has been viewed as a very natural way for multilingual people to communicate – but as a focus of research it emerged in the 1980s in Bangor, north Wales. According to Lewis, Jones, & Baker (2012, p. 643), Cen Williams and colleagues were investigating strategies for learners to use two languages (Welsh and English) in a single lesson. This led them to come up with the term "trawsieithu" to describe reading or hearing input in one language (e.g. English) and writing or speaking about it in another (e.g. Welsh, or vice versa). The term was translated into English (and popularized) as "translanguaging" by their colleague Colin Baker (Lewis et al., 2012, p. 643). Translanguaging has been defined in that you receive information through the medium of one language (e.g. English) and use it yourself through the medium of the other language (Lewis et al., 2012, pp. 643–644). According to Baker (2011, p. 288) translanguaging is the process of making meaning, shaping experiences, and gaining understanding and knowledge through the use of two languages.

The term translanguaging has also been defined in a way that stresses the flexible and meaningful actions through which bilinguals select features in their linguistic repertoire in order to communicate appropriately (Valesco & García, 2014). Ergo, Li (2011) suggests that the negotiation of repertoires involved in translanguaging creates a "translanguaging space" (p. 1223), a space for the act of translanguaging and shaped by translanguaging. It appears that Li (2011, p. 1223) has identified translanguaging as a "social space for the multilingual language user," created by networks of social relations and shared practices, which allows them to incorporate "different dimensions of their personal history, experience and environment, their attitude, belief and ideology, their cognitive and physical capacity" (Wei, 2011; Kaufhold, 2018, p. 2). In addition, translanguaging helps us adopt specific orientations that may assist multilinguals in appreciating their competence in their own terms (Canagarajah, 2015). In this context I intend to view translanguaging in writing as a self-regulating mechanism in which bi/multilingual students can engage, rather than a pedagogy to be used in the teaching of writing itself (Velasco & García, 2014). Furthermore, I will also address the way in which the students wiwll read or hear the instruction in a language that is not their home language and the way they use it in their L1 to make sense or gain understanding of the medium of instruction.

In this study students are familiar in their discipline-specific terminology in their fields, which is in the medium of instruction (English, German). However, my research intended to make students' aware of their home language and the ways they can use it to strengthen their academic writing.

2.1 Research background

This study was conducted at one university in South Africa and four universities in Switzerland. At the university in South Africa, the study was conducted on pre-service student teachers, and in Switzerland the students ranged from undergraduates to postgraduates from various faculties. The population for this study included students who were English, Afrikaans, IsiXhosa, Swiss German, and Chinese, with some from various other European-speaking countries. This was a longitudinal study and the data was collected in 2016, 2017, and 2018. The students from all the universities were given the opportunity to describe in writing what they understood under the term "good writing" and why it was important to develop this ability.

I have decided to focus on the understanding of the importance of good writing because identifying this importance was of huge value when assisting students in improving their writing skills. At this juncture, I addressed the level at which translanguaging and code-switching occur for second- or third-language speakers of English / Swiss German.

All the students that participated in this study had to answer a questionnaire that I had given them. The writing handed in by the students was largely done in English or German, with some in French. Ethical clearance for this study was provided from the university in South Africa and consent was given to collect data at the four universities in Switzerland.

Research questions:

1. What choices do students face in code-switching in their writing?
2. What considerations help them resolve their choices?
3. What composing and cognitive stages characterize the production of translanguaging?

These questions enabled me to gain insight into the processes that accompany translanguaging and code-switching, and assisted me to better teach writing techniques to students.

3. Methodology
In three successive years I polled pre-service student teachers from a South African university and under/postgraduate students from four Swiss universities by giving them the opportunity to respond in writing to four open-ended questions:

1. What is good writing and why is it important to develop that ability?

2. For English FAL (First Additional Language) students: Do you use your home language when you write? If so, how do you do it?
3. When does writing in English become challenging for you?
4. What is the most challenging part of writing for you (home language and FAL)?

However, in this chapter, I only focused on the first three open-ended questions. To analyze the data, I used a three-tiered analytic process as suggested by Miles and Huberman (1994, p. 92):

- prepare the data sets and check for completeness
- analyze the information and identify themes and categories
- synthesize the data by abstracting possible trends and linking the data to other research insights.

I looked at the word count that I noticed over the past three years from the data I collected in South Africa and Switzerland. I compared the similarities between the words that students from the two countries had mentioned in their written answers. It became clear to me that certain words and phrases were repeated in both countries and I thus decided to strengthen my analysis by using word counts. This strategy was useful to check for inconsistencies in my analysis and it also helped me not to miss anything in the wealth of data. By the third year I realized that this strategy, however, could result in me missing particular themes because I was only looking for the words that I knew had appeared in the earlier data. To overcome this problem, I only did the word searches after my initial reading of the data and this process meant that I identified new themes, which meant that I went back to the earlier data to analyze those responses again. It should be noted that all the data included in this chapter from the students' written responses to the questionnaires were not changed and are indicated in italics.

4. Results

The word counts showed the variability across the three years. In response to the question about what students think good writing is, the idea of "flow" (for example sentences or ideas "flow") as well as "cohesion/coherence/cohesive(ness)" appeared repeatedly in the data of the first two years. However, in the third year, when I had the biggest group of responses, these words and phrases were not as numerous:

Table 1. Variability of word counts over three years

Years Words/phrases	2016 (n = 62)	2017 (n = 74)	2018 (n = 243)	2017 (n = 60) Swiss
flow (for example sentences or ideas "flow"	35	14	17	7
cohesion/coherence/ cohesive(ness)	26	25	16	1

This comparison showed the degree to which conceptions are fleeting and may be influenced by a variety of factors, such as possibly the type of students who volunteered to respond. Since the responses were anonymized, I do not know, for example, whether students who majored in language teaching dominated the first groups. As seen in Table 1, only seven Swiss students indicated that the "flow" of the sentence was important for good writing.

In the discussion that follows, it is important to keep in mind that the word counts served to strengthen my initial analyses; they did not determine the coding process. Some of the words I left as they were written by the students.

Table 2. Common words used by students

Years / Words	2016	2017	2019	CH (Swiss) 2017
Clear(ly)	25	38	121	35
(in)correct(ly)	8	62	82	24
Easy, easily, ease, easier	0	21	34	13
Grammar/ grammatical(ly)/ grammar	16	71	99	21
(ideas, sentences) flow	35	14	17	7
Effect(ively)	10	18	27	1
Structure of text	9	20	63	0
Cohesion/ coherence/ cohesive(ness)	26	25	16	0

In the discussion that follows, the focus will be on the first three questions mainly in an effort to show what students value in writing and how they use their home or community languages to support their own writing. I hope to show that the focus of the students on particular features of "good writing" may have an influence on how they utilize their home languages for academic writing (in English/ German) in particular. As mentioned earlier on, I use italics to indicate students' words, which have not been corrected or adapted in any way. Since I had so much data, I had to nit-pick sentences written by the students to bring my points across. I also had to consider the word count for this chapter when writing up the results. The following sections and subsections are just an indication of some features that I noticed when writing up the results section.

4.1 Themes from Question 1: What is good writing and why is it important to develop that ability?

4.1.1 Theme 1: A focus on surface features and language mechanics
Across the data sets, students emphasize surface features of correctness and the words "(in)correct(ly)" are used mostly with the concept of grammar, but also with spelling and punctuation:

- *Good writing [...] also includes the correct and accurate use of grammar and punctuation.*
- *It also includes the use of the correct punctuation and spelling of words.*
- *Because I don't know all the words and the grammar perfectly, so it's difficult to build up a good text.*

The words "accurate" and "accuracy" is used rarely, but when they are, they link up with the issue of correctness:

- *Good writing is characterized by good diction and grammar that allows accurate presentation of thoughts.*

In the 2018 data, a few references to accuracy link to the author providing information, for example:

- *To convey information accurately and in a medium that the reader can understand.*
- *To express yourself accurately.*

- *Accurate explanation and exciting content.*

These last three statements go further than correctness of particular features of language: they constitute a link between accuracy and the degree to which a text is understood. This strand in my data links up with correctness, but in a more complex manner.

4.1.2 Theme 2: The "transparency" of language

The link between accuracy/correctness and comprehension is expressed mostly in statements about the clarity of language use, or the invocation that language should be used "clearly" to "make sense" with the result that the reader will understand:

- *Good writing commit of conveying a message clear so that the person who reads the writing understands what is being said.*
- *Clear to follow the argument.*
- *Using clear sentences and being consistent in the use of terms.*

The phrase "clear and concise" appears regularly, particularly in the 2018 and 2017 data. In the 2016 data "concise" appears 15 times with the word "coherent" as seen in Table 2. For some students, clarity of thought is the responsibility of the author and a precondition for understanding:

- *Good writing is when you have a clear understanding of the topic that you are writing about.*
- *Good writing is when the writer can clearly states his/her thoughts and arguments.*
- *Good writing is precise (defends), well-structured, presenting a particular theme.*

The same idea can be found when "clear" is used as a verb:

- *. . . your way of expressing yourself help to clear out the misunderstandings in writing.*
- *Clear to follow argument and transmit new ideas.*

Clarity is also linked to the structure of the writing and the way in which the text appears to be "coherent." However, from the way in which clarity and structure is used in the majority of the responses, these aspects function above sentence level.

4.1.3 Theme 3: The way in which the structure of a written piece coheres

For the students involved in this project, writing longer pieces of text is associated with academic writing and for that reason the quality of argumentation is an important indicator of "good writing." Two sub-themes emerge in this case: the importance of structure and the coherence of a piece of well-structured writing. Although these two sub-themes can be distinguished, they are often interlinked in the data, as the following excerpt shows (key words in bold):

- *Good writing should convey a **structured**, well thought out argument or theme that is **fluid** and **clearly** depicted through writing.*

The idea of correctness appears in this theme as well:

- *Good writing is clear and in the correct order.*

A "correct order" also appears in the guise of a "logical" structure:

- *Good writing is writing a piece or text that makes sense logically – coherent.*
- *Sentences should follow a logical sequence.*

Conceptions of "flow" and "coherence" appeared as an important feature of good writing, sometimes separately and sometimes together. "Flow" appeared to be linked to structure at and above sentence level:

- *Flowing from one sentence to the next;*
- *Also, good writing is when the writer or your writing has structure or a good flow. Usually it consist of an introduction, a body, and conclusion.*
- *When a text has a good flow and the sentences are well connected to each other.*
- *It must be logical – have a beginning, middle, and end.*

When linked to "coherence" or "cohesion," the construction of meaning is presented as a result:

- *Good writing is writing that is coherent, meaning that it is unified. It has to have flow so that reading is easy and natural;*
- *Formulate sentences coherently and effectively.*

In most of these extracts from the students' responses, it is clear that the possible impact and meaning of writing is foremost in their minds.

4.1.4 Theme 4: Good writing is the responsibility of the writer

The fact that the question focused on good writing means that the participants placed much emphasis on the responsibility of the writer to make themselves understood. In this case references to "writer" or "author" are coupled with words like good, effectively, clearly, should, (must be able):

- *In practice it would be the skill and proper use of language based*

> rules and self-ability to connect to a topic of writing, for the writer
> to fully express themselves clearly and the reader or recipient to
> clearly receive and understand the piece/story.

- *[Good writing is...] when the writer is able to write and convey
  their message or idea in a fluent and readable manner.*

An awareness of different aspects of the writing process is mentioned
throughout the data:

- Awareness of audience:
  - *As a writer you must be able to convey meaning in a way that
    accommodates the target audience.*
- Awareness of different dialects and varieties of English, linked
  to the awareness of audience:
  - *[Good writing] also enables speakers with different dialects of a
    language, to understand what is being said*
  - *Instead, there are many Englishes, all deserving of the title
    "good English". "Good writing" then should be writing that is
    understandable to the intended audience.*

As is clear from these four themes, participants had a range of ideas
about what good writing is and these ideas would naturally have
been at the back of their minds when they responded to the question
about whether they use their home or community language when
they write.

4.2 Themes from question 2: For English FAL students: Do you use your home language when you write? If so, how do you do it?

One of the aims of this project is to raise awareness of the possibilities
of using other languages as a resource when writing in English,
mostly for academic purposes. Question 2 was therefore addressed at
second language users of English in particular. I first tried to establish

how many students actually use their home language when writing in English. Over the three years, the percentage of South African participants remained more or less stable, and in Switzerland more than 80% of the students used their home language when they wrote in English, as seen in Table 3.

Table 3. Percentage of South African and Swiss students who profess to use their home language when writing in English

2016 (n = 62)	2017 (n = 74)	2018 (n = 212)	2017 (n = 60) Swiss
22 (35%)	22 (30%)	63 (30%)	53 (88%)

The majority of the students in the Swiss universities (53/60) indicated that they use their home language in some way when they write in English. Since English might not feature as prominently in European universities as it does in South Africa, and since it is a foreign language (rather than a second language), this is understandable. Generally speaking, the Swiss students seemed to use the same techniques as the South Africans, with some notable exceptions.

4.2.1 Theme 1: Using code-switching (also called "reword" or "convert" from one language to another)

In the South African data, the biggest number of students who responded to this question were Afrikaans–English bilinguals, although there were isiXhosa students as well. In the Swiss data, students with languages as diverse as Chinese, Italian, and Swiss German say that they think in their home language and translate to English.

- *I read the sentence in english and try to reword it in Afrikaans (or figure out what it should be in Afrikaans) in order to get a better*

understanding of it. I will then re-write it in english.
- *for academic purposes, I use English, but I do make use of Afrikaans translations in my head, while writing*
- *in my language [isiXhosa] . . . in order to make a point you must use a series of words, however when I think I think in my language and quickly translate into English.*
- *When my mind is block, I'll use my home language [Chinese] to think and organize my word and then translate it into English.*
- *I first think on Italian, then I try to translate it and write down a sentence.*

There is also an awareness that translation cannot be literal (bold added):

- *I will say it in Afrikaans and then try to capture **the spirit of it** in English.*
- *I often use metaphors from my home language to write in English or just translate them. The general idea is **being able to express oneself** (IsiXhosa).*
- *When I have to use difficult words or if the translation from my language in another language has not the same meaning (Swiss)*

The most widely used resource is dictionaries. Many participants refer to looking up words or getting stuck and then using their home language to look up words in a bilingual dictionary.

4.2.2 Theme 2: Planning and structuring in the home language(s)
Some participants mention that they plan or structure in their home language and then write in English. This use of the home language can be seen as a more conceptual engagement with the topic of the written text, rather than simply translating to English when stuck for a word.

- A Swiss-German participant: *first step: doing a mindmap. I often use different languages to make a difference between "german/ english – language".*
- A Swiss-German participant: *I first think in my home language and than start to write.*
- *I first get my thoughts together in Afrikaans . . .*
- *I spend most of my time speaking isiXhosa and when I'm required to write anything in English, I first have to mentally prepare myself.*

Some participants acknowledge that they do most of their thinking (for academic writing) in the home language:

- *I will always first structure my work in Afrikaans and do all my planning in Afrikaans. From there I will translate it to English, but most to all of my thinking and planning happens in Afrikaans.*
- A German participant: *for complex ideas. For organizing ideas. For arguments.*
- A Turkish participant: *to understand complex or complicated concept.*

In the data presented above there is a clear indication of translanguaging taking place. We often see that the students mention that they would first think in their home language and then start writing in English. We recognize that the students are using strategies to assist them in their writing, like the one Swiss-German student who mentioned that they create a mind map, while the other mentioned that for complex ideas, they first think in their home language (for further discussion of strategies, see also Abas, this volume). When asked this question students became aware of the way they used their home language to assist them in their writing. The isiXhosa student mentioned that they have to "mentally prepare" themselves when they have to write in English. Without students being made aware, translanguaging has become a natural tool for them to use when they are writing in a language that is not their home language.

5. Discussion

When I started with my collection of data, I was very much interested in the way that bi/multilingual writers negotiated in their minds what they would say and how they would say certain things in their writing. I was under the impression that this practice involved arguments and collaborative completion in their minds when they are writing in a language that is not their home language. I was also interested in the way that writers adjusted their writing so that it can be recognizable to audiences.

I have identified that the students' problems with writing appear in their surface features, structural problems, creativity. What students identified as features of good writing are:

- *Good writing is characterized by good diction and grammar that allows accurate presentation of thoughts.*
- *It must be logical – have a beginning, middle, and end.*
- *As a writer you must be able to convey meaning in a way that accommodates the target audience.*

Hyland (2016, p. 39) argues that we can no longer regard a "good writer" as someone who has control over the mechanics of grammar, syntax, and punctuation, as in the autonomous view of writing. He continues in saying that neither is a "good writer" someone who is able to mimic expert composing and "knowledge-transforming" practices by reworking his or her ideas during writing, as in process models. Instead, modern conceptions of literacy define an expert writer as "one who has attained the local knowledge that enables her to write as a member of a discourse community" (Carter, 1990, p. 226).

From the responses of the students, it appears that they take on board the surface and mechanical features that teachers and lecturers often focus on. We need to enhance the features of writing above sentence level (the "flow") that so many of them indicated in their responses. A focus on surface features tends to overshadow the identification of problems with writing. More attention should be placed on developing fluency beyond sentence level in the form of argumentation and structuring of writing.

Some of the code-switching choices that the students face when they have to write in a language that is not their home language may be revealed when the student states, *I do often switch between English and German when thinking how to phrase something, though.* We clearly see what Palmer et al. (2014, p. 759) has identified as code-switching taking place, where the student is switching between the two languages. The consideration that helped this student resolve their choice may be seen when the student states, *That switch often helps me sort my thoughts and get back into the flow of writing when I get stuck.* The use of code-switching was to indicate a shift in topic, person, or syntactic form (Gort, 2012). The students are in an environment where they are alternating between languages.

Some of the composing and cognitive stages that characterized the production of translanguaging is revealed when the student states, *I prefer to write in my home language, German, when I write academic texts because I feel like I know the connotation of the words better and can make more elegant sentences. When writing in English I usually don't use German.* This student is transparent in his challenges with writing and that writing in German is his preference as he feels he can make more elegant sentences. We also see that when the student writes that they "don't usually use German" when they are writing in English, my understanding is that the student does use German when they write. Subconsciously, students are not aware that they are indulging in translanguaging when they are writing in another language – in this case English, which is not their home language.

Another example of the production of translanguaging is revealed when the student writes, *I usually think in English when I write a text. But I fill up the missing words in German and look them up.* The student is not aware that they are using German even though they claim that they think in English when they write a text. It seems that the student has some myth that they are not using German, again subconsciously they are using German when they are writing and this may be the reason behind them using German words in an English text. Thus, linking to the multilingual development research on translanguaging has premised on the recognition of a full account of speakers' discursive resources, and it posits that languages are not airtight units with distinguishable boundaries nor are they capable of being placed into boxes (García, 2009, 2011; Hornberger & Link, 2012; Makoni, 2003; Makoni & Pennycook, 2007; Mignolo, 2000; Wei, 2011; Shohamy, 2006). I agree that languages should not be placed in boxes and that it should be acknowledged and recognized in the classroom by the student. From my findings I intended to make students aware that they can write without there being distinguishable boundaries. Students need to be made aware of the way they can use their home languages when they are writing in a language that is not their L1. They can develop mind maps as one of the participants mentioned, to assist them in their academic writing. It might be time-consuming, but teachers should allow the student more time when doing tasks as they are translating sentences in their head before putting it down in their L2/L3. L1 lecturers or teachers should consider speaking at a slower pace in their classrooms when giving instructions.

It appears that language accelerates the process of developing abilities for understanding and thinking and that it is reasonable to believe that bi/multilingual individuals, even emergent bi/multilinguals, will use their linguistic and experiential resources to achieve understanding and develop metacognitive skills and critical thinking (Velasco & García, 2014, p. 21). Thus, translanguaging is not solely a bi/multilingual discourse or a pedagogical strategy for scaffolding instruction, but also a way that emergent bi/ multilinguals can, and do, self-regulate and advance their learning. In addition, effective language learning, including the effective use of translanguaging strategies, requires enactment within a meaningful context, which facilitates the processing of linguistic and writing demands (Velasco & García, 2014).

6. Conclusion

I hope that various conclusions could be drawn from the data presented. One of the conclusions may be that preparation for academic literacy development at higher education levels should prepare students better to be able to manage their writing in a way that leads to fluency. We might have to consider that students should be vigilant in editing their work in terms of punctuation.

Another conclusion may be that constructing a context in which students are encouraged to draw on their various languages (even if complete fluency is not available) as resources, rather than as barriers, benefits learning, and that more emphasis on the local language enhances competence in the additional language, rather than detracting from the learning of an additional language (Brock-Utne, 1997; van der Walt & Dornbrack, 2011). I surmise that rather than forming barriers for learning, the bilingual requirements of the context stimulated the students to discover ways to negotiate it and, in García's (2009, p. 45) words, "translanguage to construct meaning." I hope that the students were appropriating the language "on their own terms, according to their needs, values and aspirations" (Canagarajah, 1999, pp. 175–179). What I discovered is that some of the participants had the opportunity and enough confidence in their bilingual competence to use their mother tongue as an academic language (van der Walt &

Dornbrack, 2011). This is seen when the student stated, *First I think in German, then translate it in English and look up unfamiliar words.* In considering how to support multilingual students' academic writing, it might be useful if academics consider focusing on the construction of identity in writing on the one side and socio-political constraints to multilingual writing on the other side (Canagarajah, 2013).

I find that, as academics, we cannot allow students to adopt any registers and conventions they want in academic writing. However, teachers can incorporate translanguaging strategies by opening up the spaces that will allow the recursive process of writing to interplay between languages a student has (Velasco & García, 2014). I am inclined to agree with Canagarajah (2015, p. 9) when he states that, as we develop teachable strategies of translanguaging, we have to consider some serious issues for assessing the effectiveness of this practice. In that, there is a place for error or mistake in translanguaging.

According to Hyland (2016, p. 30), every act of writing is in a sense both personal and individual; it is also interactional and social, expressing a culturally recognized purpose, reflecting a particular kind of relationship and acknowledging an engagement in a given community. This is demonstrated when the student writes, *First I am thinking in English. However, when I don't know a word or a formulation I write it down in German. Then I look it up in a translator. However, I think it is easier to directly think in the language we write it down.* Hyland (2010) phrases it perfectly when he states, "The way we talk and write are not simply a mimicry of community patterns but a complicated means of constructing who we are, or rather, how we would like others to see us" (p. 181). Even though there is that strong denial from students that they do not think in their home language, they are somewhat inclined to admit that they do lean on their home language when they are writing in a language that is not their home language. What the student demonstrates here is code-switching, which may be interpreted as a sign of purposive language use through which the integration of multiple codes and scripts serves to support dual language and literacy learning, produce a range of expressive effects, and accomplish particular intended meanings in two languages (Gort, 2012, p. 68).

Finally, this study hopes to describe how bi/multilingual students, when offered opportunities to engage with bilingual modes of delivery, are able to deftly and successfully use the languages at their disposal to make sense of their world (van der Walt & Dornbrack, 2011). In addition, mutual influences from the languages in one's repertoire are treated as creative and enabling, not hindering, communication (Canagarajah, 2015). As demonstrated when the student writes, *I rarely use my home language for technical texts. (only when things become emotional, I try to translate swiss expressions to English language.)* We should be more tolerant of translanguaging in writing, for example when students are using words from other languages especially in tests and examinations. Additionally, students should be made aware that they can write without there being any distinguishable boundaries.

Students are able to develop academic biliteracy and to use their languages in the powerful domain of higher education academic discourse, thereby "open[ing] up implementation spaces for multiple languages, literacies, and identities in classroom, community, and society" (Hornberger, 2007, p. 188). As a result, students are typically required to adopt a style of writing at university that involves anonymizing themselves and adopting the guise of a rational, disinterested, asocial seeker of truth (Hyland, 2016, p. 45). We need to recognize that the majority of students do not arrive at university with ready-to-use academic skills, but rather develop these skills in the course of their time spent at the institution and that an opportunity to reflect, talk through, read out aloud and discuss in their home language will facilitate the acquisition of academic skills in English (Hyland, 2016).

6.1 Suggestions/Implications

I would have to agree with Bartholomae (1986, p. 45) when he argues that students who are writing for a particular academic audience must "invent" the university, for they "have to appropriate (or be appropriated by) a specialized discourse, and they have to do this as though they were easily and comfortably one with their audience." What this implies is that students often attempt to invent the university in their writing, which is tied up with their feelings of belonging to the university and with the extent to which they identify with the label of "student" (Olinger, 2011, p. 273).

Ergo, some academic writing scholars argue that pedagogies should help students develop an awareness of how the use of the multilingual repertoire influences their writing, so that they employ their resources deliberately and strategically (Cumming, 2013; Gentil, 2005; van der Walt, 2013; Kaufhold, 2018, p. 8). The pedagogy in question should be a method that empowers students to explore their own linguistic ideologies and desires of who they want to be as writers (Canagarajah, 2013; Kaufhold, 2018, p. 8).

Van der Walt (2016, p. 15) makes a few suggestions that may be helpful in assisting students in English for academic purposes: lecturers could develop what García (2009, p. 297) calls "flexible convergence," where a variety of languages is used to produce assignments and tests in English. She continues by saying that, if possible, maybe lecturers could acknowledge other languages by using them in teaching materials (alongside English, i.e. co-languaging) and by accepting student work in more than one language, known as "flexible multiplicity" (García, 2009, p. 310). I argue that these above-mentioned suggestions could lighten the fear that many students have of a language that is not their home language when they are writing for academic purposes.

References

Abbott, R. D., Berninger, V. W., & Foyal, M. (2010). Longitudinal Relationships of Levels of Language in Writing and Between Writing and Reading in Grades 1 to 7. *Journal of Educational Psychology 102*, 281–298.

Baker, C. (2011). *Foundations of bilingual education and bilingualism* (5th ed.). Clevedon, UK: Multilingual Matters.

Bartholomae, D. (1986). Inventing the university. *Journal of Basic Writing 5*(1), 4–23.

Blom, J. P. & Gumperz, J. J. (1972). Social meaning in linguistic structures: Code-switching in Norway. In J. J. Gumperz & D. Hymes (Eds.), *Directions in Sociolinguistics* (pp. 407–434). New York: Holt, Rinehart, and Winston.

Brock-Utne, B. (1997). The language question in Namibia. *International Review of Education 43*(2/3), 241–260.

Bullock, B. E. & Toribio, A. J. (2009). Themes in the study of code-switching. In B. E. Bullock & A. J. Toribio (Eds.), *The Cambridge handbook of linguistic code-switching* (pp. 1–17). Cambridge: Cambridge University Press.

Cameron, J., Nairn, K., & Higgins, J. (2009). Demystifying academic writing: reflections on emotions, know-how and academic identity. *Journal of Geography in Higher Education 33*(2), 269–284.

Canagarajah, A. S. (1999). *Resisting linguistic imperialism in English teaching*. Oxford: Oxford University Press.

Canagarajah, A. S. (2011). Codemeshing in academic writing: Identifying teachable strategies of translanguaging. *The Modern Language Journal 95*(3), 401–417.

Canagarajah, A. S. (2013). *Translingual practice: Global Englishes and cosmopolitan relations*. London: Routledge.

Canagarajah, A. S. (2015). Corrigendum to "Blessed in my own way: "Pedagogical affordances for dialogical voice construction in multilingual student writing." *Journal of Second Language Writing*, 122–123.

Carstens, A. (2016). Designing linguistically flexible scaffolding for subject specificacademic literacy interventions. *Per Linguam. A Journal for*

Language Learning 32(3), 1–12.

Carter, M. (1990). The idea of expertise: An exploration of cognitive and social dimensions of writing. *College Composition and Communication 41*(3), 265–286.

Cloud, N., Genesee, F., & Hamayan, E. (2000). *Dual language instruction: A handbook for enriched education.* Boston: Heinle & Heinle.

Coffin, C., Curry, M.J., Goodman, S., Hewings, A., Lillis, T.M., & Swann, J. (2003). *Teaching Academic Writing: A toolkit for higher education.* London: Routledge.

Cumming, A. (2013). Multiple dimensions of academic language and literacy development. *Language Learning 63*(1), 130–152.

DeLyser, D. (2003). Teaching graduate students to write: a seminar for thesis and dissertation writers. *Journal of Geography in Higher Education 27*(2), 169–181.

Freedman, A., Pringle, I., & Yalden, J. (2014). *Learning to write: First/Second language.* New York: Routledge.

García, O. (2009). *Bilingual education in the 21st century: a global perspective.* Malden, MA: Wiley/Blackwell.

Gentil, G. (2005). Commitments to academic biliteracy: Case studies of Francophone university writers. *Written Communication 22*(4), 421–471.

Gilchrist, T. (2018). *Teachers on fire: Inquiry, translanguaging, agency, growth mindset, and more!* Blog posted June 24, 2018. https://tonyagilchrist.com/teachers-on-fire-inquiry-translanguaging-agency-growth-mindset-and-more/

Gingràs, R. (1974). Problems in the description of Spanish-English intra-sentential codeswitching. In G. A. Bills (Ed.), *Southwest areal linguistics* (pp. 167–174). San Diego, CA: Institute for Cultural Pluralism.

Gort, M. (2012). Code-switching pattern in the writing related talk of young emergent bilinguals. *Journal of Literacy Research 44*(1), 44–75.

Hornberger, N. (2007). Multilingual language policies and the continua of biliteracy: An ecological approach. In O. García & C. Baker (Eds.), *Bilingual education: An introductory reader* (pp. 177–194). Clevedon: Multilingual Matters.

Hornberger, N. & Link, H. (2012). Translanguaging and transnational literacies in multilingual classrooms: a biliteracy lens. *International Journal of Bilingual Education and Bilingualism 15*, 261–278.

Hyland, K. (2010). Community and individuality: performing identity in Applied Linguistics. *Written Communication 27*(2), 159–188.

Hyland, K. (2016). *Teaching and researching writing.* New York: Routledge.

Hyland, K. (2018). Sympathy for the devil? A defence for EAP. *Language Teaching 51*(3), 383–399.

Jaffe, A. (2007). Codeswitching and stance: Issues in interpretation. *Journal of Language, Identity, and Education 6*, 53–77.

Jamshidi, A. & Navehebrahim, M. (2013). Learners[sic!] use of code switching in the English as a foreign language classroom. *Australian Journal of Basic and Applied Sciences 7*(1), 186–190.

Johanssen, S. (2013). *Code-switching in the English classroom: What teachers do and what their students wish.* Karlstads Universitet. Department of Language, Literature and Intercultural Studies. Degree project.

Klapwijk, N. & van der Walt, C. (2015). English-plus multilingualism as the new linguistic capital? Implications of university students' attitudes towards languages of instruction in a multilingual environment. *Journal of Language, Identity & Education, 15*(2), 67–82.

Kaufhold, K. (2018). Creating translanguaging spaces in students' academic writing practices. *Linguistics and Education 45*, 1–9.

Kobayashi, M. & Rinnert, C. (2013). L1/L2/L3 writing development: Longitudinal case study of a Japanese multicompetent writer. *Journal of Second Language Writing 22*(1), 4–33.

Lewis, G., Jones, B., & Baker, C. (2012). Translanguaging: origins and development from school to street and beyond. *Educational Research and Evaluation 18*(7), 641–655.

Lillis, T. M. & Curry, M. J. (2010). Academic writing in a global context – The politics and practices of publishing in English. *Journal of Second Language Writing 19*, 237–238.

MacSwan, J. (2000). The architecture of the bilingual language faculty: Evidence from intrasentential code switching. *Bilingualism: Language and Cognition 3*, 37–54.

Makoni, S. (2003). From misinvention to disinvention of language: multilingualism and the South African Constitution. In S. Makoni, G.

Smithermann, A. Ball, & A. Spears (Eds.), *Black linguistics: language, society and politics in Africa and the Americas* (pp. 132–149). London: Routledge.

Makoni, S. & Pennycook, A. (Eds.) (2007). *Disinventing and reconstituting languages.* Clevedon, UK: Multilingual Matters.

Mazak, C. M. (2017). Introduction: Theorizing translanguaging practices in higher education. In C.M. Mazak, & K. S. Carroll (Eds.). *Translanguaging in the higher education: Beyond monolingual ideologies* (pp. 1–12). Bristol: Multilingual Matters.

Middendorf, M. (1992). Bakhtin and the dialogic writing class. *Journal of Basic Writing 11*(1), 34–47.

Mignolo, W. (2000). *Local histories/global designs. Coloniality, subaltern knowledges, and border thinking.* Princeton: Princeton University Press.

Mortensen, J. (2014). Language policy from below: Language choice in student project groups in multilingual university setting. *Journal of Multilingual and Multicultural Development 35*(4), 425–442.

Olinger, A.R. (2011). Constructing identities through "discourse": Stance and interaction in collaborative college writing. *Linguistics and Education 22*, 273–286.

Palfreyman, D. M. & van der Walt, C. (2017). Introduction: Biliteracies in higher education. In D. M. Palfreyman, & C. van der Walt (Eds.). *Academic biliteracies: Multilingual repertoires in higher education* (pp. 1–18). Bristol: Multilingual Matters.

Palmer, D.K., Mateus, S.G., Antonio Martinez, R., & Henderson, K. (2014). Reframing the debate on language separation: Toward a vision for translanguaging pedagogies in the dual classroom. *The Modern Language Journal 93*(3), 757–772.

Pfaff, W. (1979). Constraints of language mixing: Intrasentential code-switching and borrowing in Spanish/English. *Language 55*, 291–318.

Pfeiffer, V. (2015). *An investigation of L2 expressive writing in a tertiary institution in the Western Cape.* Unpublished PhD thesis. University of the Western Cape.

Rohman, D. G. (1965). Pre-writing the stage of discovery in the writing process. *College Composition and Communication 16*(2), 106–112.

Ruíz, R. (1984). Orientations in language planning. *NABE: The Journal for* the *National Association for Bilingual Education 8*(2), 15–34.

Shohamy, E. (2006). *Language policy: hidden agendas and new approaches.* London: Routledge.

Timm, L. (1975). Spanish-English code switching: El por qué y how-not-to. *Romance Philology 28*(4), 473–482.

Toribio, A. J. (2004). Convergence as an optimization strategy in bilingual speech: Evidence from code-switching. *Bilingualism: Language & Cognition 7*(2), 165–173.

Tribble, C. (1996). *Writing.* Oxford: Oxford University Press.

van der Walt, C. (2013). *Multilingual higher education: Beyond English medium orientations.* Bristol: Multilingual Matters.

van der Walt, C. (2016). Reconsidering the role of language-in-education policies in multilingual higher education contexts1. *Stellenbosch Papers in Linguistics Plus 49*, 85–104. doi: 10.5842/49-0-684.

van der Walt, C. & Dornbrack, J. (2011). Academic biliteracy in South African higher education: strategies and practices of successful students. *Language, Cultural and Curriculum*, 24(1), 89–104.

Velasco, P. & García, O. (2014). Translanguaging and the writing of bilingual learners. *Bilingual Research Journal 37*(1), 6–23.

Vivian, B. & Fourie, R. (2016). Non-curricular postgraduate writing interventions at South African universities. *Journal for Language Teaching 50*(1), 145–165.

Wei, L. (2011). Moment analysis and translanguaging space: discursive construction of identities by multilingual Chinese youth in Britain. *Journal of Pragmatics 43*, 1222–1235.

Woolard, K. (2004). Codeswitching. In A. Duranti (Ed.), *A companion to linguistic Anthropology* (pp. 73–94). Malden, MA: Blackwell.

Zentella, A. C. (1997). *Growing up bilingual: Puerto Rican children in New York.* Oxford, UK: Blackwell.

CHAPTER 13

Implementation of a Bilingual Model Based on the Integration of Translanguaging, English, and Content

Enrique Arias Castaño and Isabel Cristina Sánchez

1. Introduction

English has become a universal language and a necessity for people all over the world; this is true for areas ranging from business, education, and communication, to social networks. Since long ago, different methods and approaches for teaching second languages have been implemented; those methods and approaches have evolved in constant search of improvement of bilingual education. However, it has been a privilege restricted for the elites and is not a guaranteed right for all citizens. As a reserved advantage, it is now important to start looking for different alternatives and to implement different models that allow everyone access to bilingual education; this is an outstanding need in Colombia where there is an urge for developing different ways of instruction in which teaching a language focuses on using it in meaningful contexts for the students, rather than just learning about the language.

In a more local perspective, the Ministry of Education in Colombia (MEN) has proposed making Colombia a bilingual country by means of the implementation of a number of programs to educate students from the public sector in a foreign language: English. The main goal of all these programs has been raising high school students' proficiency in English so that they can communicate effectively in real-life situations.

For this reason, the MEN has set the B1-intermediate (according to the CEFRL) as the proficiency level that students are expected to reach in 11th grade. Along with the different levels of proficiency established, the MEN has produced material and has promoted a series of strategies in order to grant the improvement of the English proficiency in students from the public sector.

However, the challenges faced in terms of public bilingual education, as established by Amador-Watson (Linares, 2011), seem huge. The author argues that there are generalized factors that hinder the achievement of the proficiency levels expected; these factors also impact the teaching and learning of English in the public sector in Colombia in a negative way. Among the factors she mentions are the large number of students in classrooms, the few educational materials, and the lack of student motivation. More importantly, the author says that a big problem, as well, is the classroom methodologies inclined to developing mere linguistic knowledge and the implementation of traditional teacher-centered pedagogical models (Linares, 2011) (see also Busic & Sullivan, this volume). The above information evidences that public education in Colombia in terms of the English language has a huge gap. According to Zuleta (2015), bilingual education has corresponded with the elites in the large majority, so they have managed to build and maintain teaching approaches that are different to the ones maintained in public schools. This is supported by the results of the *Pruebas Saber 11* (a standardized test administered by ICFES, the Colombian Institute for the Evaluation of Education, to 11th graders) as reported by the MEN in Colombia Very Well! (Ministry of National Education, 2014): only 1% of the students who graduate from the public sector reach a B1 level. In contrast, 52% of the students graduating from bilingual private institutions reach the same level when they finish high school.

Another issue relevant to the present study is the role given to the students' first language. Although the Colombian program is named "bilingual," Spanish has not been integrated with the English language process. The first language of the students is not given a central role or is forbidden in several cases. Cummins (2000) remarks that many educational contexts favor the isolation of languages. This language separation seeks to avoid the L1 interference in the L2 development; this comes from the idea that the more exposure students have in the L2, the better it is for achieving high proficiency in the language (Lasagabaster & García, 2014).

However, Cummings (2000) asserts that the knowledge and the integration of the knowledge coming from the students' first language into the learning of another language can enhance and speed up the acquisition process. In the same line, Lewis, Jones, & Baker (2012) assert that the incorporation of the students' L1 will help to increase learners' linguistic and cognitive development in the language being learned.

In Colombia, there is a generalized view that Spanish (the L1 in our context) can prevent students' learning of English (the L2); another view is that the level of competence reached in one language does not affect the other. Thus, the teaching and learning process of English does not regard the importance that Spanish, the students' L1, and the Spanish level of competence have in the performance in English.

In search of this articulation, the present study proposes the use of translanguaging, a pedagogical strategy for schools, educators, and students, and the implementation of CLIL (content and language integrated learning) in two public schools in Pereira. The question the study intends to answer is in regards to what can be seen in the integration of content and translanguaging as a dynamic bilingual pedagogy in 5th graders of two public schools in Pereira.

2. Important concepts to the research

In this section, two important constructs to the work will be discussed. First, the types of bilingual education will be explored in the light of García (2011) and Baker (2001); then, the concept of translanguaging will be defined following Lasagabaster and García (2014), García and Li (2011), and Baker (2006); and the types of translanguaging will be explored following Williams (2012) (cited by Lasagabaster & García, 2014).

2.1 Types of bilingual education

According to García (2011), bilingual education in the 20th century was perceived to be exclusively for the elites. With the colonization around the world, the powerful and prestige languages used to be part of the curriculum of private institutions. Later in the same century, social activism made people aware of the importance of preserving native, less prestigious, languages around the world, which included using them in the school curriculum. However, the 21st century requires a more complex vision toward bilingualism; the idea that only the languages in power should be taught and that the minority languages should be preserved, should be changed.

According to the different perceptions of bilingualism in the 20th and the 21st centuries, two different language ideologies can be recognized: monoglossic and heteroglossic. The first one refers to transitional or immersion programs, which approach the languages from a monolingual view; in this type of program, the languages are separated from one another by the subject or the teacher. This separation is not beneficial for the learners, as when it is time for instruction in one language, only that language is allowed in the classroom. This means that the learners learn one language and lose the other or keep that language and add another. The monoglossic ideology is divided in the subtractive and additive types (for more on the monoglossic ideology, see Hornberger, 1991, cited in García, 2011).

Different to the monoglossic ideology, García (2011) presents the heteroglossic one. This ideology involves language shift, language maintenance, and language addition, which give the teacher the opportunity of using all of the students' language resources in the classroom. In this way, learners keep their mother tongue and add the new language to their repertoire; this is the main reason this ideology is call heteroglossic. It has two different divisions: recursive and dynamic. Because of the purpose of the research and the chapter's length, only the dynamic type will be presented (for more on the recursive type, see García, 2011). García (2011) states that the dynamic type of bilingualism accepts the integration of both languages in communication and the combination of cultures. One of the characteristics of dynamic bilingual education is that learners can bring these different contexts into the classroom and promote enriching cultural experiences with the coexistence of their different languages. This type of bilingual education is distinguished for accepting translanguaging; this term will be expanded on in the following sub-section.

2.2 Translanguaging

Lasagabaster and García (2014) highlight that it is necessary to change the role given to the first language (L1) of the students in the second language (L2) classroom. The authors argue that the change of role should be focused on "simultaneous use of both languages [. . .] one which supports the coexistence of languages in the classroom without their arbitrary separation" (Lasagabaster & García, 2014, p. 2). Cen Williams (1994) (cited by Lasagabaster & García, 2014, p. 2) was the first to use the term translanguaging in order to "refer to the planned and systematic use of two languages in the same lesson." He presents an example that helps visualize the use of both languages: "One is used during the introduction phase and the other during the production phase." It is important to emphasize that the author proposes a "systematic use" (p. 2), which means that the use of the languages is integrated by having a prior fixed plan in mind. Thus, translanguaging is the pedagogical strategy that allows a change of paradigm: from one that supports the separation of the language codes and that sees the use of one of the codes negatively, to one that uses them as a resource and that accepts the complexities of bilingual individuals.

García and Li (2011) add to the discussion of translanguaging that, by its implementation, bilingual learners take control of their own learning by means of using the different languages that make up their repertoire. The learners develop the ability to use any of the languages depending on their needs; this ability lets students use the languages available as a single language repertoire. Baker (2006) also adds that both languages are used in a single, dynamic system in order to develop language skills and to learn the content of a subject matter.

The contributions by Lasagabaster and García (2014), García and Li (2011), and Baker (2006) discussed above converge in the use of a linguistic repertoire for bilingual learners so that the academic community stops seeing the learning of a second language as separated from the first one and vice versa. This is specifically carried out in the classroom in two ways according to Williams (2012) (cited by García & Li, 2014): official translanguaging, which is the planned integration of the students' linguistic repertoire in the classroom, and natural translanguaging, which is the spontaneous use of the languages that make up the repertoire of the students. The use of the different languages may happen by the teachers or by the students, and it may be planned or unplanned.

In discussing translanguaging, code-switching may emerge to cause confusion or be used interchangeably with translanguaging. However, as presented above, in translanguaging the languages are used in a social, cultural, and political context (García & Leiva, 2014). Instead, code-switching refers to just going from one language code to another without a pedagogical use (see also Pfeiffer, this volume). The distinction between these two concepts is expanded by Lewis et al. (2012) who argue that translanguaging accepts the flexibility of the process of learning two or more languages, while code-switching is associated with the use of the two separate languages. As a result, translanguaging implies more advantages over other uses of the languages of the linguistic repertoire because it allows the methodical or unmethodical integration of the codes in order to enhance the process of a language and content learning.

3. Literature review

The systematic integration of first and second languages has been an issue widely researched. In the following section, two of those studies will be explored. The first research by Arias (2017) sought to determine the impact of the integration of content, language and translanguaging as a dynamic bilingual education model in two public schools. The second one by Garza and Langman (2014) analyzes students' reactions toward the integration of Spanish and English in their classes.

Arias (2017) conducted a study on the analysis of the implementation of translanguaging and CLIL through the use of a dynamic bilingual education model. The participants were six preschool and primary school teachers from two public institutions in Pereira, Risaralda, Colombia; four of them were women and two were men.

Four important findings emerged from the study. The first result presents that Spanish was used not because of a lack of competence in English; the data demonstrated that students used their L1 in order to integrate their prior knowledge and to support the learning of the content in the L2. In the second finding, it was evidenced that the students used Spanish not only because they felt more confident, but also because the use of both languages facilitates their understanding. The third finding shows that through the implementation of translanguaging and CLIL, students' participation increased because the dynamics in the classroom allowed them to use their whole linguistic repertoire; this possibility made students more confident and interested in the class. The fact that students already know the content in Spanish helped them use the L2 more efficiently.

In a related study, Garza and Langman (2014) aimed at exploring how students from a Latin Bilingual Community use translanguaging in two classes: Social Studies taught in Spanish and Science taught in English (English as a second language). This qualitative study was carried out during the school year 2012–2013 with the 5th grade of the Lagos Elementary School located in San Antonio, Texas, USA. The authors found that translanguaging was used in the classroom as a strategy to improve the "fluidity and movement of teaching and learning" (p. 37), which means that the processes carried out in the classroom by the teachers and the students is more effective and practical. Another finding points out that by the use of translanguaging, meaning in the classroom is constructed collaboratively. Translanguaging, then, creates an environment where the use of both languages is honored and valued. The implementation of translanguaging has been proven to enhance the understanding of the content of the lessons.

Both studies converge with the idea of using the two languages in the students' linguistic repertoire (in these specific cases, English and Spanish) in the classroom. The implementation proved to be beneficial in helping students to make meaning of the content by creating connections between the languages. In the studies conducted by Arias (2017) and Garza and Langman (2014), it is evident that the integration of the students' mother tongue to support the learning of new concepts and topics in the second language is advisable because of the positive results obtained. The findings agree on the idea that the first language does not impact the language learning process negatively.

4. Methodology
4.1 Type of Research and study
The research design was a qualitative case study. Firstly, this study has a qualitative approach as Flick (2009) establishes that this type of research functions in natural settings based on realities configured by perceptions, beliefs, thoughts given from investigators who do not define them as "absolute truths" (p. 13). Additionally, Rudestam and Newton (2001) argue that qualitative research centers its attention on the socially constructed reality and the context that influences it. The study was conducted in two state schools, which means the context was completely natural, as was its impact in the teachers' and students' behavior toward translanguaging implementation.

Secondly, the research focus is a case study. Lodico, Spaulding, and Voegtle (2010) say that the case study focuses on an individual, on a small group, or on a specific person in a group; it aims to document the experiences of the subject(s) who is immersed in a specific scenario. The main purpose of the study was to systematize the experiences of the implementation of a dynamic bilingual model that integrated content and the translanguaging strategy in two public schools in the city of Pereira, which are individual units among a group of institutions.

4.2 Context and Setting
This study was conducted in two public schools in Pereira, Risaralda, which offer primary and secondary education. They are located in the Comuna (commune) Villa Santana and Comuna (commune) del Café. According to the *Informe General de Estratificación* [*Strata General Report*], a document produced by the Town Hall, 96.8% of the people who live in Comuna del Café and 99.9% of the ones in Comuna Villa Santana, belong to the bottom socio-economical strata. The former school has approximately 1,440 students and the latter approximately 1,050.

At the time of the research implementation, the English curriculum in these schools was being guided by the Guide 22nd, Basic Standards in the Foreign Language Competences established by the Ministry of Education of Colombia (MEN). In these institutions, English is taught from 1st to 11th grade with an average of three hours for secondary and two hours for primary students. In Colombia, English primary level is not taught by an English teacher; it is guided by the regular teacher of each group who teaches all the subjects. However, each of the schools has an institutional agreement with the language teaching and bilingualism program from Universidad Tecnológica de Pereira; the language program provides English language practitioners who are pursuing different semesters to teach English to the different groups at the school.

For the purposes of the research, the authors did not separate the data collected as coming from two different schools because both schools provided a similar setting, and the practitioners who were making the implementations conducted very similar procedures at the institutions.

4.3 Participants of the study

The participants of the study were six practitioners of the Language teaching and bilingualism program from Universidad Tecnológica de Pereira who, at the moment of the study, were in their 7th semester. They were chosen to be part of the investigation because of their high academic performance and GPAs. Before taking the first Teaching Practicum course, the students took an Applied Linguistics course, which prepared them in theoretical and practical teaching aspects such as bilingual education frameworks and types, methods and approaches in language teaching, and current bilingual models and strategies. The roles the practitioners played in the study were those of lesson planners and implementers of the classes. They were also asked to reflect on specific issues after each of the classes and to collect the students' artefacts such as worksheets, notebooks, board production, etc. They were supported in their lesson planning by one of the investigators. The lessons were carried out with students from primary schools: three from each of the two public schools.

4.4 Data collection and data analysis

Regarding the instruments used to collect the data, the study used stimulated recall, teachers' journals and reflections, and students' artefacts implemented for assessment of the class's outcomes. Stimulated Recall is a research method that allows the investigation of cognitive processes through inviting participants to recall their thinking during an event when prompted by some other form of visual recall (Fox-Turnbull, 2009). As the author mentions, educators recorded the classes in order to recall decisions and their performance in the classroom as well as reactions to different situations that were not detailed in the lesson plan. The stimulated recall focused on student and teacher reactions toward the implementation of the classes. Additionally, data was collected through journals; as Wiegerová (2013) suggests, they are useful in analyzing student practices, reactions, and class development, in making reflections based on those practices, and in collecting meaningful notes to bring conclusions with their interpretations. Moreover, professional aspects were considered as well as students' responses and outcomes, so we could reflect on the positive and negative aspects evidenced through this process and to see if the students' language proficiency was affected positively. Finally, artefacts as Hancock, Ockleford, and Windridge (2007) define, are useful to understand events that are part of the context or produced by it. Thus, student responses to teacher productions were used as reference for classroom events and the pupils' development.

In order to analyze the data, content analysis was used for the systematization and interpretation of the data. The sequence followed for the purpose was (1) Transcription and digitalization of class observations, the practitioners' reflections, and the students' artefacts, (2) Coding of the events depending on who were the main actors – practitioners, students, students, and (3) Analysis of the data to find repetitive incidents; it was coded accordingly to reflect the data source (the data collection instrument, the instrument number, etc.). According to the repetition of the incidents, categories were chosen and were assigned a title that reported the general concept of the category.

4.5 Instructional design

At the beginning of the whole process, one of the researchers worked with the practitioners and reviewed the theoretical framework of the investigation: the dynamic bilingual education model. The researchers instructed the practitioners in the lesson plan design that would reflect and include the theoretical and practical characteristics of the model, including translanguaging. The lesson planning was systematic in that it included specific content from the Science class that was chosen based on the *Guide Basic Standards for Natural Science Education* (Ministry of National Education, 2006a), and English competencies came from the *Guide 22 Basic Standards for Language Education* (Ministry of National Education, 2006b). In addition, they reported the lesson plans and material design for classes, which were constructed with in-service-content teachers. Thus, the practitioners were asked to reflect on the implementations after each of the classes, which were scheduled to happen three times per week during one academic semester; they were also asked to collect the students' artefacts. After every class section was implemented, the researchers analyzed the videos with the practitioners in order to ponder the process and the decisions made in the implementation.

5. Findings

Since the purpose of the study was to use translanguaging in classes, the teachers assumed it as a pedagogical strategy in which the coexistence of both languages was not seen as a problem that needed to be eliminated; instead, it was used as a resource to enable emergent bilinguals to make meaning by using all the features of the first and second language. Spanish was used systematically in the English content class; that is, teachers used it with specific purposes, which were previously planned. There were also some other times in which they used the languages spontaneously, promoting flexibility in the students' language use. In this way, the teachers and the students took part in a translanguaging classroom where the students could interact in any of the languages that made up their repertoire in order to demonstrate what they knew and what they could do with the language and the content being taught. Thus, this paper reports the specific results found in the class implementations.

5.1 Pedagogical use of Spanish by means of translanguaging

As it was mentioned before, teachers used translanguaging as a strategy in the classroom to help emergent bilinguals understand the content and develop proficiency in the second language. Spanish was used as a resource to clarify doubts, to recall or activate previous knowledge, to explain complex input, and to manage the class; there is also evidence that the use of Spanish was planned in advance.

To illustrate the official use of translanguaging, the artefact 1 shows evidence of how the pre-service teacher indicated in the lesson plan that an analogy between the functions of the cell organelles and the operations of a mall was going to be developed in Spanish. This analogy was previously planned to be carried out during the study stage of the lesson with a specific goal. By using a comparison with an aspect that the students already knew in Spanish, in this case the operations in a mall, comprehension of the topic was to be promoted.

Artefact 1. Study procedure from lesson plan with analogy in Spanish registered

Study 2:40 –2:50	T will give an example in Spanish of a mall shop in order for them to understand better the functions of each structure of a cell. For example, the mall is similar to a cell, and so on. Then, Ss will match the part of the cell in English with each example given in Spanish. *(The example will be given in Spanish so they relate a difficult input in English with something that is real for them and in a language they can understand. In this way, they'll use the example in Spanish as a resource to remember the functions and parts of a cell.)* Finally T will practise in English the functions by showing them the part and they will have to answer using it is the . . .

In the previous piece of the lesson plan, it is evidenced that the use of Spanish was pre-planned; that is, it was conceived before the class was implemented. It is also evidenced that the purpose of the pre-service teacher was to promote understanding of the topic and of a specific aspect being taught as well as to activate the students' previous knowledge by means of an analogy. Besides including the Spanish use, it is important to highlight that the teacher is aware that the use of the language will ease understanding, which is explicitly said in the lesson plan.

In the following excerpt, taken from the video recording of a class related to the lesson plan explored above, there is evidence of how translanguaging happened in the classroom discourse.

Transcription 1. Interaction teacher and students using an analogy in Spanish

S5:   Cell membrane

T: Cell membrane y luego tenemos el director, el que manda todo el centro comercial. [Cell membrane and then, we have the director who controls all the mall.]

Ss: Nucleus, nucleus!!! [*students gave the correct answer*]

T: Y luego tenemos unos tanques de agua que llevan el agua a todo el centro comercial. [And then, we have some water tanks that distribute the water to the whole mall.]

Ss: Vacuole . . . vacuole [*students gave the correct answer*]

The teacher implemented the pre-planned use of Spanish to help students make connections between what they know about the operations in a mall and what they were learning about the cell in the target language. In the instances where the analogy is being made, the students actually provide the correct answer as the analogy is part of the students' background knowledge in their mother tongue. It is important to note that, although the pre-service teacher was using Spanish, the students correctly answered in English.

The data explored evidences that translanguaging was conceived before its actual implementation in order to promote understanding of the content of the class and to activate the students' background knowledge. In addition, the use of translanguaging was a resourceful practice from students who spontaneously used the language to accomplish their immediate needs in the class. García and Li (2014) assert that the use of translanguaging with emergent bilinguals is important because it helps language learners to engage with and understand difficult content and texts, and to develop new language and knowledge. In the same line, Snow, Burns, and Griffin (1998) state that for language and content learning to happen, the background knowledge needs to be activated as it helps learners to compare the new information with the information they already have.

Besides the implementation of translanguaging in the teacher's speech and lesson plans, it was identified through the analysis of the data that another use of the pedagogical strategy is in the design of the activities that students do as part of the practice of the content of the class. The teacher designed a handout in which the questions were in Spanish and the answer options in English (the exercise was originally hand-written by the teacher; because of the formatting, it was typed). Given that the activity was prepared to be developed orally, the class was divided into two small groups; the members of each group first discussed in Spanish and then shared their ideas with one another. Students took turns to answer the questions in front of the whole group. The following sample shows the design of the exercise.

Artefact 2. Multiple choice questions in Spanish with options in English

¿Cuál es el proceso que las plantas usan para hacer la comida?
What is the process the plants use to produce their food?
a. Germination   b. Photosynthesis   c. Pollination

¿Qué hacen las plantas con el dióxido de carbono y el agua?
What do plants do with the carbon dioxide and the water?
a. Light   b. Sugar   c. Minerals

¿De dónde consiguen energía las plantas para hacer su comida?
Where do plants get their energy to produce their food from?
a. From light   b. From soil

¿Para qué usan las plantas la clorofila?
What do plants use chlorophyll for?
a. To take water   b. To trap energy   c. To take air

¿Para qué usan las plantas sus raíces?
What do plants use their roots for?
a. To take air   b. To take carbon dioxide   c. To take water

Depending on the specific purpose that teachers have with the implementation of the strategy, the design of the exercises can vary. In this particular case, the teacher's purpose in having the questions in Spanish and the options for the answers in English is to promote comprehension of the content as facilitated by the questions and to enhance the key vocabulary learning of the topic provided by the answers. It is important to highlight that the use of the strategy in this particular case is official as the teacher planned the activity and the use and roles of the languages in advance. In addition, teachers can modify the use and role of the languages depending on the particular needs. In the following interview excerpt, the teacher confirms the purpose of having the questions in Spanish and refers to the success of the design.

Reflection 1. Use of questions in Spanish

For the practice of the topic, the students solved some questions that were in Spanish and it helped them to understand the topic and then look for the answer in English. The students answered most of the questions appropriately and they did it in English.

The teacher makes clear the purpose of having the questions in Spanish; it effectively fosters students' comprehension of the topic. The teacher also comments that the students did well in answering the questions correctly; this reaffirms that translanguaging has a very important role in promoting comprehension of the input and in helping the students accomplish language goals and language development. During this implementation, the English classes were focused on incorporating activities that promoted the coexistence of both languages but the main purpose was to measure the students' performance in English at the end of the activities to see whether they understood the new input. The reason for giving them some resources in their mother tongue, in this case questions in Spanish, was to obtain the appropriate answer in English, promoting the thinking and use of the target language.

Through this section, the researchers have presented some of the principal samples and evidence that the implementation of this project has reached in terms of using translanguaging systematically with different pedagogical purposes as a way to facilitate content understanding, recall previous knowledge, and promote language development. This shows that there are different ways in which this strategy can be used by the teacher as a tool to facilitate the teaching process. Besides the teacher's implementation, we also found evidence that the students translanguage in the classroom to fulfil different purposes.

5.2 Students' use of Spanish as a learning strategy

After the analysis of the data collected, it was identified that not only teachers translanguaged in the classroom; students also do it as a resource to make meaning of new content and to reinforce and help themselves with their own learning process. The next fragment of a class sequence shows the use of the Spanish language by students with the purpose of participating in class interactions and of proving their comprehension of the content studied in class. The topic was about photosynthesis; it was explained in English by using a drawing on the board of a plant engaging in the process. After the teacher finished explaining, she wanted to confirm whether the students had understood since the explanation was carried out using the vocabulary specific to the topic.

Transcription 4. Spanish use by student to prove understanding

T2: No one can explain the process?

Ss: Ah que si no aprendimos? [What if we didn't learn it?]

T2: Juan Manuel, yes?

S24: ¿Que sí entendí el proceso? [What if I understood the process?]

S9: ¿Lo repito? [Do I repeat it?]

T2: Yes

S9: Primero las plantas por las raíces toman el agua . . . [First, the plants take the water through the roots . . .]

Ss: La absorben . . . [They absorb it . . .]

T2: Yes

S9: Luego les llega la energía solar y la clorofila combinada con el dióxido de carbono que ellas respiran, sueltan el oxígeno y los frutos. [Then, they get energy and the chlorophyll combined with the carbon dioxide they take in, they release oxygen and fruits.]

T2: And they produce sugar that is their food. The sugar is the plant's food. What they eat.

The role given to the English language in this particular class event was that of introducing the content of the class. The whole explanation of photosynthesis was in L2. Then, Spanish started playing a role as the teacher intended to confirm the understanding of the presentation of the topic, which was successful as the students could recall step by step the different stages of the process. She asked the whole class, and one student started to answer the teacher's questions; her answers were complemented by the responses of the other students. The teacher wraps up the interaction by reintroducing the last stage of photosynthesis in English.

García, Johnson, and Seltzer (2017) state that translanguaging works as a way to decrease both the students' fear of participating in the classroom and uncomfortable silence during lessons. In addition, García and Li (2014) also assert that translanguaging helps learners to create meaning in what others are saying and to act as mediators to help their classmates understand what the facilitator is saying or teaching. By integrating both languages, Spanish and English in this specific case, the students were exposed to new content in English, confirmed their understanding of the content in Spanish, and produced content in English.

Besides translanguaging to understand new content and demonstrate its understanding, the students translanguaged to confirm that they had comprehended the teacher's instructions and to help the partners who have not.

Transcription 5. **Student using Spanish to reinforce instruction given in English**

    T2:   It is not drawing. It's writing the name of the word. [*modeling with her hand*]. So, I'm gonna tell a word of a part of the plant to Yeison, Miguel, and Juan Sebastian and they are going to whisper.

S1: A los últimos de cada fila, ahh como la vez pasada. [To the last of each row, like the last time.]

T2: Right, now, listen. Federico come here, can you explain everyone the game. Explain.

S1: Vamos a jugar teléfono roto, que el último de cada fila le va diciendo al que sigue y después el primero escribe en el tablero. [We are going to play Chinese whispers, the last person in each row says to the next and then the first writes on the board.]

When the teacher gives the instructions for the activity in English, she models it in order to foster comprehension. In addition, she asks one of the students to explain the activity to the whole class without specifying the language to do so. What the student decides to do is to paraphrase the teacher's instructions in Spanish, which is a well-received practice seeking to help the successful realization of the activity. It is noticed that when the student says, "a los últimos de cada fila, ahh como la vez pasada [to the last of each row, ahh like the last time]" he is also associating the explanation with a past activity. Lee, Hill-Bonnet, and Raley (cited by Wright, Boun, & García, 2015) state that translanguaging enables students to act as language brokers because they help their classmates to understand instructions given in the second language; this action provides them with more opportunities for understanding, developing activities, and comprehending class content, besides students growing collaboratively.

As it has been developed in the previous section the integration of the two languages, English and Spanish, with the content classes provides several advantages in the teaching and learning process. The role of the teacher as planner and controller of the appropriate use of the strategy played an important role in this implementation apart from the confidence the teacher provided to students to use any of the languages as part of the learning environment.

5.3 Integrating translanguaging, content, and language as bilingual pedagogy

The teaching of content has a fundamental role in this project because it was through the teaching of Science that the researchers could explore different teaching strategies that were directed to helping the students comprehend the content. The analysis of the data shows that translanguaging facilitated the comprehension of the topic and encouraged the students to use the target language; at the same time, in analyzing the specific difficulties the participants had, other advantages (and some challenges) in the implementation of translanguaging were identified.

During the implementation of these classes, the teachers looked for ways to strategically incorporate Spanish and English; they also incorporated visual aids, charts, analogies, mimics, and other resources that were helpful for content and language instruction. In the following sample, it is evidenced how the teacher used a strategy related to the levels of organization of a living thing to help students understand the content of a topic; the teacher integrated the students to exemplify how a cell, tissue, organ, and organ system are formed.

Transcription 6. Teacher using strategy to facilitate concepts comprehension

> T: If we have many cells . . . Let's put an example, Valentina!! Come here [*calling Valentina to the front*] Pay attention . . . Valentina is a cell . . . she is a cell.

S26:   ella es una célula. [She is a cell.]

T: [*teacher is calling other student*] now we have, Valentina is a cell right? Valentina, Erick, and Laura are cells and if we put all of them together [*teacher is organizing them*]. They are a tissue.

S26:   Conjunto de células. [A group of cells.]

T: yes! Many cells working together . . . It is a tissue [*organizing other groups of students*].

In the previous specific example, the teacher is using English during the whole interaction, and the students are confirming their comprehension with the use of Spanish. Additionally, the teacher integrated the students in the explanation when she asked them to come to the front and simulate that they were a cell, which is then part of a tissue; the point was to help the students understand that a tissue is formed when several cells are joined together. By means of the analogy and the interaction with the group of students, the teacher was able to concretely illustrate the explanation. The strategy is identified as successful given that one of the students could confirm her understanding in Spanish: "S26: conjunto de células."

Instead of viewing the use of Spanish as the students' difficulty to express in English, the use of the mother tongue is to be seen as the students' ability to comprehend messages in English and to follow the thread in an explanation, and as a resource in comprehending and conveying messages in class. Corzo and Robles (2011) found that Spanish played an important role in the process of understanding lesson content; it is the way in which the students can express themselves freely and the way in which the teachers can confirm that the students are following through.

This sample also shows how the different strategies used by the teacher in a classroom can help the students understand the content being taught and make connections with the linguistic aspects being used. In providing the opportunities for these connections, it is important to consider different aspects given the linguistic repertoire of the students. Students need to be exposed to information that is known or real for them; better, easier, and stronger connections are made when the input they are being exposed to can somehow be associated with their background knowledge. As evidenced above, this can be achieved by using strategies such as translanguaging, analogies, and the teachers' paralinguistic features. According to Paris and Glynn (2004), using analogies strategically during a lesson can promote the building of conceptual bridges to connect their previous knowledge with the new input.

Additional to the use of analogies and the integration of the students in the dynamic of the class, it was also found that images and cognates in the vocabulary to be learned were two outstanding resources to accompany translanguaging in the CLIL classes. In the sample below, the teachers used images of people developing different activities in order to teach the functions of the animal cell organelles. The images in this activity were displayed with the purpose of helping students to infer the meaning of the vocabulary being used (words such as "to transport"). Many of the words used in the content presented and in the activities planned were cognates, which also helped in facilitating the students' understanding and learning. After inferring the action, the students were able to conclude the function developed by each organelle like "the smooth endoplasmic reticulum transports proteins." In the following sample of a reflection, the teacher expresses how the words in Spanish that were selected to infer effectively helped the students in making relations between the two languages and in facilitating the comprehension of the content.

Reflection 4. Use of images by the teacher to facilitate content and language understanding

They [students] provided the name of the organelles already learned in English and in addition the translanguaging strategy was implemented with some images where the students could infer a main verb in Spanish and conclude the functions in English. This strategy was good to help students understand the meaning of the new input in English; they show understanding filling a chart with all the functions of the organelles and participating in English and Spanish.

It is important to draw attention to the fact that the implementation of translanguaging was purposeful and systematic: the vocabulary was taught in English, inference was carried out in Spanish, and the functions of the organelles were expressed in English. In addition, in its implementation there are other elements involved. The first has to do with the importance of using images or other visual input to facilitate comprehension and acceleration of the students' connections between form and meaning. The second has to do with the use of cognates as they also contribute to fostering comprehension and production. The use of translanguaging, accompanied by strategies such as the use of cognates or materials such as images, supports the students' comprehension of the content and their production in the second language.

With regard to the use of cognates, it gives students valuable opportunities to learn a word in English based on a similar word in Spanish by being the clue to conclude a complete function developed for an organelle. As Corzo and Robles (2011) state, using the first language encourages students to associate concepts in Spanish with the content in the second language. Therefore, once the students identified an action in their first language, they established that action as belonging to the organelle and started thinking of a way to express it in English. In this part, the students made connections between the new word in the target language and its definition.

6. Conclusions

The current study intended to analyze the general impact on students in the integration of content, language, and translanguaging within a dynamic bilingual education model being implemented in two state schools in Pereira. This research built on the idea of giving access to bilingual education to the state-school populations by using a model that fits the characteristics of the setting in which the study was developed.

Firstly, the study aimed to determine what was evidenced from the implementation of lessons where the integration of language, science content, and translanguaging was used as dynamic bilingual pedagogy. There was no prohibition of the first language in the classroom; in other words, there was systematic and unsystematic use of the languages that could foster not only content processing and its acquisition, but also second language development. Teacher-participants of the study applied translanguaging to give instructions or manage classroom situations, thus translanguaging worked as a bilingual pedagogy to foster students' processing of the content and understanding; besides, it activated the students' previous knowledge on the topics, and facilitated the students' expression of meaning and knowledge. Thus, translanguaging practices should be promoted in class so as to make the language learning process integral, where all languages are used to boost improvement and development not only of the first but also of the second language, as well as specific content.

Limiting the students to the single use of the L2 in the classroom means limiting their expression of meaning and knowledge. The systematic and unsystematic use of both languages allowed in the classroom a way to cope with the requirements or needs of the teaching/learning moments. In this way, the students are more prepared at the time of developing the specific activities planned by the teachers.

Content, language, and translanguaging are recommended to be accompanied by visual aids, which proved effective in fostering the students' acquisition of the content, their language development, and the expression of meaning. Translanguaging, then, is proven to work more effectively if there are other elements involved such as analogies or cognates, which may be used as a way to integrate the students' knowledge of the world into the class to help the students make connections between language and content.

Some recommendations could be established toward the integration of L2, L1, and content. Firstly, what students have built in L1 leverages the L2 development through the integration of content, thus learners are empowered in not only linguistic but also general knowledge repertoire. Secondly, content development articulated with L2 permits the second language to acquire a different role in the learning process; it becomes a source, not the aim of the process. Finally, current bilingual education models could fit in contexts similar to the Colombian one, under the consideration that there should be an explicit and systematic articulation between two languages as part of that context.

References

Arias, E. (2017). *Translanguaging and Language Integrated Learning as a Dynamic Bilingual Education Model*. Tesis doctoral. Rudecolombia, Pereira.

Baker, C. (2001). *Foundations of Bilingual Education and Bilingualism*. Third edition. Clevedon: Multilingual Matters.

Baker, C. (2006). *Foundations of Bilingual Education and Bilingualism*. Fourth edition. Clevedon: Multilingual Matters.

Corzo, X. & Robles, H. S. (2011). Approaches to scaffolding in teaching mathematics in English with primary school students in Colombia. *Latin American Journal of Content & Language Integrated Learning, 4*(2), 13–20. doi: 10.5294/laclil.2011.4.2.2 ISSN 2011-6721

Cummins, J. (2000). *Language, Power and Pedagogy: Bilingual children in the crossfire.* Clevedon: Multilingual Matters.

Flick, U. (2009). *An introduction to qualitative research.* Chenai: Sage publications, 13.

Fox-Turnbull, W. (2009). *Stimulated Recall Using Autophotography - A Method for Investigating Technology Education.* University of Waikato, Hamilton, New Zealand: Centre for Science and Technology Education Research (CSTER) Graduate Conference, 8 Jul 2009. (Conference - Other - Oral presentations)

García, O. (2011). *Bilingual education in the 21st century: A global perspective.* Malden, MA: Wiley-Blackwell.

García, O. & Li, W. (2014) *Translanguaging: Language education and bilingualism.* New York: Palgrave McMillan.

García, O. & Leiva, C. (2014). Theorizing and Enacting Translanguaging for Social Justice. In A. Blackledge & A. Creese (Eds.), *Heteroglossia as Practice and Pedagogy* (pp. 199-216). Dordrecht: Springer.

García, O., Johnson, S., & Seltzer, K. (2017). *The Translanguaging classroom. Leveraging student bilingualism for learning.* Philadelphia: Caslon.

Garza, A. & Langman, J. (2014). *Translanguaging in a Latin Bilingual Community: Negotiations and Mediations in a Dual-Language classroom.* University of Texas, San Antonio. Retrieved from http://amaejournal.utsa.edu/index.php/amae/article/viewFile/225/180

George, A. & Bennett, A. (2004). *Case studies and theory development.* BCSIA Studies in International Security. Massachusetts: Harvard University.

Hancock, B., Ockleford, E., & Windridge, K. (2007). *An introduction to qualitative research.* The NIHR RDS EM / YH. Retrieved from https://www.rds-yh.nihr.ac.uk/wp-content/uploads/2013/05/5_Introduction-to-qualitative-research-2009.pdf

Lasagabaster, D. & García, O. (2014). Translanguaging: towards a dynamic model of bilingualism at school / Translanguaging: hacia un modelo dinámico de bilingismo en la escuela. *Cultura y Educación: Culture and*

Education, 26(3), 557-572.

Lewis, G., Jones, B., & Baker, C. (2012). Translanguaging: developing its conceptualization and contextualization. *Educational Research and Evaluation, 18*(7), 655–670.

Linares, A. (1 April 2011). El inglés se enseña todavía de forma muy arcaica. *El tiempo*. Retrieved from http://www.eltiempo.com/archivo/documento/MAM-4479844.

Lodico, M. G., Spaulding, D. T., & Voegtle, K. H. (2010). *Methods in Educational Research: From theory to practice*. San Francisco: Jossey-Bass. 2nd edition.

Ministry of National Education. (2006a). *Estándares básicos de competencias en lenguaje, matemáticas, ciencias, y ciudadanos*. Bogotá, Colombia: Imprenta Nacional.

Ministry of National Education. (2006b). *Estándares básicos de competencias en lenguas extranjeras: Ingles [Cartilla 22]*. Bogotá, Colombia: Imprenta Nacional.

Ministry of National Education. (2014). *Colombia Very well! Programa Nacional de Ingles 2015-2025: Documento de Socializacion*. Bogota, Colombia: Imprenta Nacional. Retrieved from http://www.colombiaaprende.edu.co/html/micrositios/1752/articles-343287_recurso_1.pdf

Paris, N. A. & Glynn, S. M. (2004). Elaborate analogies in science text: Tools for enhancing pre-service teachers' knowledge and attitudes reference. *Contemporary Educational Psychology, 29* (3), 230–247.

Rudestam, K.E. & Newton, R.R. (2001). *Surviving your dissertation: A comprehensive guide to content and process*, 2nd edn. London: Sage Publications.

Snow, C.E., Burns, M.S., & Griffin, P. (eds.) (1998). *Preventing reading difficulties in young children*. Washington, DC: National Academy Press.

Wright, W. E., Boun, S., & García, O. (2015). *The handbook of bilingual and multilingual education*. Hoboken, NJ: Wiley Blackwell.

Williams, C. (1994). *Arfarniado Ddulliau Dysguac Addysguyng Nghyddestun Addysg Uwchradd Ddwyieithog*. Unpublished PhD thesis. Bangor: University of Wales.

Williams, C. (2012). *The national immersion scheme guidance for teachers on*

subject language threshold: Accelerating the process of reaching the threshold.
Bangor, Wales: The Welsh Language Board.

Zuleta, A. (2015). El tema del bilingüismo en Colombia. Blendex. (Publicado 17 diciembre de 2015). [Citado 23 de abril de 2016]. Disponible en: http://idiomasblendex.com/el-tema-del-bilinguismo-en-colombia/

Conclusion: Reflecting on Trends in Translanguaging across Educational Contexts

Corinne A. Seals and Vincent Ieni Olsen-Reeder

This book arose from a shared interest across the contributors in locating discussions of multilingualism in education. For some, this discussion has been most salient at the policy level, while for some salience has arisen from within classroom interactional practice, and there are many other places in between where multilingualism in education has drawn researchers' attention. Regardless of exact context, however, there is a shared agreement across all chapters that embracing students' multilingual resources within the learning environment is crucial for success.

Furthermore, we are talking about equitable access to the learning space when students' full multilingual repertoires are embraced in educational spaces. This argument, made across chapters, further adds voice to the same argument made by researchers such as Menard-Warwick (2009) when looking to immigrants' access to language and education in the United States, and García and Wei's (2014) analysis of increased classroom participation of Spanish language–dominant students in an English class in New York. By adding further cases from contexts around the world to those already published, the chapters in this volume add strength to our empirical proof of the value of embracing multilingualism across educational contexts.

In the following section, we present core themes that emerged as salient across chapters. By discussing these and the connections between them, we can uncover notable directions for future research in line with what we are learning about translanguaging in education.

Emergent themes: Education

The first set of themes that emerged across chapters as salient were those addressing the topic of education directly. This is not a surprise, as the volume specifically focuses on educational contexts. However, it was interesting to find specifically which aspects of education were viewed as playing a major role across chapters: teacher strategies, teacher education / professional development, literacy, and curriculum/materials.

Many chapters focused on the importance of representing teachers' experiences in applying translingual and multilingual teaching models. For instance, in Chapter 2, Amosa Burgess and Fiti, as teacher-researchers themselves, looked to how teachers in their educational center draw upon a variety of strategies in working the translingual book into their teaching practices. Likewise, Plöger and Putjata in Chapter 9 seek to understand more about the experiences of multilingual staff who have been employed by the school administration specifically to support multilingualism within the educational environment. In Chapter 11, Abas adds to this conversation by considering an exploratory environment and the ways that teachers facilitate connections with the students and community members to create a transformative experience. Finally, Castaño and Sánchez in Chapter 13 look to the experiences of pre-service teachers in particular, seeking to uncover strategies that they employ when utilizing translanguaging in diglossic educational spaces.

Additionally, Chapters 2 and 13, mentioned above, show a focus on teacher development, as they look to ways that teachers overcome the challenges they face in working toward a translingual pedagogy in their respective teaching contexts. Likewise, Purkarthofer in Chapter 7 considers how explicit teacher education in flexible multilingual pedagogical practices equips teachers with the skills to facilitate acceptance of heritage language education. Additionally, Chapter 10 by Busic and Sullivan examines how pre-service teacher education can serve a major role in equipping teacher trainees with the skills to negotiate the use and value of translingual pedagogy in spaces where their managers may have very different language ideologies.

Another theme that arose is that of the importance of fostering literacy in multilingual education. This is examined in Chapter 2 when discussing book literacy in the Samoan aʻoga amata in New Zealand, as well as in Chapter 11 when the author discusses the development of community literacy through multilingual practice in the schoolscape. Chapter 4 by Tamati also looks at the role of literacy, specifically in the development of academic English for Māori students to reach greater equity with their English monolingual peers. Finally, Pfeiffer also considers the ways the students' academic literacy (specifically writing) is enhanced in South Africa and Sweden through a multilingual approach.

Following on from the emergent importance of literacy in multilingual education, a number of chapters also looked specifically to the role of a multilingual curriculum or multilingual teaching materials. Chapter 2 focused on the value of using a specially created translingual resource and how they created lessons in their curriculum around this to extend the benefits it offered. Chapter 7 analyzed Austria's curriculum to uncover how a shared curriculum across schools actually allowed for the integration of more languages and the status of heritage language education. Chapter 10 likewise examined a national curriculum (Sweden) to demonstrate how it actually makes space for and encourages the use of translingual teaching practices. Finally, Chapter 8 by Rosén, Straszer, and Wedin looks to how the Swedish curriculum has been implemented across various schools in Sweden, including the victories and challenges that have arisen when attempting to support the revitalization of home languages in this space.

As this first set of emergent themes show, the issue of teachers' experiences and realities on the ground has come to the forefront in considerations of multilingual and translingual education. This is a commonality across countries and across contexts. While there are many instances of translanguaging being supported from the top-down, teachers' realities are often much different, as they struggle to negotiate this paradigm shift while balancing parents' concerns, managers' expectations, and the ideologies of many. As shown in these cases, many teachers across contexts have found value in working together and also working with researchers to create materials and techniques for incorporating translanguaging into their teaching. Teachers also remind us that literacy is just as important a concern for student achievement as is speaking, so this is not to be left behind. As we continue to move forward in translanguaging research, we must center the experiences of teachers in the process to be relevant, helpful, and accountable in on the ground practice.

Emergent themes: Investigating attitudes and ideologies
The second set of emergent themes from across chapters focuses on investigations of attitudes, beliefs, and ideologies. Specifically, these topics included attitudes and beliefs, ideologies, an ethnographic approach, and interview methodology.

Attitudes and beliefs proved a chosen focus for chapters such as Chapter 5 by Hammine and Chapter 12 by Pfeiffer. For Hammine, attitudes and beliefs were a major contributing factor to the lack of maintenance support for Indigenous speakers of Yaeyaman in Japan. Additionally, Hammine shows how the dominant societal attitudes and beliefs in favor of monolingualism are embodied in the monolingual educational practices that ill fit the multilingual communities of the Ryukyus. Pfeiffer also shows the important role of attitudes and beliefs for language maintenance, focusing on how positive attitudes toward heritage languages are important in students' maintenance of them, which will in turn contribute positively to their academic writing.

Relatedly, ideologies play an important role as well across chapters in this volume. In addition to the ideologies present in Chapter 5's look at Indigenous language maintenance efforts in the Ryukyus, Chapter 6 by Chen also highlighted the centrality of ideology when it comes to language shift versus language maintenance for the Indigenous Paiwan speakers of Southern Taiwan. Rosén, Straszer, and Wedin also investigate the role of ideologies in Chapter 8 when examining Swedish language policy regarding heritage languages as well as home language instruction in compulsory schools. Furthermore, all of the chapters in this volume touch upon language attitudes, beliefs, and ideologies in some way, with those chapters listed above highlighting these issues as particularly central in their investigations of multilingual education.

It is also interesting to note that there is a majority presence of an ethnographic approach and interview methodology across chapters, which speaks to how issues such as attitudes and ideologies, as well as more broadly work with multilingualism in education are often being investigated in this space. This makes sense, as an ethnographic approach to data collection focuses on "the behaviors (including the linguistic behaviors) of the members of a particular community by studying them in naturally occurring, ongoing settings, typically while they participate in mundane day-to-day events" (Dufon, 2002, p. 42; cf. Garcez, 2008). Through an ethnographic approach, we can make the familiar strange, learning more about the *hows* and *whys* of language and interaction in everyday spaces such as education.

The ethnographic approach appears in Chapter 3 by Seals, Pine, Ash, Olsen-Reeder, and Wallace in their investigation of translanguaging practices within the everyday operations of a Māori puna reo in New Zealand. Through this approach, they stress the value of being able to work alongside the community to reach a deeper understanding of translanguaging in practice. Likewise, Hammine in Chapter 5 finds the use of an ethnographic approach important when working with the Indigenous Yaeyaman-speaking community of Japan and establishing trust with the community members as they discuss issues of language and identity.

Contexts in additional language settings (outside of Indigenous language settings) also find great value in the ethnographic approach to research. Chapter 7 by Purkarthofer sees a long-term ethnography of Austrian heritage language education providing detailed insight into the pressures that heritage language speakers face. Chapter 8 by Rosén, Straszer, and Wedin applies the ethnography of language policy approach (cf. Hornberger & Johnson, 2007; McCarty, 2011) to examine how language policy is "interpreted and appropriated by agents in a local context" (Johnson, 2009, p. 142). In Chapter 9 by Plöger and Putjata, the multilingual linguistic marketplace of a school is investigated via the ethnographic approach of ongoing participatory observation, allowing the researchers to see how the multilingual staff become agents situated between policy and practice (cf. Shohamy, 2006). Furthermore, Chapter 11 by Abas utilizes a community-based ethnographic approach to more deeply investigate the role of pedagogical translanguaging in a community educational space. Finally, Chapter 12 by Pfeiffer provides an account of a longitudinal qualitative investigation into heritage language use in schools in South Africa and Switzerland, showing how heritage language knowledge contributes an excellent foundation upon which students can strengthen their academic writing skills.

In addition to the ethnographic approach, many chapters made use of interview methodology. Interviews help us gain further insight into interlocutors' social and conceptual selves and experiences, while also empowering our interlocutors by giving them a space to talk where they will be heard (cf. Talmy, 2010; Tembe & Norton, 2008). Chapters 8 and 9, mentioned above, were both able to add more detailed understandings of participants' experiences, ideologies, and expectations by additionally applying interview methodology to their ethnographic investigations. Furthermore, Chapter 6 by Chen showed the value in semi-structured narrative interviews for uncovering families' experiences with Indigenous language use across domains and the families' perceived connections between language and identity. Lastly, Busic and Sullivan in Chapter 10 made use of semi-structured focus group interviews to better understand the challenges faced by teacher trainees when facing work environments that do not meet the trainees' own ideologies regarding translanguaging in education.

The emergence of ideological themes across the chapters speaks to how ideologically loaded discourses involving multilingual education are across contexts. This is part of what makes researching in this area at times very difficult, whether procedurally or interpersonally – people have very strong feelings about how and why multilingual education should exist and what form(s) it should take. A rise in ethnographic and interview research, as evidenced by the strong presence of these across chapters, speaks to the importance that researchers are putting on reaching a deeper understanding of the attitudes and beliefs that drive these ideologies. This deeper understanding is necessary to then understand the basis for current practice and the not-so-obvious constraints often placed on progress in multilingual education. By delving deeper into attitudes and ideologies, we can seek to understand how to better advance the needs of multilingual speakers, especially speakers of minority languages.

Emergent themes: Sustainability
A final set of themes that emerged across chapters has to do with the topic of linguistic sustainability. In particular, these covered

Indigenous knowledge, cultural and linguistic sustainability, language shift and loss, and the cognitive, emotional, and social benefits of translanguaging.

First, Chapter 3 by Seals, Pine, Ash, Olsen-Reeder, and Wallace, as well as Chapter 4 by Tamati, directly addressed the need to value and focus on Indigenous knowledge when working with Indigenous communities. Both of these chapters focus on Māori educational settings, and New Zealand scholarship has seen a rise in awareness of the importance of upholding the value of mātauranga Māori (the Māori way of knowing) and kaupapa Māori (the Māori way of doing) (cf. G.H. Smith, 1990; L.T. Smith, 1997, 2012; Ka'ai, 2008; Awatere, 2010; Hikuroa, 2017). Both chapters draw upon this rise in awareness to emphasize the centrality that Indigenous knowledge should play in research with Indigenous peoples.

Furthermore, chapters 3 and 4 also focus on the need to establish multilingual education that promotes cultural and linguistic sustainability, which responds to Cenoz and Gorter's (2017) call for more research into sustainable translanguaging as a means by which to protect endangered languages and language maintenance efforts. Chapter 3 discusses ways in which translanguaging in a Māori puna reo facilitates the incorporation and use of more Māori cultural and linguistic resources, and Chapter 4 looks at how translanguaging in a kura kaupapa is able to enhance students' English language mastery without taking away from their te reo Māori proficiency and usage. Additionally, Chapter 5 by Hammine also looks to cultural and linguistic sustainability in an Indigenous context – showing how embracing a translanguaging pedagogy shows promise for Yaeyaman language maintenance efforts in Japan. Finally, Chapter 8 by Rosén, Straszer, and Wedin considers the connection between embedded ideologies in Swedish national curriculum and home language maintenance, arguing that similar challenges in sustainability are faced in each domain.

The need for measures of cultural and linguistic sustainability is further evidenced by the chapters discussing the realities of language shift and loss. Chapter 5 argues that a focus on sustainability is important due to the very real language shift and loss taking place within the Indigenous communities of Japan. As Hammine argues, the current dominant educational practices are harming, rather than helping to sustain, the Indigenous languages, but a translanguaging pedagogy offers hope. Additionally, Chapter 6 by Chen also looks at language shift and loss within an Indigenous language community – this time among speakers of Paiwan in Southern Taiwan. As Chen shows, there has not been much space made in the linguistic marketplace of Taiwan for Indigenous languages, leading to increasing language shift among younger generations. Chen concludes that for language maintenance to succeed, there needs to be the establishment of more linguistic support for Indigenous language education and family language maintenance efforts.

Finally, all of the chapters argue for the cognitive, emotional, and social benefits of multilingualism and multilingual education. Many of these chapters focus specifically on these benefits within a translanguaging pedagogy. For example, Chapter 2 by Amosa Burgess and Fiti shows empirical proof of increased participation and minority language use among both heritage language speakers and new speakers when a translanguaging pedagogy is utilized. Chapter 3 demonstrates via discourse analysis how translanguaging in education allows for sociocultural knowledge bridge building by weaving cultural and linguistic practices together in the classroom. Chapter 4 provides empirical evidence of increased language performance in English and te reo Māori following a translingual pedagogical intervention. Finally, Chapter 11 by Abas shows how translanguaging in the schoolscape and through interaction allows for a transformative educational experience that supports the development of community literacy.

All of the above chapters argue for the essentialness of making multilingual education a space of cultural and linguistic sustainability to support families and individual speakers in resisting language shift and loss. Some of the chapters have specifically drawn upon Indigenous frameworks in making this argument, and others have argued for this more broadly, but all have highlighted the central role of multilingual education. As all chapters in this book have argued and demonstrated empirically, there are huge benefits to be gained through multilingual education, including through the specific application of a translanguaging pedagogy. The fact that this evidence is shown empirically across contexts around the world further speaks to the necessity of supporting the linguistic and cultural needs of communities through community-specific multilingual education.

Concluding comments

This volume sought to add understanding to how translanguaging is done around the globe in contemporary times, and how it looks and feels within the multi-faceted educational contexts. It is hoped that a dedicated focus on heritage languages has exemplified how translanguaging can best service both Indigenous and immigrant languages, for their continued revitalization and maintenance in a time when linguistic diversity is constantly under threat by languages perceived as more powerful.

This book has also privileged the voices of both researchers and practitioners, and their work. While it remains true to the academic integrity of the university in which its editors reside, there has been a particular focus on allowing a wide range of community scholars to have a voice on the subject. Since language exists in many places and spaces, this collection has sought to amplify the voices of those working in a variety of settings where language education occurs.

As the door on this publication closes, its authors have opened several more for us to walk through in the future. It is important to understand translanguaging as more than an alternative term for other sociolinguistic terms such as code-switching. It is also pertinent to empower Indigenous language revivalists to integrate elements of translanguaging into their work, should they deem that important. This is particularly relevant to those Indigenous groups working to provide immersion language education. Heritage languages are still in competition for space, including an internal competition within speakers. To that end, emphasizing translanguaging as a way to educate generations through those internal struggles, is very useful indeed. Kia mau tonu ngā reo – good health to our languages!

References

Awatere, S. (2010). What is the degree of Mātauranga Māori expressed through measures of ethnicity? *AlterNative: An International Journal of Indigenous Peoples, 6*(1), 1–14.

Cenoz, J. & Gorter, D. (2017). Minority languages and sustainable translanguaging: threat or opportunity? *Journal of Multilingual and Multicultural Development*, 1–12.

Dufon, M.A. (2002). Video recording in ethnographic SLA research: some issues of validity in data collection. *Language Learning & Technology, 6*(1), 40–59.

Garcez P.M. (2008) Microethnography in the Classroom. In N. H. Hornberger (Ed.), *Encyclopedia of Language and Education* (pp. 257–271). Boston: Springer.

García, O. & Wei, L. (2014). *Translanguaging: Language, Bilingualism and Education*. New York: Palgrave Macmillan.

Hikuroa, D. (2017). Mātauranga Māori—the ūkaipō of knowledge in New Zealand. *Journal of the Royal Society of New Zealand, 47*(1), 1-6.

Hornberger, N. H. & Johnson, D. C. (2007). Slicing the onion ethnographically: layers and spaces in multilingual language education policy and practice. *TESOL Quarterly, 41*(3), 509–532.

Johnson, D. C. (2009). Ethnography of language policy. *Language Policy, 8*(2), 139–159.

Ka'ai, T. (2008). Te Ha Whakawairua, Whakatinana i te Mātauranga Māori i Te Whare Wānanga: The validation of Indigenous knowledge within the university academy. *Te Kaharoa, 1*(1), 50-85.

McCarty, T. L. (2011). *Ethnography and Language Policy.* New York: Routledge.

Menard-Warwick, J. (2009). *Gendered Identities and Immigrant Language Learning.* Tonawanda: Multilingual Matters.

Shohamy, E. (2006). Imagined multilingual schools: How come we don't deliver. In O. García, T. Skutnabb-Kangas, & M. E. Torres-Guzmán (Eds.), *Imagining multilingual schools: Languages in education and globalization* (pp. 171–183). Bristol: Multilingual Matters.

Smith, G. H. (1997). *Kaupapa Māori: Theory and praxis.* Unpublished PhD thesis. Auckland, NZ: The University of Auckland.

Smith, L. T. (1997). *Ngā aho o te kākahu mātauranga: The multiple layers of struggle by Māori in education.* Unpublished PhD thesis. Auckland, NZ: The University of Auckland.

Smith, L. T. (2012). *Decolonizing methodologies: Research and Indigenous peoples,* 2nd edn. Dunedin: Otago University Press.

Talmy, S. (2010). Qualitative Interviews in Applied Linguistics: From Research Instrument to Social Practice. *Annual Review of Applied Linguistics, 30,* 128–148.

Tembe, J. & Norton, B. (2008). Promoting Local Languages in Ugandan Primary Schools: The Community as Stakeholder. *The Canadian Modern Language Review, 65*(1), 33–60.

Contributors

Editors
Corinne A. Seals
Victoria University of Wellington
corinne.seals@vuw.ac.nz

Vincent Ieni Olsen-Reeder
Victoria University of Wellington
vini.olsen-reeder@vuw.ac.nz

Chapter 2
Feaua'i Amosa Burgess
EFKS A'oga Amata Newtown
efksaogaamata@xtra.co.nz

Sadie Fiti
EFKS A'oga Amata Newtown
sadiefiti@yahoo.co.nz

Chapter 3
Corinne A. Seals
Victoria University of Wellington
corinne.seals@vuw.ac.nz

Vincent Ieni Olsen-Reeder
Victoria University of Wellington
vini.olsen-reeder@vuw.ac.nz

Russell Pine
Victoria University of Wellington
russell.pine@vuw.ac.nz

Cereace Wallace
Victoria University of Wellington
cereace.wallace@vuw.ac.nz

Madeline Ash
Victoria University of Wellington
madsash22@gmail.com

Chapter 4
Sophie Tauwehe Tamati
The University of Auckland
t.tamati@auckland.ac.nz

Chapter 5
Madoka Hammine
University of Lapland
madoka.hammine@gmail.com, mhammine@ulapland.fi

Chapter 6
Chun-Mei Chen
National Chung Hsing University
chench@dragon.nchu.edu.tw

Chapter 7
Judith Purkarthofer
University of Oslo, Norway
judith.purkarthofer@iln.uio.no

Chapter 8
Jenny Rosén
Stockholm University and
Dalarna University, Sweden
jenny.rosen@isd.su.se

Åsa Wedin
Dalarna University, Sweden
awe@du.se

Borglárka Straszer
Dalarna University, Sweden
bsr@du.se

Chapter 9
Simone Plöger
University of Hamburg
simone.ploger@uni-hamburg.de

Galina Putjata
University of Münster
putjata@uni-meunster.de

Chapter 10
Vesna Busic
Umeå University, Sweden
vesna.busic@umu.se

Kirk P. H. Sullivan
Umeå University, Sweden
kirk.sullivan@umu.se

Chapter 11
Suriati Abas
Indiana University
sabas@iu.edu

Chapter 12
Verbra Frances Pfeiffer
Stellenbosch University, Cape Town
South Africa
vfpfeiffer@sun.ac.za, verbrapfeiffer@gmail.com

Chapter 13
Isabel Cristina Sánchez Castaño
Universidad Tecnológica de Pereira
icsc88@utp.edu.co

Enrique Arias Castaño
Universidad Tecnológica de Pereira
earias@utp.edu.co